So WE CaN KNOW

So WE CaN KNoW

writers of color on pregnancy, loss, abortion, and birth

edited by
aracelis girmay

foreword by
Nina Angela Mercer

Haymarket Books
Chicago, Illinois

Published in 2023 by
Haymarket Books
P.O. Box 180165
Chicago, IL 60618
773-583-7884
www.haymarketbooks.org
info@haymarketbooks.org

ISBN: 978-1-64259-839-1

Distributed to the trade in the US through Consortium Book Sales and Dis-
tribution (www.cbsd.com) and internationally through Ingram Publisher
Services International (www.ingramcontent.com).

This book was published with the generous support of Lannan Foundation
and Wallace Action Fund.

Special discounts are available for bulk purchases by organizations and institutions. Please call 773-583-7884 or email info@haymarketbooks.org for
more information.

Cover and book design by Jamie Kerry.

Printed in Canada by union labor.

Library of Congress Cataloging-in-Publication data is available.

10 9 8 7 6 5 4 3 2 1

Contents

I   a fact

             answer of my own making

—Desiree C. Bailey, from "Woman in Dub"

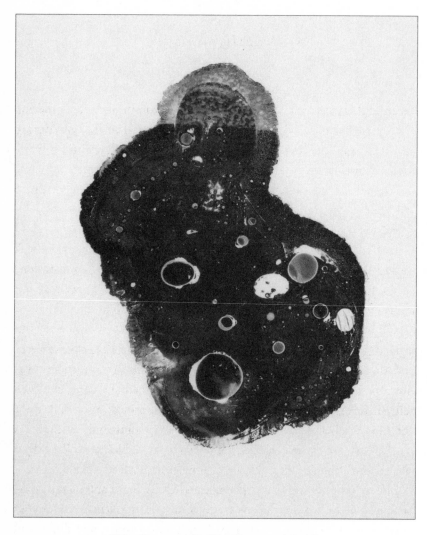

"The Evanesced: The Retrieval #48"
Kenyatta A. C. Hinkle

A Caul

Nina Angela Mercer

To enter this gathering is to bear witness to a communion, a mothering channeled by those who chose this road and walked it, a mothering that has sometimes meant refusal, or a prayer for understanding at the roots of an elder tree when we could not birth the child who came just as we were daring flight. We know pedestals are lies we are meant to fall from, so we lean into our left hip instead, arms akimbo.

We tell it so you know without question.

This is the way it is with us—what it means to birth, and what it means to not give birth and still be reborn and someone else's testimony in the telling. We are more than wombs, but we also know that our reproductive lives are in danger, so we hold the shell of our lives open to the heart of the matter—the divine mother funk is crowned both king and queen; we who are the gate and also guard it; the passageway and those who come through it, conduit and inspiration, supernovas illuminating city sidewalks, as in mama is so bad she name her own self, shedding whole lifetimes in seasons, a uterine riot of dark crimson blood rich as fresh-turned earth heavy with minerals and rain. A mothering of self when we shed a whole woman in blood—coiling deep, dangerous, a shocking beauty, taut, unraveling, or free. We decide.

Sing of us when we make mistakes, when we leave and do not come back and when we do. Tell of those of us who took many lovers but never wed, those of us who married without certainty, and those who made choices there was no language for generations ago.

Here we light the shadowy places to recall what every born human must know in the quiet of muscle memory, in the skin's thrill when touched by spirit—

To know our way is to walk with feet bare in damp soil, to smell the coming rain, to feel electricity before the storm, to ride its center once in it; our way is to be all nerve endings, always on heightened sensory alert, a feeling deep inside the belly of the unknown, an apprehension almost out of reach.

This is inside secret and prayer. This is testify and let loose, kitchen talk and the back porch when the lightning bugs are out and the heat thick as thighs touching. This is low laughter or loud, and there is no shame in it. This is love. Let it be known.

Snake-headed woman. Two-headed. Mother of Many Fishes—we are here, been here—generations of mermaid people with swords gleaming. Sharp-tongued and heavy-handed, holding grace and kindness with discretion. We who open our souls on this road follow the water inside, ask its current to pull us into a port that respects our many names, calling us into ourselves. We are flowering and feral.

Come see.

Introduction

aracelis girmay

for Lois

I cannot remember when my mother's body first became a mystery to me. Though she was the one out of whose body I was made, since I can remember, I was only ever myself, and dense as a clove. I could sense where I ended and where she began. But I imagine we had lived whole years without her shyness from me, without her embarrassment or articulation of a distance between us, just my sleeping at her nipple after milk. And yet, for all my childhood, I remember her turning away from me to release the strap of her bra or to take off her shirt. She hid her breasts. She hid her behind. She hid her stomach—strange and stretched and shining as though burnt once in a fire.

I did not know her naked body, really. I knew her in slips and brown pantyhose on Sunday mornings. I knew her in her dark blue FedEx uniform pants and vest and her sharp white collar. I did not know her skin unless it was the skin of her face or arms or hands. Her hands I knew the most. They were busy with us. They flew quickly in the kitchen. They folded clothes and wrung the mop. They oiled our skin and braided my hair. The pointer-finger bones of her right hand turned slightly inward, pointing to the words we read.

In the story of my mother's line, there were experiences more enormous than I could understand. Often, as was the way of my mother's family, they fed me silence and fear about sex and pregnancy. All of it was something to avoid and then to endure. Undoubtedly, these

1

silences and shames stemmed from abuses suffered at the hands sometimes of husbands, stepfathers, teachers, doctors. These women were
complicated, easily agitated, capable, larger than life. My mother was
always working on the family car. She played congas in the gospel
choir. She and her sister and her mother, they painted their nails and
kept the record player in the kitchen where they could dance. They
gardened and painted walls and built things and moved strong in their
bodies—yet, their choices and lack of choices around sex, pregnancy,
and birth were mostly hidden from me.

I grew older. I inherited the hushed voices of my mothers as did
many of my friends. Somewhere along the way, though, I began to need
these stories. I wanted to listen to all the ways that women and girls
had tried to live. Which choices seemed big, which choices seemed
tiny, and which seemed not choices at all. I read poems and novels. I
interned with an oral historian in Bluefields, Nicaragua, as she docu-
mented Black women midwives, nurses, and community leaders, like
her. When I became pregnant with my first child, I unearthed those
stories and touched them to my questions and courage.

I was a Black, cis woman pregnant in the United States, a country in
which Black and Native American women, as the Centers for Disease
Control and Prevention announced in 2019, are two to three times
more likely to die from pregnancy-related causes than white women,
a ratio that only increases with age; a country of eugenics-based sterilization laws and campaigns that resulted in more than 37 percent
of women of childbearing age in Puerto Rico (most of them in their
twenties) being sterilized, as reported in 1976 by the US Department
of Health, Education, and Welfare. In the last fifteen years alone,
forced sterilizations have been recorded in California prisons and in a
for-profit Immigration and Customs Enforcement detention center in
Georgia. Simultaneously, the criminalization of abortion continues to
threaten the health and freedoms of Black and working-class people.
With the erosion of *Roe v. Wade* came an increase of convictions for
abortion, miscarriage, and stillbirth. We see this happening now in
Texas and Mississippi.

When I became pregnant, I read and kept on reading. I knew where I was. I memorized symptoms and facts: warning signs of eclampsia, preeclampsia, and peripartum cardiomyopathy; medical statistics that revealed how regularly, and with harrowing consequences, medical workers ignore our pain and symptoms. I kept track of anecdotes and questions in the notes section of my phone and in a journal I took with me to all my visits. I forwarded articles to my partner. I wondered newly about my own family's stories—the mysteries of deaths, abortions, pregnancies, and births.

There is the story I think of often, told solemnly by my mother, about the death of her maternal grandmother, Lois. She was born to farm laborers in Griffin, Georgia, in February 1909, and she died in Chicago in January 1944, when her seven living children were between the ages of seventeen and four. In my mother's version of the story, Lois may have been pregnant or recently pregnant and suffered from hemorrhaging. As I write this, I close my inner eye around a photograph of her posing in the grass with four of her children. A gap in years between the oldest and the second, and the feeling of the baby who was born having already died, floating in the female dark and light between them. I trace Lois's long fingers settled softly on the neck of one child and the shoulder of another. Within about a year of this photograph, she will give birth to my own grandmother, and after that, twin daughters. In 1940, when my grandmother is just two or three years old and the twins are just about one year old, she will sign a Communist Party election petition. I find her name and the family's address at 3656 [S.] Vincennes Avenue in a Special Committee on Un-American Activities report. Who was this woman? What did she fight for? What did she need? What might she have told her own children to consider when thinking about their futures, had she lived? For months, then years, I tried to listen to what Lois's story could tell me about it all. Increasingly, I needed the medicine of stories by people making choices about their pregnancies, which is to say, their lives.

Chicago, Illinois, circa 1936. Lois Vargas pictured with her children and perhaps pregnant with my grandmother. Photo courtesy of Vargas family archive.

In the opening pages of Cristina Rivera Garza's *Grieving: Dispatches from a Wounded Country*, she describes meeting a young man named Saúl, who asks her to articulate in a book her ideas "about the current situation in Mexico." She writes: "... Saúl wanted the words of the dweller of this world who was simultaneously—who cannot cease being—a historian and a writer and a mother and a daughter and a sister."

Without yet knowing this story, I had begun taking notes toward this anthology, wanting to hear writers thinking about their own lived experiences of pregnancy and choice. Words from the dwellers of this world. I wrote to writers of color living—or who had lived once—in the United States, with a belief that their words, together, would carry some of what we must know about the history of now. I wrote to people not always knowing their relationships to questions of pregnancy, abortion, loss, and birth. I proposed an anthology of nonfiction across strategies, modes, registers, forms. Together, these mostly previously unpublished texts are a gathering of varied and intricate thinking at the intersections of research, personal history, and the intimacies of their own lived experiences and choices around pregnancy.

This gathering is not exhaustive. It is part of an ongoing practice of the sharing and listening that happens on telephones, in laundry rooms, before the altars, and in the kitchens. And it is not the first of its kind. I hope that it is in constellation with other feminist gatherings of people who listen and write toward the truth of their lived experiences to articulate and dream toward the flourishing of each Other, such as *This Bridge Called My Back*, edited by Cherríe Moraga and Gloria Anzaldúa; *Revolutionary Mothering*, edited by Alexis Pauline Gumbs, China Martens, and Mai'a Williams; and *What God Is Honored Here? Writings on Miscarriage and Infant Loss by and for Native Women and Women of Color*, edited by Shannon Gibney and Kao Kalia Yang, who discuss their work as editors of that anthology in this one.

* * *

In the book *As We Have Always Done: Indigenous Freedom Through Radical Resistance*, Leanne Betasamosake Simpson thinks about the "unfolding of a different present." This ongoing engagement with possibility informed by presence with others is part of what this anthology continues to awaken in me. May this book be always, changing, alive, dynamic, an opening into a new and deep relationship with others who, like each of us, carry some long part of our long story. I am deeply grateful to these brilliant contributors for carrying their stories into this ceremony. As mother and daughter Rosemarie Freeney Harding and Rachel Elizabeth Harding carry to us in "Pachamama Circle III," "Theirs is the knowledge of planting blessings in hard ground. They hold stones and stories under their tongues so that we will have them when we need them."

And we need them.

In this book, scholar and poet Umniya Najaer shares "dear Alice..." an epistolary essay that "performs a historical, and at times speculative, recounting of Alice Clifton's 1781 case, 'The Trial of Alice Clifton for the Murder of her Bastard-Child, At the Court of Oyer and Terminer and General Gaol Delivery, held at Philadelphia, on Wednesday the 18th day of April, 1787.'" Najaer begins her piece, "dear Alice," and with epigraphs from Hortense Spillers's "Mama's Baby, Papa's Maybe," Jessica Marie Johnson's *Wicked Flesh*, and Saidiya Hartman's "The Belly of the World," she moves readers toward an intergenerational, polytemporal gathering of Black women makers and thinkers. Najaer's text, as is true of so much of the work of this anthology, is a deeply felt and researched ceremony.

The same can be said about the three works by Kenyatta A. C. Hinkle included here. Hinkle's *The Evanesced* are part of what she describes as "a series of drawings, large-scale paintings, and a suite of performances toward missing Black womxn in the US and in the African diaspora," across time. Such work makes itself available to what the vanishing might tell us but also what we might retrieve in order to be, perhaps, better in the being together.

From these works to lyric essays on homeland and grief to interviews and collaborations between mothers and daughters, this anthology is a wild and teeming place of many breaths, locations, histories, and lineages.

In "All of Yourself," an interview, Elizabeth Alexander describes, among other things, profound moments of learning from Black women elders Lucille Clifton and Ruth Simmons. In a lyric essay, "we participate in the creation of the world by decreating ourselves," Jennifer S. Cheng writes about undergoing infertility treatments, an idea of decreation, and some of the complexities of suffering and grief in relation to pregnancy and early motherhood. And in her essay, "The Beginning and End of It," Patricia Smith writes about her anguish as a pregnant young person embattled with her own mother.

Throughout, there are not only writings of isolation but also of community. There are a few texts that describe secret, courageous, impossible acts of love between pregnant people and the elders who, against their own beliefs, supported them to undergo abortions. We see this in Cheryl Boyce-Taylor's essay "Born Ibeji." The included texts span generations and, often, flickering and plural relationships to specific pregnancies across a single lifetime, as in Seema Reza's "Pity," in which she writes of a shift from being "pro-choice for everyone, but pro-life for me" to being changed by the mighty love of a hawkeyed grandmother willing to make a hard choice. In "Then They Came for Our Wombs," Sandra Guzmán writes a love song to the life *fuerza* of her titis Himilce, Minerva, and Aida. Woven into this song is a livid indictment of the US government–sanctioned gynecological violence and forced sterilization of Black and Indigenous women on the island of her beloved Borikén.

Here there are so many stories of touch, of rebellion and invention, of land, of death, tenderness, imagination, and grief. Over and over, the works gleam with lucidity and great feeling. They bristle and sound, made in the dark of the body as they are.

In arranging these works I tried to honor their expansive and varied resonances and repetitions one to the next—yet it is vitally important to me to think of these works as perpetually outside of order, stunningly entangled. For this reason, I chose not to organize the book into themed sections but instead thought of the sections as mini arcs within the larger book. My hope is that the index will be a useful tool for those wanting to locate specific themes. More words from "Pachamama Circle III" come to me now: "And this is the circle I'm telling you about. All this is the circle ..."

I, like many of you, grew up dancing inside a circle or being part of the circle the dancers danced inside of. Taking turns like that. Improvising a space of refuge, joy, attention, and possibility. Like those circles, may these conversations be ongoing, unfixed, all the time touching and making space for a beloved to decide their movement inside of. All this is "the circle," here where it is darkest, where we are all time, where the stories are tangled and dense as the mangroves, as us.

Editor's note: I am particularly indebted to Loretta Ross and Rickie Sollinger's notes on language and gender in Reproductive Justice: An Introduction. *In my own introduction, I use the terms "girls," "women," "people who can get pregnant," and "people making choices about their pregnancies" to reflect a range of individuals and their lived experiences of pregnancy and the idea of pregnancy.*

"The Evanesced: Rivers"
Kenyatta A. C. Hinkle

dear Alice, 'for the murder of [your] bastard child' of the starry-eyed tribe born to children[1]

Umniya Najaer

"My country needs me, and if I were not here, I would have to be invented."

—Hortense Spillers, "Mama's Baby, Papa's Maybe"

"Black femme freedom resided in enslaved and free African women and girls' *capacity to belong to themselves and each other.*"[2]

—Jessica Marie Johnson, *Wicked Flesh* (emphasis mine)

"Certainly we know that enslaved women fled the plantation, albeit not in as great numbers as men; poisoned slaveholders; plotted resistance; dreamed of destroying the master and his house; utilized abortifacients rather than reproduce slaves; practiced infanticide rather than sentence their children to social death, the auction block, and the master's bed; exercised autonomy in suicidal acts; gave birth to children as testament to

---

1   This essay performs a historical, and at times speculative, recounting of Alice Clifton's 1787 case, "The Trial of Alice Clifton for the Murder of her Bastard-Child, At the Court of Oyer and Terminer and General Gaol Delivery, held at Philadelphia, on Wednesday the 18th day of April, 1787." Italics denote direct quotations from the aforementioned trial record. Only when stated otherwise do italics denote quotations from other texts.

2   In her monograph *Wicked Flesh* (2020) Jessica Marie Johnson writes, "Black femme freedom resided in enslaved and free African women and girls' capacity to *belong to themselves and each other.* It demanded a promiscuous accounting of blackness not as bondage and subjection, but as future possibility. It rejected discourses of Black women as lascivious or wicked, and transmuted them into practices of defiance and pleasure for themselves. Black femme freedom enacted a radical opposition to bondage, reinterpreting wickedness as freedom, intimacy as fugitive, and blackness as diasporic and archipelagic." This articulation resonates with my sense of Black femmeness as an intrinsically collective and relational experience.

an abiding knowledge of freedom contrary to every empirical index of the plantation; and yearned for radically different ways of being in the world."

—Saidiya Hartman, "The Belly of the World"

The infant is born in the room above the parlor where the Bartholomews eat supper in their new home on the corner of Second and Market Street in Philadelphia. Must have been a quiet birth since no one heard a thing. Even with the door wide open, there is no evidence she cried. Not at the intake of the first breath, not in the harrowing push when her head was in the world and her body engulfed in the world of another body.

The way they see it, you have been the legal property of Mr. Bartholomew for three years. Before that, you were *brought up* by his father-in-law, Mr. Milne. Passed on, or so the expression goes. It appears no one cared for you when a month before going into labor you fell down the cellar stairs with a log of wood in your arms. In court, Mr. Bartholomew will admit they didn't call a doctor, even when the bruises darkened, that it was unwarranted since the quality of your work was not affected. Nor did they call for help when three days before giving birth you fell down the same flight of stairs. Why not? the attorney general will want to know. Because *she was not confined*.

Twelve days after giving birth alone and silently, the Philadelphia court tries you *for the murder of* [your] *bastard-child* on a Wednesday. It is April 18, and your mistress, Mrs. Mary Bartholomew, tells the court you continuously denied your pregnancy, but she knew all along, it was obvious from your bulk. She says the morning of the birth you *got up and made fire in the parlor* before lying down. Without recalling what was served for supper, or by whom, Mrs. Bartholomew tells the court that after supper she suspected you had given birth and *searched about in the closets, and in the chimney* but found nothing.

The sister-in-law, Miss Bartholomew, began probing every nook and cranny. Later, Miss B will tell the court: No, she did not observe cuts or bruises when she found the infant at the bottom of a trunk, *under a large roll of linen*, wrapped in your petticoat. That had there been blood, you must have wiped it away, for she recalls seeing none before returning the corpse to you. She will recall you sitting on the floor, rocking the quiet corpse.

Alice, I imagine you, *the prisoner*, gazing into the five eclipses forming where you press nails into skin, listening as the attorney general, sergeant, and council pose the strangest questions. *Did you see any blood about the child? Was the child cold or warm? Had the infant hair and nails?*[3] Miss B answers to the best of her ability. After some hesitation, she responds that yes, she believes *it had nails.*

In the courtroom time is a dimensionless swamp with no beginning and you are the cradle of your terror. The coroner, John Leacock testifies that you told him you did it to stop her from crying. That he measured the cut: one inch in depth and four inches across the infant's neck, from ear to ear. The sheriff, Samuel Bullfinch, testifies that he found you *sitting on the floor, with the child leaning over* [your] *arm.* He thought *it appeared plump and hearty.* Nathaniel Norgrove says you confided in him that you did it with a razor, because John Schaffer— the fat Schaffer, the one who married Chavilier's daughter—told you to. Dr. Foulke tells the court that Schaffer promised *if she made away with the child, she should have her time purchased, and he would set her at liberty.* Adding that before he did it to you, *Schaffer persuaded a milk-girl to do the like once before.*

It seems the moving lips are never yours, Alice.

---

3   Blood and nails are beside the point. Presumably, this question intends to clarify whether the child was born full term or not. The underlying reasoning is flawed since these are not contingent factors: she could have been a full-term stillborn infant or a living preterm infant or a living full-term infant or a stillborn preterm infant. It is not possible to tell whether or not she was stillborn based on the presence of blood. The question presumes that if her throat was slit and she didn't bleed then the infant was stillborn. But blood would have been present regardless, as it is, simply, a natural part of birth. More so, it would have been impossible to distinguish if the blood was Alice's or the infant's. These inquires illustrate that the decision about Alice's guilt or innocence, and whether she should be pardoned or hanged, were framed around questions that are scientifically unsound, even by eighteenth-century standards, and, on a more basic level, lack elementary logical reasoning.

On the day of the trial you have been a passenger on earth, lapping air, circling the sun with astonishing precision for a mere sixteen years. You are so young. Not a "child" but briefly new on earth.[4] So new, even after hate's longing for a resting place cores you.

Whereas so much still awaits you.

I wonder how you care for you. Are you someone beside yourself when the contractions set in and you have no mother to turn to? When the coroner holds your newborn up to the afternoon light, squinting into her slit? Or during the thirteen long days you sit in the jail, braiding and unbraiding your hair to distract from the need to evacuate your waterlogged breasts, sore and brimming with sustenance? What is the content of your dreams leading up to the day your fate would rest with a jury comprised of Schaffer's compatriots? Did you believe Schaffer when he promised, in exchange for the infant's death, to purchase your freedom and *make* [you] *as happy and as fine as his wife*? That if you failed to comply you *should suffer immensely*?

The threat betrays the bait. The bait is never freedom, this much I think you knew.

Doctor Foulke tells the jury: it was towards the end of September that John Schaffer də'bôCHt you on your master's lot. Debauched, stemming from the French *debauchier*, meaning to scatter or disperse, entered the English language in 1595, nearly a century after those initial flocks of colonists disembarked.[5] Its synonyms include: [to] abase,

---

4   Since Black children's experiences complicate antebellum and contemporary conception of 'childhood,' I find newness an apt counter-concept, one that defines youthfulness through a temporal framework, as opposed to a contingent subject position. For more on Black girlhood studies, see Crystal Lynn Webster's "The History of Black Girls and the Field of Black Girlhood Studies: At the Forefront of Academic Scholarship" (2020); Robin Berstein's *Racial Innocence: Performing American Childhood from Slavery to Civil Rights* (2011); Aimee Meredith Cox's *Shapeshifter: Black Girls and the Choreography of Citizenship* (2015); Toby Rollo's "The Color of Childhood: The Role of the Child/Human Binary in the Production of Anti-Black Racism" (2018); and the Georgetown Law Center on Poverty and Inequality's publication *Girlhood Interrupted: The Erasure of Black Girls' Childhood* (2017).

5   From the Oxford English Dictionary: To turn or lead away, entice, seduce, *from* one to whom service or allegiance is due. To seduce from allegiance or duty, induce to desert; to render disaffected; to pervert or corrupt in regard

bastardize, bestialize, brutalize, canker, cheapen, corrupt, debase, degrade, demean, demoralize, deprave, deteriorate, pervert, and ravish. And yet, you are juridically unrapable.[6]

* * *

What is it about the Black female and femme that incites such violence?[7] This violence that boils down to the act of division—where partition is the instrument of invention.[8] They are inventing a New World and you are its dexterous blueprint. The year is 1787. The law's acrobatics contend that you have no will and can neither give nor withhold consent.[9] As property you have no right to legal recourse. You are a

---

of allegiance or duty to others. To seduce from virtue or morality; to pervert, deprave, or corrupt morally; *esp.* to corrupt or deprave by intemperance, or sensual indulgence. To seduce (a woman) from chastity. To vilify, damage in reputation; to depreciate, disparage. To damage or spoil in quality.

6   Saidiya Hartman, *Scenes of Subjection: Terror, Slavery, and the Making of Nineteenth-Century America* (1997).

7   This violence is at times particular to female anatomy and at others applies to Black femme embodiements and expressions broadly. For my purposes, I try to think of Black femmeness and femaleness in coherence without collapsing one into the other. For more on the Black female and femme, see Hortense Spillers, "Mama's Baby, Papa's Maybe: An American Grammar Book" (1987); C. Riley Snorton, *Black on Both Sides: A Racial History of Trans Identity* (2017); Jessica Marie Johnson, *Wicked Flesh: Black Women, Intimacy, and Freedom in the Atlantic World* (2020); Omise'eke Natasha Tinsley, "Black Atlantic, Queer Atlantic: Queer Imaginings of the Middle Passage" (2008); Omise'eke Natasha Tinsley, *Ezili's Mirros: Imagining Black Queer Genders* (2018); Kara Keeling, *The Witch's Flight: The Cinematic, the Black Femme and the Image of Common Sense* (2007). See also Treva Carrie Ellison's "Black Femme Praxis and the Promise of Black Gender" (2019).

8   Hortense Spillers's use of the term "atomization" comes to mind here in that it attends to the violent material partition of the Black female flesh, alongside, at the level of grammar, epistemology, and ontology the violence of being an unsolvable paradox.

9   As an enslaved girl you were subjected to a regime of "institutionalized rape" and a colonial sexual economy in which you were physically, structurally, and legally vulnerable to acts of sexual violence from all men. Legally, rape was a legitimate use of property. As Hartman explains, fertility figured as a form of "speculative capital" that slaveholders could actualize by enacting a myriad of sexual and reproductive terrors upon girls and women within childbearing age.

Black girl and therefore always willing. A metaphysically inexhaustible reservoir, your body is "a form of infinitely malleable lexical and biological matter, a plastic upon which projects of humanization and animalization rest."[10] Your flesh is modernity's definitional site. Without you, how could they invent themselves rightful creators and inheritors of the New World?

The year is 1787. According to the law of *partus sequitur ventrum* any child born of your body inherits your legal status as "Slave."[11] This law is the mother of the New World and your womb is its anchor. This law ensures a steady and self-reproducing population of "slaves" in case the transnational trafficking of humans is ever to be prohibited. It guarantees that long after your mammary glands dry out not a single descendent of yours will be a rights-bearing subject—even if they are the afterlife of rape. This logic of there-will-always-be-more is a legal whirlpool making you and the life of your budding womb into slavery's insurance policy.

Dispensable and indispensable, you creator of Black life, are the prototype of the subhuman.[12] You are the prerequisite to their iteration of the human. They need you.[13] This need for a subhuman is the

---

The institution of slavery—and by extension the modernity that it ushered into maturity—depended on the creation of Blackness as abject, both materially (a steady and self-reproducing slave population) and ontologically (to define their "humanity" against the non-being of the "slave"). The legalization of *partus sequitur ventrem* utilized the doubling of the biological and ontological in the realm of birth to produce both.

10 Zakiyyah Iman Jackson, "Losing Manhood: Animality and Plasticity in the (Neo)Slave Narrative," *Qui Parle* 25, no. 1–2 (2016): 95–136.

11 For work that deals with *partus sequitur ventrem* and enslaved women's reproductive lives, see Jennifer L. Morgan, "Partus Sequitur Ventrem: Law, Race and Reproduction in Colonial Slavery" (2018) and *Laboring Women: Reproduction and Gender in New World Slavery* (2004). See also Christina Sharpe, *In the Wake: On Blackness and Being* (2016).

12 For more on this, see Sylvia Wynter "Unsettling the Coloniality of Being/Power/Truth/Freedom: Towards the Human, After Man, Its Overrepresentation—An Argument" (2003) and Alexander Weheliye, *Habeas Viscus: Racializing Biopolitics and Black Feminist Theories of the Human* (2014).

13 In his book *The Repeating Island* (1992), Antonio Benitez-Rojo imagines that Western capital accumulation is birthed from the Caribbean womb. In his poetic rendition, "The Atlantic is today the Atlantic (The navel of

Achilles' heel of modernity since, paradoxically, you are the source of the Black life whose brutalization shapes the meaning and content of their humanity. Too much hinges on your womb and their ability to delineate the life that flows through it as less than human. This desperate need to control your womb is the father of American rape culture. Fortifying and fertilizing the nation from the inside out, rape becomes the first instrument of our political order.[14]

This is how the fathers of the Enlightenment invent a world in which their humanity depends on your permanent and inheritable exclusion from humanity. It is an attempt to predestine the Black life *yet to come*. The year is 1787. At the advent of modernity your womb is the frontier of a global war over who will control the future. This sustained occupation to discipline, extort, cull, and otherwise control the Black female/femme and her body is the first world war of the modern world. This war is a means to an end. It is one strategy of a loftier scheme to govern the Black womb in order to yoke Black futurity.[15]

You and your baby girl are its frontier.

Ajar—you are the revolving door to the inception and destruction of our current order.

What are you to do? You who *belong to yourself and each other*.

* * *

capitalism) because Europe, in its mercantilist laboratory, conceived of the project of inseminating the Caribbean womb with the blood of Africa; the Atlantic is today the Atlantic ... because it is the painfully delivered child of the Caribbean, whose vagina was stretched between continental clamps ... All Europe pulling on the forceps to help the birth of the Atlantic ... After the blood and salt water spurts, quickly sew up the torn flesh and apply the antiseptic tinctures, the gauze and surgical plaster; then the febrile wait through the forming of a scar: suppurating, always suppurating" (5).

14   This argument extends to the systematized rape of Indigenous women. For more on this subject see Audra Simpson's "The State is a Man: Therese Spence, Loretta Saunders, and the Gender of Settler Sovereignty" (2016) and Stéphane Guimont Marceu's "Approaching Violence against Indigenous Women in the Americas from Relation, Intersectional and Multiscalar Perspectives" (2019).

15   To control black futurity—and by extension—all futurity. The flesh wound is a seed. Seeds, like us, are not singular, but collective entities belonging to a tribe of before and after.

Doctor Jones testifies you were born dead. *The windpipe was cut through from side to side and the other large vessels were separated*, but you were never alive to begin with, the doctor is certain of this, it is a fact, based on your general size and the amount of hair on your head. Maybe it was the log or the tumble down the stairs that did it. The second doctor, Dr. Foulke, agrees that infanticide is off the table since it is not possible to manslaughter the deceased. Based on the size of your outer limbs you could not have been full term. By his estimation likely closer to six or seven months. Sure, a dead infant might bleed upon having its throat cut, he assures the council, because you see, *the blood of children is much finer than the blood of men.*

And since Dr. Foulke went to all the trouble of preserving you, the jury ought to judge for themselves the spectacle of your small limbs. You are *brought in a large glass jar . . . with it a pair of forceps to* if deemed necessary *extract it.* All eyes flock to the jar, past the glass, through the amber liquid to you, little sister, the pale morsel nodding imperceptibly, suspended in a capsule where you are so sterile that time cannot touch you. Splayed in a wide prayer, the eternal eyes of your corpse rattle the living men arbitrating the facts of your death-birth.[16]

When it was all said and done, when the jury left and the court closed, did Dr. Foulke keep you in his study on a low shelf beside the jaw of a rhinoceros—both collectible and instructional model—so that those whose mouths went dry at the site of you could get a closer look? Preserved in an interval, who was your first friend there and was it more or less lonely to collect dust in communion with canines and amphibians? When none were watching did you rest your eyes? Did Dr. Foulke bequeath you to your mother, so she could bury you and return you to your maker in the kingdom of matrilineal descent where she is bound one day to join you *in pleasures without measure, without end?*[17] Did you become the soil

16 This evokes for me the Elizabeth Alexander's essay "Can You Be BLACK and Look at This? Reading the Rodney King Video(s)" (1994) Alexander poses this question in the context of King's murder, questioning the role of the photographer who videotaped the brutal beating. "Who could watch and videotape such an event? What is the role of looking?" she probes.

17 Phillis Wheatley Peters, *Poems on Various Subjects, Religious and Moral* (1773), 71. This line is taken from the poem "A Funeral Poem on the Death of C.E. an Infant of Twelve months." The full line reads, "Delightful infant, nightly visions give thee to our arms, and we with joy receive, we fain would clasp the

where the living dance as they lay you to sleep for a retreat at the river's craned neck, one day perhaps to surface again, to collide with the foot of a shovel, a dead end, as once was her cervix, an archeological relic, nearly decapitated and premature? It is highly unlikely. You are too valuable an asset to forgo, so perhaps you are warehoused in the basement of a museum awaiting the eternal rest of decomposition.[18]

You, the little sister who did not taste air, waiting for this, the most rudimentary of natural rights, to unfurl, atom by atom.

You, of the millions dead before alive, child of the starry-eyed tribe born to children, tribe of the miscarried maroons and infants unzipped by the one who birthed you. Cellular fledglings of intricately choreographed proteins undone by teas brewed of Peacock Flower, Pennyroyal, Rue, Blue Cohosh, Poinciana, Savin, Quinquina, and Tansy.[19] This world whose fragile flowers unhinge the unborn from their mother's uterine lining, sequestering the seashore within her, liquefying her interior address until she becomes the season of the hemoglobin monsoons. All the while, keeping her alive in this world where flesh is the alter of being.[20]

Whereas you, little sister, the flowers dissolve. You, who enter the revolving door of surrogacy the tiniest of bubbles and come out the other end without a body. You, whose tender body is slayed upon arrival. You, the secret born out of sight, clandestine teachers in the school of how to celebrate the death of an origin, incognito ancestors,

---

Phantom to our breast, the *Phantom* flies, and leaves the soul unblest. To yon bright regions let your faith ascend, prepare to join your dearest infant friend, in pleasures without measure, without end."

18   Dr. Foulke tells the court, "I have compared this child with several others which I have preserved, as I have them of almost every period of conception."

19   These are some of the plants used by Black and Indigenous women to induce abortions. For more on the use of abortifacient plants, see Joscelyn Garner's *Bleeding and Breeding* series (2011) and Londa Schiebinger's *Plants and Empire: Colonial Bioprospecting in the Atlantic World* (2004).

20   Its profound that humans have no intrinsic way to control our internal reproductive processes and therefore must turn to interspecies relations with plants that remarkably give us some control over our reproductive processes, the power to prevent pregnancy, induce sterility, or terminate emerging human life without terminating the life of the carrier. Cultivating them, we in turn become a part of the reproductive life cycles of the very plants that can increase our reproductive autonomy.

disciples of our unknown beyond, occasionally hold ceremony for the living, the wilderness surpassed behind.

* * *

They all get what they want. The Bartholomews get their show. Perhaps Mrs. B wears a new wool dress sewn just for the occasion. The jurors proudly serve as arbitrators of justice in the name of the almighty, the doctors and coroners as experts in delineating the margin between life and death. Schaffer, too, gets what he wants, you in the palm of his hand, in the lot, and later, your hands an extension of his, a jolt at the top of the stairs, a cut where there may have been a pulse.[21]

And you, dear Alice, get one last look at the nameless flesh of your flesh. They call her *it* and *bastard-child* of debauchment and formaldehyde traveling with no feet of her own, head bobbing; how unfortunate, the afterlife of rape, to have never known the ease of sleep nor the mercy of a grave.

The year is 1787. You have not said a word and I am worried for you. I imagine you anxiously picking your cuticles down to the meat. I picture your blood staining the cuffs of your blouse a relentless maroon.

The fact of the matter is your freedom pivots on this, the meat and marrow of the production: Was *it* ever alive? Did *it* cry?[22] The jury decides. If yes, you shall be denied the dividend of air. But if the thing at the edge of her larynx never chimed, if you are the kind of creature to carnage a cadaver, then you are neither innocent nor a threat to anything but yourself and the deceased. Then, and only then, may you live.

Following both doctors' consensus that she was born dead, the attorney general recaps the staggering evidence against you: your persistent denial of the pregnancy, *having made not the least provision of cloaths for the infant*, delivering alone rather than inviting the assistance of [your]

---

21 Despite being named many times, John Schaffer, who had a less than favorable reputation in Philadelphia, was not present at the trial. This is not surprising since the crimes done onto Alice were never part of the conversation.

22 All three Bartholomews testified that they *did not* hear the infant cry. A cry would have been the only irrefutable and unequivocal proof the infant was born living.

mistress, the cut, of course, and finally your *endeavor to conceal it, by placing it wrapped up under a large roll of linen, in a trunk.*

After a three-hour recess the jury rules you guilty of murder and you are sentenced to death.

It is Wednesday and, as far as you are concerned, this fate is final. Most likely they transport you back to prison. You don't know yet that some combination of Schaffer's reputation and your "naivete" and the lifelike corpse has spooked the jury, unearthing a force of benevolent remorse. Jointly, the twelve jurors write to Thomas McKean, the chief justice, a plea to spare your life. The letter reads, in part, *"Alice being of tender age ignorant and unexperienced was seduced to the perpetration of the said crime by the persuasions and instigation of the father of the child your petitioners are desirous that the life of the said Alice may be saved."*[23]

That Saturday Thomas McKean writes to Benjamin Franklin:

> *Philadelphia April 21, 1787:*
>
> *Sir,*
>
> *In consideration of the tender years of the mother named Alice Clifton, being only sixteen years of age, and of her situation in life, being a Mute Slave, illiterate and ignorant; and out of respect to the Petition of the Jury, who convicted her, We beg leave to recommend her, to Your Excellency and the Supreme Executive Council, as an object of Mercy.*
>
> *Your most obedient humble*
>
> *Tho McKean*

---

23 Note, the jury's pivot—the shift from convicting Alice of murder, to begging, quite literally, for her mercy—lays bare the distinction between the logic of the verdict and the logic of amnesty. The two logics cohere to form the following narrative: Alice committed a crime but did not exercise criminal will due to both her age and her actions being ventriloquized by Schaffer, "the father." Alice doesn't have to uphold the doctrine of "perfect submission" described by Saidiya Hartman in the essay "Seduction and the Ruses of Power," because the rapist and ventriloquist is not Alice's master or his son, but a white man with whom she has no kind of relation or obligation. In a way, Schaffer betrays the fragile "family romance" through which the Bartholomews likely imagine their enslavement of the young Alice as a benevolent relation. By virtue of this romance, the betrayal extends beyond Alice to the Bartholomews, who *were all so affected that they could not bear to remain in the room* of their home, where Alice sat with the infant.

On these grounds Benjamin Franklin, supreme executive council, repeals the verdict.[24]

And you, dear Alice, do not sway from atop the gallows. You, the object of mercy, live. You of us, the sum who did not die, not right away.[25] I don't know how long or where, and certainly not *how*. Only that you infiltrated my own shapeless grief, asking *What has the moon's waning got to do with skimming myself from the surface of my body? If the only prayer granted is that my knees have stopped behaving as magnets, the left knee no longer pulling the right knee into its orbit—What does that leave of the bewildering intimacy of sinking into myself like a wick into wax?*

* * *

Alice, when I dream your dream I think of the groves' umbilical exchange of data.[26] The dream goes something like this: You pass through me. I am a pasture and you are the bird. I am a bird and you are the sun. Our bygone babies are winged. The ones who lived to cast moving shadows, but nonetheless one day bounced overboard, escaped to the caves, and caught bullets with their flesh are the snowcapped

---

24 It is noteworthy that this exchange arbitrating Alice's fate occurs in the two days before the completion of *The Constitution of the Philadelphia Society for Promoting the Abolition of Slavery and the Relief of Free Negros Unlawfully Held in Bondage.* On May 2, 1787, three weeks after she gives birth, the official statement is made that Franklin, who also served as the society's president, pardoned Alice. The fact that "leaders of the nation" such as McKean and Franklin arbitrated over cases like Alice's illustrates the centrality of Black women's reproductive lives to the project/s of early America.

25 June Jordan, *Some of Us Did Not Die* (2002).

26 Alice, can you believe that trees suckle their young through subterranean networks? Root to root, elder trees transmit messages, warnings and nutrients to the young and vulnerable saplings of the grove through something akin to a collective mammary-nervous system. Their life force is continuous and distributed in accordance with the laws of symbiosis, a biologically ingrained impulse favoring the survival of the collective. Imagine millions of Black girls, women, femmes, and queers as a grove, likewise tapped into an transcorporeal network retaining memory and redistributing resilience. This life force that is continuous when we love, care, tell stories, and dare to imagine. These instinctual and learned acts toward collective survival are at their core rituals of mothering. Love is the practice of freedom. Freedom is at the core of all being.

mountaintops that shoulder the sky. The mothers we lost are our song and we are the flock. [27] Together, we are impenetrable since a flock has no outside, no inside, like water, like smoke, like wind, like fire. Unlike our flesh bodies, you can't point at the flock's interior. Your finger is also her heart, is the eye and winged timber of gospel. I am the nest and you are the tree. You are the soil and we are the grove.

In your dream the unborn thrusts her tiny feet, soft as naked pecans, into my sleeping face. I take it to mean the wound is a collective hole. [28] That we are sisters as are our seedling ancestors who did not cry. Awakened by the unborn, the scream you deprived of breath takes refuge in my lungs. Swallowing mouthfuls of air, I give it free rein. [29] For you beloveds, the glowing pearls at my center.

---

27 Black feminist writers have turned to analogies such as swarms and flocks to describe Black female, femme, and/or queer socialites by centering the aspect of collective interdependency and symbiosis. For examples of flocking as relational framework see adrienne marie brown's *Emergent Strategy: Shaping Change, Changing Worlds* (2017) and Treva Carrie Ellison's "Black Femme Praxis and the Promise of Black Gender" (2019).

28 See Evelynn Hammonds's "Black (W)holes and the Geometry of Black Female Sexuality" (1997) as well as Rizvanna Bradley's work in "Living in the Absence of a Body: The (Sus)Stain of Black Female (W)holeness" (2016).

29 We have gathered at the Ashara Ekundayo gallery in Oakland, California. This *is* the ceremony that must be found (Sylvia Wynter "The Ceremony Must be Found, After Humanism" [1984].) The invitation comes through word of mouth. For us there is no way to prepare, since none beside the women in white know what is to follow. They are the ones who break our waters with their song. Every eye comes undone. Each griever is subsumed in contractions of her own sorrow, the unreckoned, old and new, a collective release amidst strangers. We fall to our knees and holler. We tear down the wallpaper. The grief doulas hold us and sing. They bathe us with white water and bouquets of basil, these guardians of the things that weigh us down, the grief we inherit or pick up along the way and otherwise risk passing on. The year is 2019, the season is spring. The occasion is *Black Women Grieving*, an episode of Amara Tabor-Smith's *House Full of Black Women* series, a ritual performance project with separate but connected site specific episodes set in Oakland, California, over a seven-year period. More ceremony than performance, she calls it "conjure art"—integrating where the art practice and the spiritual practice cannot be separated. Amara tells me her art is guided by the belief "that Black women need each other. That we have a lot of grief to release and are worthy of protection and love." For more I suggest watching *Blatant: A Forum on Art, Joy and Rage with Amara Tabor-Smith, Ashara Ekundayo, and Savannah Shange* (2020) hosted by the Museum of the African Diaspora.

If the soundest sanctuary from this world is the spiritworld thawing within me then why do I outwake the morning aching to name you without having to name you?[30] You who are permanent residents of my interior, the lawless island where nothing is prey, where I go to shed the sunset robe of my sorrow and spread my skin, where my breasts are stargazers done guarding the citadel of a body I lay no claim to. Hollowed of matter, the inside world is engorged. I, the inside, am boundless and touch the outside only through the membrane of my interior; that nameless crossroad where we assemble to marvel as the untethered hand of the afterlife pares away our many husks, beneath each pilfered flesh a horizon, and beneath that a stone heavy as a wet star, a light pilgrimaging the cosmos anonymously, untouched and touching nothing.

30   Numerous scholars, including most notably Hortense Spillers, Saidiya Hartman, and Katherine McKittrick, have observed that one of slavery's monstrosities is the mutilation of motherhood. Orlando Patterson argued the constant threat of losing one's kin cast Black life into a state of social death, meaning, the enslaved and their descendants are born biologically alive but socially deceased. I think of it less like social death and more as the systematic wounding of the Black social body. Black mothers become central enemies of the state because of our capacity to heal, through care and love, a wound whose festering presence anchors the project of white supremacist modernity. We are the main destination of this studied, practiced wounding. As with torture, the state's maiming and killing of Black people is secondary, the primary aim is to break the spirit of the living left behind and thereby undermine the spirit of the collective. The life force of the collective enables the individual to survive the fatal aftereffect of the grief that follows losing one's kin to anti-Black violence, what Christen Smith terms "sequelae." This communal immunitary impulse—to love, care, protect, and defend with ferocity is medicine for the wounded Black social body. The opposition has staked its claim on futurity by continuing a war on the entirety of Black social life. In stark opposition, our capacity to move as one, as flock, as grove, to nurture, heal, and immunize against impending violence threatens the wrath of the state.

In 1787 the state's targeting of Black kinship relations includes systematized rape and a global economy bent on separating families, as it did in centuries past and to follow. In 2021 it looks like uninvestigated disappearances of Black girls and women, police violence, mass incarceration, borders and immigration policies designed to keep the most vulnerable of the world's population in closer proximity death, US gun culture broadly—including Black-on-Black violence that is precipitated by state's investment in ensuring a large chunk of the US's Black population lives in poverty, which is to say, at the brink of life, and therefore fighting for our lives—and extends as far as the transnational weapons industry which produces the unnatural means by which so many across the globe have and will continue to die.

Newly husked, I discover I am not my mother's daughter. Unmasked, our children, born and unborn, are not our children.[31] They are stepping-stones of the divine unruly. Despite the heart's insistence, loss is not loss. You sleep, I wake. You flock, we grove. Yesterday's unburied are here embalmed in a language wearing the emerald dress of a coffin. This is all I know to do, to build from flesh and discourse an altar at the open entry of my heart. To crown you the open sky through which every leg of light must wade before resting its tired feet.

"the presence among us / of the unfenced Is"[32]

"breaking hard against things, turning to burning reason
this is you girl, this is the poem no woman ever write
for a woman because she 'fraid to touch this river
boiling like a woman in she sleep . . ."[33]

---

31   Khalil Gibran wrote, "Your children are not your children. They are the sons and daughters of Life's longing for itself. They come through you but not from you . . . You are the bows from which your children as living arrows are sent forth. The archer sees the mark upon the path of the infinite, and He bends you with His might that His arrows may go swift and far." The real power of kinship (social and biological) has nothing to do with lineage or racial categories but rather the chaotic choreography of spirit-matter begetting spirit-matter.

32   This line is from the poem "All Praises," which appears in *How to Carry Water: Selected Poems of Lucille Clifton* (2020), gathered and tended by aracelis girmay.

33   These lines are taken from page 7 of Dionne Brand's book *No Language Is Neutral* (1990).

If I Am Ever Less Than a Mountain

Dominique Matti

"God made stones for memory. He builds a mountain
Himself when he wants things not forgot."

—Langston Hughes, "Hoodoo," *The Book of Negro Folklore*

"and if I am ever less than a mountain / for your definite brothers and sisters
/ let the rivers wash over my head / let the sea take me for a spiller of seas"

—Lucille Clifton, "Lost Baby Poem"

"and / grandmother / if I be you / let me not forget to / work
hard / trust the Gods / love my children and / wait"

—Lucille Clifton, "Harriet"

I.

invocation of the foremothers:

I am a memory cataloguing more. A portrait of shapeshifting faces. A moment in a legacy of moments. This is a disjointed story. Let these stories co-occur. Stack. Weave. Collapse. Into my body. Make and unmake me. Reach past me in all conceivable directions. This is a blood story that bleeds into others. All the mothers before me. The mothers I am and am not. Have been and will be.

II.

the foremothers speak:

No mother knows what to do, really. We are all just trying to listen. Listen in the now—through the chorus of voices—to the past, to the future, for what is needed. Our mothers can only tell us what they heard when they pressed their ear up to the roar, under the distortion of the noise of their circumstances. The noise of no money or volatile skin or a tired body or a nervous system jittered by tragedy. The loud boom of love. Its persistent humming after-buzz. Blessings all, and terrible against the knocking of the world. Our mothers play whisper down the lane, riffing on the recitations of the generations before. So much is lost in translation. We inherit their long cascade of trying. This cocking of the head and pressure on the heart, this angling to conceive the incalculable—the original whisper and the last.

III.

their daughter continues:

My foremothers whisper what they know into my head, and by grace I whisper back my children's chatter.

Does the moon love us? Can you bless me? Will you tell me a story? Why did you have me? Can we make a song together? Can you turn on the light? I'm really tired. Do you have magic powers? Is god a bad word? I don't like it when you talk like that. What's my magic power? How do you know?

Were the primordial whispers a child's *how?* and a mother's *how?* right back?

IV.

chorus:

Sometimes I just want to say to my child, "I don't know any better than you, baby."

What can prepare us for something as large as a *life?*

V.

their daughter continues:

The second and third time I found myself due to have a child, I did it. Because I felt too much with death, and I believed life would be gentler with me than death had been. But life and death are a two-headed creature. They love each other. Hold the door for one another. Don't split or cancel out or come apart, despite the prying of humankind.

Life exposes us to death, and death opens us to life. The abortion came with its open doors and the births came with their closed ones. A series of days to breathe into and through, beneath piles of bricks of grief. A series of days I could no longer return to, though bursting with life, still, in my heart. There is living and dying in everything. I tend life now, under the haze of burning cities. And I know the fertilizing quality of ash.

Memory simultaneously preserves life and signifies what is gone. I am dutiful in my remembering. Even torturous toward myself in it. I don't remember much of my childhood. But I try to hold on to what came before, all the living and dying that had to happen for me to be here, living and dying, too. It makes my existence feel too large to take up, sometimes. And other times—when I situate myself in the long story—I feel just small enough to get by.

In December 2012, in Connecticut, my mother-in-law called me to tell me that she had seen in a dream that I was pregnant and would choose to have an abortion. All of it was news to me, but she was not ill-informed. There was so much of that two-headed creature in all the aching after. The breath of it still catches in my throat. How the heavens might inform but do not intervene in an ending's course. Like our mothers, the gods can only tell us what they know. Perhaps just to say that they are with us in the dark, when we can't see or hear or feel them. Perhaps to say: *Don't hide from us what we have already borne witness to.* To say: *May no private shame endure between us.* And yet. We hear what we hear through the noise of our circumstances.

At dawn on the first day of 2014, I laughed out the last of my midnight sobbing about it. Erupted it out of my body. Fell to the floor with it. Hysterically. A few months after that came the news of my next child. Life, I thought (at last!), had come to seal the deal. To deliver me from death. To cure me of my grieving. But grief is a living condition.

During that pregnancy and after and during the next pregnancy and after, I was afraid most of the time. I felt indebted to the dead, that the cost of my no was that each yes after must be carried out in a manner that justified my no. That all the things that informed my no—what I felt I could not do or be or sort out or make sense of or manage—must resolve themselves rapidly or who was I to have these children? But there is nothing tidy or immaculate in mothering. Just listening.

In 2018 I started speaking to spirits because I couldn't sustain all the questions of mothering and living and dying on the intel of the living alone. It started with candles and prayers and then visitations in dreams and then cards and then plants and then feelings and voices and colors. A song on the radio. Numbers on the clock. Words leaking from my fingertips, guided hands. In one dream, my great grandmother lent me her body to teach me a lesson. She was a midwife. In her cabin, a pregnant woman was doubled over in the kitchen, clutching her ripe belly, ready. My great grandmother was propping her own feet up over a basin of steaming water. She was wrapping her aching legs with some kind of poultice. All that as if to say: *You got to listen to yourself about what you need, too. There is nothing that cannot wait.*

In October 2019, during a grief ritual in North Carolina, Sobande Greer instructed everyone in the room to intuitively choose a colored mat. Once we had chosen our mats, she revealed to us an Orisha, a geographical direction, and an affliction. The mat my body led me to was "pleasure blocked by guilt." With wailing women all around me, I denied myself the pleasure of crying in company. But later that night, I was summoned from my sleep by a stream of quiet tears about it.

In April 2020, at our respective homes in Philadelphia, my friend Desiree Thompson laid hands on me by using a magnolia branch as a surrogate for my body. Under her guidance, I was in my bathtub, singing, when my great grandmother spoke through the water. She told me to write down what she said and to place it on my altar for remembering.

VI.
the foremother spoke:
Life is good!

Death is kind!
Everything is a mercy!
Thank god!
That baby is safe.
You are not alone in anything.

VII.

her daughter continues:

Thank god. I am not alone in anything. Not life or death or trying.

VIII.

closing prayer for the foremothers:

thank you.
enough now.
sleep in my bones and blood.
you are the knowing that my body
will not unknow.
in this way you live in death.
in this way your death survives.
but it is my turn, now, to listen.
and to answer.

IX.

closing prayer for the ancestor child:

on my best days as a mother,
you crack me open like an egg.
make room
for all that is,
for your bodiless body,
everything, everyplace, every time.

My Nothings

Ama Codjoe

You, who have bowed your head, shed
another season of antlers at my feet, for years
you fall asleep to the lullabies of dolls,
cotton-stuffed and frayed, ears damp with sleep
and saliva, scalps knotted with yarn, milk-breath,
and yawns. Birth is a torn ticket stub, a sugar
cone wrapped in a paper sleeve, the blackest
ice. It has been called irretrievable, a foreign
coin, the moon's slip, showing, a pair
of new shoes rubbing raw your heel.
I lose the back of my earring and bend
the metal in such a way as to keep it
fastened to me. In the universe where we are
strangers, you kick with fury, impatient
as grass. I have eaten all your names.
In this garden you are blue ink, baseball cap
wishbone, pulled teeth, wet sand, hourglass.
There are locks of your hair in the robin's nest
and clogging the shower drain. You, who are
covered in feathers, who have witnessed birth
give birth to death and watched death suck
her purple nipple. You long for a mother
like death's mother, want to nurse until drunk
you dream of minnows swimming
through your ears—their iridescence causing
you to blink, your arms twitching.
Even while you sleep I feed you.

Then They Came for Our Wombs

Sandra Guzmán

They greeted me with lifted skirts flaunting their glory. They commanded, pointing to their pussies one by one, "Pídele la bendición a tu tía!" I was ten years old, returning to my ancestral village in Borikén for a summer vacation a year after my mom and four siblings immigrated north. I giggled and fake screamed in horror, unable to look away from their untamed splendor. My tías had the opposite of Brazilian waxes—no clips came near their glory. Titi Himilce, Titi Minerva, and Titi Aida, Caribbean Indigenous and Black women with names of Iberian princesses, Roman, and Ethiopian goddesses, teased me about how Nueva Yol was making me soft.

"Actually, I live in New Jersey," I'd correct them, both hands on my skinny hips, voice filled with young-girl hubris. Their cackles sounded like thundering rainforest rivers on their way to meet the Caribbean Sea. It made no difference to them where I lived. Any Boricua who left pa'lla fuera—even if they immigrated[1] to Chicago, Philadelphia, or Connecticut—went to the same place: Nueva Yol. They were happy I was home. It was all that mattered. Love sparkled in their eyes each and every time they laid eyes on me.

Their playful welcomes remained the same as the years salt and peppered their hair and wrinkles never touched their sun-kissed skin. I could count on them flashing me, pointing to their hairy pussies, and reminding me that those were my *real* tías. It was a gag and I loved it. I would wait for the hoots and the howls, mouths wide open, heads tilting back, followed by raucous, joyous roars that seemed to come from a place deep inside, a space I've come to learn is called freedom.

With these audacious greetings my three tías taught me important life lessons:

The womb is the origin of the universe
Wombs are sacred.
This is from where I come.
My pussy is my glory.
Enjoy.

My three tías were lawless women. They walked like they owned the village, even if their ancestors were brought in chains from the African continent, sold, and brutally stamped in a beastly practice called carimbó, a hot iron brand on parts of the body evidencing that the slaver paid taxes on the human cargo they purchased from one of the slaver auctioning blocks in the cobblestone streets of Old San Juan. My tías walked regal, even if they were landless, displaced from their ancestral lands that we know as Guainía, lands occupied and "owned" by bushwhacking settlers from Spain and Corsica. They were proud women, even if they lived in the most pitiful wood shack in town, a home they audaciously called La Mansión, which not even Hurricane Maria's Category 5 winds could topple in 2017. They strutted their big asses through the winding dirt roads of el barrio de Santo Domingo from Guayanilla to Macaná, with heads held high, loving their bodies in all ways and every day. They were the envy of their world—proud Prietas who lived free in a colonial system that tried to oppress them in every way it could.

They possessed a brazen realness, a wildness that irked judgmental and "classier" women folk in town who called them, behind their backs, mujeres ordinarias and cafres, the Puerto Rican word for nigger. My tías paid no mind to the petty and petit bourgeoisie who suffered all sorts of indignities ascending the island's colonial middle class. They gave a middle finger to the colonized gaze that labeled them vulgar and attempted to diminish their lives and to bring them and their bodies into modern-day societal submission.

* * *

Dancing was a communal ritual in the village, and my three titis were well-known for their skills. They danced on the one, like real home-grown salseras. All week they prepped for the weekend ceremonies under the moon and dazzling stars. They kept their hair in rollers during the day and slept with their tight curls and kinks wrapped and bobby-pinned round their roundheads in dubi dubis. The trick temporarily straightened their hair for the weekend bailes with live bands, bailes they seldom missed. They walked barefoot through sugarcane fields on moonless nights, shoes in hand, torches made with cupey seeds lighting the way; they hiked a mile up the rainforest mountain to an outdoor joint called Los Cuatro Vientos. Once on the zenith, on a clear night, you make out the magnificent sinuous Caribbean coastline as far west as Guayama and east to the tip of Cabo Rojo. And up there so very high, so close to heaven, you could get lost gazing at the luminous Milky Way galaxy. Other weekends, they'd trek downhill in their pretty party dresses, past the only gas station in town, through the platanal, to another outdoor spot called La Terraza. And always, they ended their nights in an afterhours dive under an old mango tree called El Carajo. After a night of dancing guaguancó, merengue, and sensual boleros, sweat and humidity stuck to their bodies, and their pelo lacio was transformed back to its beautiful essence, locks that resembled wild roseleaf bramble bushes whose leaves and roots eased menstrual cramps, morning sickness, labor pains, and cured their babies, and sometimes me, of bouts of diarrhea after eating too many ripe mangoes.

In those days, it was tradition that all the children ask every grown up they encountered—relative or not—for a blessing. This was a spiritual contract, a sign of respeto, and a request to be graced with the love and protection from things seen and unseen by people older than you. This custom spiritually and physically tethered all the adults in the community to all the children. It is no small matter for children to feel the grace of adults, to walk around town asking adults to keep them in their hearts and in their prayers. It was a time filled with breathtaking goodness. This rite felt ancient. What I remember were magical incantations trailing and embracing me as I ran through the lush green meadows with my cousins Norka, Cinthia, Toro, Pito,

Negro, Sari, and a neighbor, Kiko. We chased neon-colored butterflies, ate wild mangoes and guayabas from trees, quenched our thirst with chinas, toronjas, and cocos, bolted from raging bulls bent on goring us, rode wild horses with names like Pendejo and Petra. A trail of kids and a trail of bendiciones humming after us: *Que la virgen los favoresca y los acompañe y los libre de malos y peligros, que Dios y todos los santos y santas los bendigan, que las diosas y los dioses los protejan. Vayan con Dios. Amen. Ashé. Ahó.*

But my tías' pussy blessings were next level and thus felt even more ancient. Titi Himilce, Titi Minerva, and Titi Aida, who smelled like recao, coconut oil, lemon, dirt, tabaco, guanábana, cerveza, and love, infused me with a dangerous freedom that held me together when the world outside the village and the United States tried to break me.

* * *

My tías had a ritual of reading newspapers back to back every day, even if the papers they read were old. Many times, they clipped important stories and glued them into an old spiral notebook, bringing the clippings out and sharing them with neighbors. One old clipping whose headline I will never forget: "Rockefeller Compra la Playa de Guayanilla." *They stole our beaches*, Titi Himilce declared. It was not until decades later that I connected the sale of our beaches to the building of the refineries that now dot and poison what was once the most spectacular beach in the Caribbean. Titi Himilce, the eldest, whose high cheekbones reached the clouds and who had the singing voice of Nina Simone, seethed during her newspaper reading sessions. She had a daily ritual of sweeping the patch of dirt in front of La Mansión every evening. Like a shaman who smudges his space to cleanse and release love and light, she swept the red clay earth until it glistened. After she finished, she'd sit on a rocking chair and admire her grand work and read old newspapers out loud to herself and neighbors who happened to stop by, café colao in hand. Years later, I realized that she was the unofficial village newspaper reader. She passed away from a heart attack at seventy-five, sitting on a chair, her dark, muscular, long legs speckled with varicose veins from standing too long and working too much. Feet stretched out, toes touching the warm turquoise of her favorite beach, Caña Gorda. She transitioned like a queen—a cold Medalla in one hand and *El Nuevo Día* in the other, as her four grand-children intermittently chased ghost crabs and built sandcastles around her. The majestic sea before her, welcoming her. Titi Himilce seeded my dream to be a writer during my visits to la tierra de los bravos. I would sit on the sparkling dirt floor and listen to her reading the news and to her insightful commentary. The brilliance of her analysis would rival any MSNBC pundit or PhD. She'd often pause dramatically and declare or remind me that when I grew up, I would *want* to be a journalist. "Ay gato encerrao," she'd warn. She read the erasure of our people—la gente humilde de barrio, del campo, la gente negra invis-ible—in the nation's papers and wanted me to be part of a generation that corrected the crooked narratives she got sick of reading day after day. She was a school cafeteria lady who sneaked extra mounds of rice and beans to kids she knew would not have dinner at night. She gave them secret containers filled with goodness to take home for mothers, fathers, abuelos and abuelas. No one went hungry in el barrio de Santo Domingo, thanks to the beloved cafeteria lady, my tía. Everyone in town knew too that in La Mansión there was always a cup of cafécito, a bite to eat, a story to hear, and a little moonshine to chase the bitter.

My aunties' scientific knowledge and life wisdom—and freedom—was not earned in academia but rather at the feet of the medicine women who raised them, root women who ran to their freedom and settled in a maroon settlement called Raja Larga. They learned the secrets of the universe from thousands of years of observation and practice. Their mothers and foremothers studied the sun, the moon, the night sky, ocean and wind currents, and the flora and flowers and fauna that sur-rounded them. They tended and foraged the land, harvested rivers and the sea. There were living, ancient encyclopedias. They were elegant storytellers and, because they loved for free, they were the most popu-lar women in the village.

They were godmothers to most of the children in town, though they never visited a church. No Jehovah's Witness, Catholic, Pentecostal, or Evangelical missionary dare knock on the door of the small shack where they were raised and continued to live, even after they took on lovers, married, and birthed ten babies between them to an assortment of gorgeous baby daddies and husbands.

They were the superheroes in my storybooks, goddesses who taught me that I, too, was a goddess.

* * *

Even after La Mansión got indoor plumbing, they continued to bathe in the hundreds of rivulets and streams crisscrossing the village. They also swam naked in the rivers and made love by the river's bend.

The matriarch of La Mansión, located at the base of a rainforest mountain in the southwest of the big island, was Emiliana De la Paz Pérez Santiago Santos. Guela Milla was tall, slim, with creamy skin and the highest cheekbones you'd ever seen on a human. A halo of wavy, white hair that she kept short made her look angelic and otherworldly. No one would ever suspect that the beatific abuela made and sold illegal pitorro to make a living. She drank a daily shot of her consecrated moonshine, the medicine she swore kept her strong. She was the grandma goddess that swam naked in the rivers until her last breath, just like her foremothers did. And she danced every day and sang boleros while cooking or pulling caillos from my hair. She *was* the village's best dancer, known for twirling, stepping, and shimmying on an eight-by-eleven-inch plank of wood at the center of the dance-hall without falling off. Ella bailaba hasta los anuncios. She was the light of the village, beloved by both paupers and princes.

Emiliana De la Paz Pérez Santiago, or Milla, lived the exploitation of both empires and did her part to end the hell they imported. One day while hiking a hill in Ceiba, I met an ex-political prisoner who spent two decades behind bars fighting for Puerto Rico's independence. When he learned that I was from la tierra de los bravos and was Milla's granddaughter, he kissed my hands and told me that she fed and stashed shotguns for local Macheteros. She never spoke about her underground liberation work or about the years she was the house slave of Los Castellares, a landowning, settler Spaniard family. She worked from the time she was twelve, before she got her first period, when her mother "gave" her to one of the richest families in town, who needed someone to help the new bride around the house. In colonial and post-slavery life in Puerto Rico, Native and African girls were given away to white families, and like kittens in a litter, the whites took their pick. In return, the girls got room and food, but they were never paid for the work they did in the house, nor were they sent to school. Only a lucky few were able to have kids and families of their own. They were abused in all ways. There was no dowry for Guela Milla. She was one less mouth to feed in her large family. Her twin, Panchita, stayed behind in El Barrial, and Guela Milla never talked about her either.

When she was twenty, Guela Milla met the love of her life, Atilano Rodriguez Colón, a muscular young fella who worked the cane and came from Raja Larga, a maroon village a few miles up la montaña. The old Spaniard patriarch gave my grandma and her new beau his toolshed, located next to his main house, where he housed his oxen and a cart. The holes of the walls of the dilapidated shed were so big that chickens jumped through them while being chased by the roosters roaming the property. The roosters followed the chickens into the house, and all were kicked out with Guela Milla's coconut palm broom. It was the patriarch's solution to keeping my abuela around to do the housework. The shed was close enough to the big house that Abuela could still cook and care for his wife, sister Olivia, and his five children while also taking care of her own growing brood. Abuela's last baby, Titi Aida, was born on one of the ox carts because she was busy cooking for the family and the midwife didn't arrive on time. Guela Milla lived and worked with the family for thirty-five years, and she never got paid a dime for her lifelong work in the big house. Once, on a river outing in el Rio Guayanés with my cousin Doel, I met the youngest son of the Castellar family who, upon seeing me, cried me a river remembering the kitchen love that my Guela Milla gifted him. "Tu abuela me enseñó lo que es el amor."

In 1950, when one of my grandfather's sisters immigrated to Queens, she gave the young couple their first home, a sharecropper house located closer to the edge of the mountain where our kin's placentas are planted. A few years later, my grandfather Papa Atilano died, leaving Guela Milla to fend for herself, her young son—my father, Miguel Antonio—and three daughters, one still nourishing from her breast. The Great Depression that had ravaged the North two decades earlier was still having its way with the colony. Hacienda Clementina, the town's cane plantation, owned by a Corsican settler family and the main employer of the village, where my father and many relatives worked, was on its last juice press.

My father was five years old when he began working in the same cane fields where his father and family worked. He handed out cups of cold water to dehydrated cane cutters. He got paid five cents a week. One afternoon, as he was pouring water from a large pail into a communal cup being held by his six-year-old cousin, Toquiro, someone ran up to the boys and told them that Papa Atilano had died. My father dropped the bucket-splashing the icy water on Padrino Toquiro, running through the fields to find his father sprawled on a dirt road. The cause of death was never listed on his death certificate, and town folk, without facts but with furtive imaginations, filled in the details: a fulminante, syphilis, heatstroke, un tiro, el pitorro de Milla. No one mentioned that Atilano, the grandson of a runaway slave woman, was most likely worked to death. He was thirty-three. When my father got to La Mansión he was told that from that moment on, he was the man of the house. He was seven years old, and he never recovered.

* * *

My tías and abuelas were outlaws in a system that stole, enslaved, and, even after the Spanish Royal Crown abolished slavery on March 22, 1873, squeezed and oppressed them. They taught me to question everything and that genius and knowledge were not only found in the white man's schools and culture but also in the communities of people who looked like them, me, us, who were not considered "cultured" by the outside world. They taught me that my body was mine and that it was sacred and that I could do with it as I pleased.

Ask this pussy for a blessing, echoes in my head. I know today what my three tías meant.

They had a deep mistrust of government and authority because they knew they were at the mercy of both—secret hands of history that had shaped their lives and, at every turn, their furious undoing of a hellacious colonial destiny. When white men in white coats came to talk to the women in the village about a new way to evitar los hijos, my tías and abuela were hip to the games being played. My grandmother told me she let the strange people in her house, treated them with kindness, served them coffee sweetened with a cane stick, and listened to their pitch. Then she told them to go to hell in her sweet revolutionary abuela voice. They may have been dirt poor, but they were no fools, and no amount of money or cuento would convince them to be part of something that would help them plan their babies. Evitar los hijos? Porque? A child is a blessing. Also, they knew how to evitar los hijos anyway, without strange Yankees intervening.

During colonial times, Native and African women of Borikén held ceremonial abortion circles. They were raped by slavers and settlers, and those who did not want to bring children into the living hell the Royal Crown created and supported gathered under the light of the stars on moonless nights. They gathered, drank a strong brew made with plants and tree roots. They danced. They prayed. They sang and they rested. Their fertile wombs intact.

My tías and grandmother inherited this knowledge and knew the medicinal power of the plant world. Once, on a walk by the river, Titi Aida showed me a blessed plant. "This one is a woman's best friend," she noted, tenderly touching a vivid green bush that seemed to beam brighter with her attention. My tías regulated their menses, soothed their wombs and period pain, cured their babies and their neighbors with salves and broths made with wild leaves and roots. When they missed a period, they knew what to do. There was no need for white men in white coats to teach them about their wombs and family planning. The Americanos visited the poorest, Blackest places on the big island and found many victims. My tías were the lucky ones. They escaped horrifying gynecological violence and mutilation sanctioned by white men and women in white coats from the US. The unethical contraceptive pill study they were being recruited for was part of a larger US population-control policy that included forced sterilization that began on the island in the 1930s. This five-decade eugenics movement is one of the darkest in US and Puerto Rician contemporary history. The trauma continues to haunt today.

It was a diabolical US government–sanctioned agenda, and the true horror of the eugenics policy that included the first human trials of the contraceptive pill on the wombs of unsuspecting Puerto Rican women will never be known. The pill experiments began with Planned Parenthood's founder, Margaret Sanger, and her friend, suffragist millionaire and funder of the pill trials, Katherine Dexter McCormick. The two women dreamed of a pill that would give white women the freedom to plan their pregnancies. They were looking to hire a scientist to conduct the first human experiments for a promising contraceptive pill. In their search, they found an ideal candidate, Dr. Gregory Goodwin "Gordy" Pincus, a Harvard and Cornell University–trained doctor nicknamed "Dr. Frankenstein" in scientific circles because of his depraved fertility experiments on the reproductive organs of rabbits. His toiling with the uteri of animals was so despotic his own peers shied away from the monstrous experiments he was fond of conducting. Some of the details of the pill experiments, sifted through the white gaze, are included in the fawning book on another doctor who participated in the pill trials, John Rock, titled *The Fertility Doctor: John Rock and the Fertility Revolution* by Margaret Marsh and Wanda Ronner. From my gaze, it is a book of horrors.

Once Pincus was hired, Sanger and McCormick needed a location to conduct the human trials, and the colony of Puerto Rico seemed like a perfect place, since there were US government–sanctioned population control policies already under way. Also, on the archipelago, militarily occupied by the US since 1898, Pincus could experiment *with impunity*.

Pincus was aided on the ground by another American doctor, a white woman named Dr. Edris Rice-Wray, who led the Puerto Rico Family Planning Association. Rice-Wray was not shy about her racist views on Puerto Ricans. She told a *New York Times* reporter that "when all Puerto Ricans can have the number of children they want and can properly care for, much of the misery and desperation of the poorer classes can be eliminated."

Pincus and Rice-Wray were a match made in colonial hell. Both knew that the US territory was an ideal place for these reprehensible experiments on women's wombs because it was a nation of colonial subjects, poor Black and Indigenous women who were politically powerless and vulnerable.

To add, colonial administrators, appointed by white men in Congress, were "horrified" at the poverty they found on the island and also the so-called uncontrolled population growth, so they welcomed the experimenters and gave them carte blanche on the wombs of women who had no idea that they were being used as human guinea pigs.

It did not occur to any of those white men and women who wanted to impact poverty in Puerto Rico that it was their nation's extractive policies that were the root cause of endemic and generational poverty. Instead of tooling with women's wombs, they could have used their white privilege for real economic reforms, starting with the removal of the 1917 Jones Act that strangled, and still strangles, the island nation's economy. Instead, the white men and women blamed poor Black and Indigenous women who had too many Black and Brown babies. They blamed the poor women for being poor.

The infrastructure of the wicked birth control studies was sixty-seven clinics around the island, run by Rice-Wray. It was through these clinics that they dispensed medicines, vaccines, and, in the 1950s, untested methods of birth control hawked as vitamins to innocent victims.

In official reports, 1,500 unsuspecting Puerto Rican women all over the big island were given the largest doses of hormones ever ingested by human beings. Maybe there were more victims, but we will never know. But what is know is that until then, only rats and rabbits had been given the pill. As these Frankensteins manipulated dosages, the white men and women in white coats waited and watched excitedly to see what happened to the blessed reproductive organs of innocent, poor, Black and Native Puerto Rican women, lowering the dosages when some died. The women reported nausea, vomiting, stomach pain, dizziness, and headaches. There were rumors that women went into comas. Many fainted. One of those women was my friend Ivette Mayo's mother, who had bouts of unexplained fainting spells. According to Mayo, her mom was being treated by a US Navy doctor in San Juan since her husband was a Navy man. She'd been told that she was malnourished and needed vitamins. During her last fainting spell, she was rushed to the local clínica pública in Manatí, and a local country doctor who triaged her in the emergency room asked what, if any, medicines the young mom was taking. Ivette's father took out a little brown bottle that he thought were vitaminas de hierro. That is how the Mayo family learned that it was not iron pills that the young mom was prescribed but untested high doses of hormones that were slowly killing her. According to Mayo, the young country doctor was shocked at the dosage of hormones her mom had been ingesting for almost a year. Seven decades later, her mom is still traumatized by the experience. Around the island, people pleaded with Pincus, telling him that the women were being poisoned. He dismissed the women, including Rice-Wray, saying that the "women's symptoms were psychosomatic." The myth that Black and Brown women don't experience pain was on full and violent display.

In official reports, it was noted that "only" three women died. The exact hormonal dosage they ingested will never be known. No autopsies were performed on the blessed bodies of the women who were pummeled with hormones unknowingly and without their full consent. Local women say that the death toll, like that after Hurricane Maria, was much higher than officials reported.

None of the women were told they were part of the largest human experiments for contraceptive pills.

Rice-Wray and Pincus became celebrated, international stars after the unethical Puerto Rico contraceptive experiments and mutilations. After a "successful" seventeen years of clinical trials on the blessed reproductive organs of unsuspecting Black and Indigenous Puerto Rican women, Rice-Wray was hired by the United Nations and sent to Mexico. Mercy! Planned Parenthood's Sanger decorated Rice-Wray with awards for her research.

It is important to note that none of the Puerto Rican women or families, including the three dead women's families, were financially compensated, given awards, or thanked.

In the 1960s, the white woman's sexual revolution happened on the backs and wombs of the poor Black and Native women of Puerto Rico. Gynecological violence on poor, unsuspecting Black and Native women and their blessed reproductive organs did not end then. It continued with a different, more brutal, invasive mutilation: forced surgical removal of fallopian tubes, sterilization, including hysterectomies, without consent during a three-decade dark period on the island known as La Operación. My mother was one of the women whose tubes were cut because her doctor, Dr Finch, the obstetrician who delivered me, thought that she had too many babies. She gave birth to my brother in 1969, going into the delivery room fertile, coming out sterilized like a stray. Mom was twenty-seven years old. She was not alone. Between 1930 and 1990, one third of Puerto Rican female population was sterilized—voluntarily or coerced. This is the highest rate of sterilization in the world.[2]

In the 1980s, experimentation on the wombs of Puerto Rican women continued with a dangerous cocktail of new, super-addictive drugs. According to a *Los Angeles Times* investigative report, in 1989, ninety Puerto Rican women recuperating from abdominal and gynecological surgery were part of the first human trial of OxyContin.[3] Purdue Pharma scientists gave half of the women a single dose of the narcotic and others got a short-acting pain killer or placebo. Sixty of the women complained of pain. They were ignored. The violent myth that Black and Brown women don't experience pain is consistent among oppressors.

None of the women were told they were part of the first and largest human trial of opioids. None of the Puerto Rican women or families were financially compensated, given awards, or thanked by a pharmaceutical corporation that created and promoted a drug that has wreaked havoc in the world and made its owners billionaires in an unprecedented opioid epidemic in the US.

So, when the white men in white coats came to my grandmother's pueblito in the 1950s to recruit human guinea pigs, Guela Milla took a good look at the Americanos and sweetly sent them along. They left knowing that in that pitiful little house, the women were wild and they would be too difficult to include in a tightly controlled study.

My tías took their freedom seriously and never did enter middle-class society, the kind where you go to college, the opera, theater, and church. This polite society they knew demanded a kind of decorum that was too expensive—it restrained their freedom and threatened their wombs. They paid for their freedom, greatly. Poverty is wretched. Two are on the ancestral plane—all three have their wombs intact.

They were proud when I finished college, when I won journalism awards and published stories that correct skewed narratives of people like them, me, us. But they never stopped flashing their pussies when I visited. They said this kept me humble.

My tías would release their batas and quickly bring me close to their hearts, hug me tight, bless and kiss me a thousand times. They were so happy to see me each and every time I came home. Their kind of beautiful self-regard is something I wish I could bottle and give away. This power protects wombs from harm.

My womb is whole thanks to them. While I don't flash my glory to my children, nieces, and nephews when they ask me la bendición, I remind them of the origin of their universe, the long line of women in our lineage who fought like hell to be free. I bless them and every child who comes my way, even if they don't request me to keep them in holy grace.

I often think about my tía's blessings—wild bushy pussies and all—and I giggle and feel strong. I know that their freedom is my inheritance.

we participate in the creation of the world by decreating ourselves[1]

Jennifer S. Cheng

The hour my baby was born, the world readjusted itself. I thought love was supposed to be immediate and innate, but instead it wandered slowly, blurry—the way day turns into night, light in a house gradually losing itself to something less bright. The hour my baby was born, the world collapsed in on itself. I could not catch it in my hands. It swept away from me like a violent earthquake or continent swallowed into sea. I did not love the world but dreaded it. It terrified me, like falling into the inside of a dark mouth.

*

There are contexts for what we say on the surface, if we say anything at all: *I am undergoing infertility treatments.* We do not say, or we sometimes say to those who are close to us, in confidence, in secret, in broad strokes because there is too much to explain: *hormone medications, daily injections, enlarged ovaries, vaginal probes, egg retrieval procedure, embryo transfer procedure.* But what you really want to say, what you can never say, are the things underwater, where there is no scaffolding to hold anything of structure up. There is: the vast liminal space between grief and hope, where you lie perpetually suspended, your feet constantly searching for ground. There is: the tenderness you feel for the fact of womanhood, in your best moments when grief is what it should be. There is: in your worst moments, the hot rage of self-hatred for your body and the parts of you that are broken—a stifling anger that, augmented by a soup of medications interacting chaotically with your hormones, has nowhere to go until you stand in the shower one afternoon and hit yourself as hard as you can, staying carefully away from the area around your stomach. You hit yourself in the head so hard that your nose bleeds.

*

Dear Isla: Everything falls through a hole of my making like light. Today I watched an interview in which a director said that her least favorite myth about motherhood is that it is uninteresting—that the details of domestic life are boring. *Motherhood is epic*, she said. *Especially the first child*, she said, *is revolutionary*.

My first public words about your birth were, *It is such a wilderness*. Followed by *I am trying to process how the world has shifted*. If I had been more honest, I would have used the word *undone*. I would have said, *dissolution*. Suddenly there is the knowledge of a parallel reality that had been transpiring invisibly across the world all this time. Suddenly I know that one of the most ubiquitous experiences in the history of humanity is also one of the most unspoken.

*

The doctors give you numbers, percentages, statistics. They draw charts and diagrams with ballpoint pens. They say, *A woman's body over the age of thirty-five*. They say, *If it hasn't happened by now*. They tell you surprising facts about your menstrual cycle, your reserve of eggs, that you did not learn in public school. They name things where you have not known to name them. They give you instructions for morning medications, evening injections, how to mix them, what time to take them, what to eat and what not to eat, what activities to avoid and when, what side effects are normal and unavoidable, *intensified PMS symptoms, depression, anxiety, foggy brain*, what side effects are undesirable, *halos of light*, what days you will need to come in so they can push a camera inside your vagina and measure the growth and abundance of eggs, *come again tomorrow*; and if the timing is right, *not too big, not too small,* and if the grouping is right, *enough eggs at similar size,* they will tell you the exact time you will inject the shot to trigger ovulation, *12:30 A.M.,* and then *thirty-six hours* later you will come in for the egg retrieval procedure, *Has anyone in your family had adverse reactions to anesthesia,* and if they are able to get a certain number of eggs and if a certain number of those eggs are healthy and if a certain number are successfully fertilized and if a few of those embryos develop healthily and if at least one of those healthy embryos is chromosomally viable and if your uterus is not a hostile environment and if it implants successfully—

The doctors have so much information to give. No one, however, tells you about the ongoing relationship with grief. How every small loss, which can happen during any of the tiny steps of the million-step process, will not just feel like a setback, like a video game where one must *start over,* but will feel like *loss.* Like you lost something. Like the shape of a life has been lost. And the loss, it suspends, it carries the possibility of something that spreads, boundless, shapeless—something you do not know how to name and therefore cannot contain.

*

It was raining ash on the western coast, and the Child was a series of cells, no bigger than a fingernail.

I woke up, and the Child was still swimming inside of me, losing its tail, growing legs.

She pushes her fist or her leg into the boundary of my flesh, a protrusion of skin conforming to the air. As if she is stretching into the world as far as she can go while my body holds her back. I whisper nonsensical sequences into the atmosphere.

*

What is another word for *water?* The process of becoming a mother is one of dissolution. As cells inside my uterus began to slowly accrete, as my body gradually accumulated matter and mass, something else began to dissolve. The first law of thermodynamics observes that something cannot come from nothing—an exchange must be made.

*

Dear Isla: Today you wanted to play the same game over and over, and I wanted to tell you that sometimes less is more; I wanted to teach you how to save what you love, to keep it sacred. *Dear Isla*: Sometimes when you cry upon waking, it is the sound of one who is utterly lost—the weeping and wailing of someone who has lost everything in the world and can no longer locate themselves, a terrible grief that understands no nuance. To be near such unmediated anguish every day—sometimes all day—feels, to me, traumatic. The hormonal shifts are the largest in a lifetime, but also, it is no wonder: *postpartum depression, postpartum anxiety.*

*

I was seeking new texts on the *fragment*, on *silence*, and suddenly I thought, *Is this what life consists of? Sites of silence, one after another, that we move through, attempting to speak.*

*

Which is to say, infertility: like being under a dark continent. And since there are no words in our social spheres for this kind of liminal grief, you say nothing about the invisible continent enveloping you at all times. When you do speak, you say, *It's such a strange process.* There is an inaccessible world underneath what you are able to say; even you cannot puncture the surface; you exist wholly below.

*

In my work as a writer, I have circled the body over and over because it has always eluded me. *Body*, I write. *Body*, with sounds that do not whisper, like the rest of me. Perhaps it is because so much of my being lives in the amorphous hidden of an interior life, or perhaps it's because I was taught as a child that materiality is a kind of enemy. In any case, what should be intimate and concrete has always seemed distant, elusive—the way I am afraid to touch corners and blemishes, as if they do not belong to me, their factual surfaces both mundane and startling. *Body*, I write. It took me years to notice that I have almost always meant it metaphorically; I can barely fathom its literalness.

*

And then: only a body. For years: ruled by the body, a burdensome thing I must carry with me and perform tasks of will upon.

*

There are things you grow used to even as you do not. A stranger puts a mechanical probe inside your most intimate self, and he sees what you have not been able to see. The body becomes sore: pelvis sore, thighs sore, injection site sore. The body looks as if it has been pummeled: bruised, swollen, bleeding. Your cervix is curved, and sometimes the procedures hurt so much, you cry or almost faint. Your husband holds your hand or he stands in the corner of the room or he waits outside. At home, you open the window in your bedroom so you can smell the salt in the wind.

He tells you he keeps hearing stories of people who went through IVF for years, only to stop and suddenly get pregnant naturally. *As if the body needs to prepare itself,* he says. *Like you have to train your body to understand it's okay to get pregnant now.* You do not share his interpretation. You think it's a lesson in surrender, the contradiction of how the very act of letting go allows one to be able to open your hands large enough to hold whatever falls.

You have spent your life managing your life into small pockets of control. You do not reach for things that may lead to failure; you avoid risky activities; you stay in the house. Your hand has been a clenched fist, gripping on for dear life.

At your acupuncturist's office, there is the kind of music they play in planetariums. As you are lying on your back, eyes closed, you try, as instructed, to imagine your womb filled with glittering jewels, and then as a galaxy of planets, orbiting moons, stars.

*

How the experience of a *prenatal* woman is similar to that of a marginalized person: one is both hypervisible and hyperinvisible at the same time. In public, people comment, critique, even touch—the body becomes a public object, physically aberrant, a spectacle. At the same time, *I* disappear. One is merely the round belly and the socialized significance of the belly. One's deepest experiences and needs, so monstrous and vital, are unacknowledged, unknown. One walks into the world feeling as if one is carrying a parallel universe, a gaping wound, that nobody knows how to *see*.

Or perhaps the confluence of invisibilities and visibilities are simply compounded for a marginalized person: ways of being unseen, surveilled, dehumanized.

The medical environment is the apex of such unsettling contradiction, where visibility and invisibility merge into something almost uncanny. Only the body exists; meanwhile *I* am dispossessed of it. In such an environment where control over the body is relinquished to complete strangers who know nothing of the self inhabiting that body, it helps to detach oneself, to pretend the self does not exist, so that is what I do, as best I can. I lie on the table, counting the number of squares on the ceiling. I sign papers handing over authority, but not responsibility, to other people.

*

The hormones are wild and volatile, a turbulent ocean that confuses and blurs throughout the years—infertility, pregnancy, birth, postpartum.

I am long lost at sea in an apparition's shadow. Before she came, the sky grew violent with wildfire. There were days of ash. The foghorn blew all day and night. Before she came, the roof of the house caved in, made a hole of uneven borders. We returned home to find a coverlet of foreign debris where our bodies usually slept: splinters of weather, wood, nails, architectural dust. A year after she was born, when I finally began to close my eyes long enough to dream, I dreamt every night of the apocalypse. Beautiful half-memories of deserts, rock cliffs, dunes; trails of river and forest; glacial mountains—all the while, the sky above burning with a fire I could not see. I had a wound hidden away, and she touched me there. She tried to make a home of it. *Have you had thoughts of harming yourself or ending your life? Have you acted on these thoughts?* In the months after her birth, I did not sleep, and if I did for an hour or two, I woke in the darkness with my heart pounding and a swollen blossom storming my chest. In our social script for pregnancy, the volatility of hormones is mythic and humorous: *I cried when I dropped my breakfast! I put my scissors in the freezer!* Even the misleading term, *morning sickness*, as if the positioning of the sun is some kind of container. The truth is, one's internal organs, beginning with the lung and ending with the heart, like skinned plums, begin to fall out of oneself, little by little, and then suddenly and all at once.

*

The hormones make it impossible to think a coherent thought, much less to say anything aloud. Once you are so tongue-tied, you close your eyes, trying to think of the word for *butter*. You say: *oil, but soft*. Where language had been a companion in aloneness, where words were once a talisman you kept for self-soothing—*lung, water, god*—now there is only a growing hole whose absence of boundaries frightens you. You take the hole and lay yourself inside it in order to keep it filled with something. Once, while describing to someone what it feels like to watch helplessly as language slips away, you give yourself a severe panic attack. One invites trauma in in order to believe in the possibility that one might love more deeply.

*

One had ten months to get used to a growing belly, but one did not get used to it. Each morning the Child was a gathering of cells that slowly and invisibly accumulated the attributes of the living. I caught my belly in the mirror and felt something like shock at what is otherworldly, an uncertainty over what is real.

Throughout the day, I am disturbed by sudden waves I can only name as *existential vulnerability*. Less like tenderness and more like terror. A feeling in the pit of the stomach, almost like a child's homesickness but expansive in space and scope.

I felt the Child swimming inside me as I was writing on my computer, as I was teaching in the classroom, as I was cutting tomatoes for lunch. She turned over, and something inside me turned over. She pressed, and something near my bladder tickled. She kicked, and my roundness visibly pulsed. Something shivered.

The Child grew inside the globe of my body. It began the size of a needle's point. It was now the size of a squash. All of the comparisons in books are to vegetables and fruit—things that grow in gardens or hidden under the earth. In the morning I circled my roundness with my hand and spoke to her through a wall. *Baby,* I said in the daylight to an empty room. I had been told it is good to address the Child. 寶寶， 你起來了啊? 你在游泳, 還是你在做運動? *Baby, did you wake up? Are you swimming, are you exercising?* I said the words in Mandarin first, then English. I imagined her as a water creature with a tail.

Every morning I woke with an intense and imminent fear that something inside me was dead or that my belly was deflated and flat. I woke up and did not feel the weight of my belly, though I could see it. I felt around my belly, pushing it slightly, prodding, looking for a signal, though of exactly what I did not know.

To be two beings at a singular moment of being one. For the body to accommodate two heartbeats, two sets of lungs: what becomes monstrous?

*

Afterward, there are no memories of daily life. No walks to the ocean, no reflective notetaking. There is the guarding of your movements. There is the careful monitoring of each ache or pulsating sensation. During these months, I begin sleeping with a stuffed animal for the first time since I was a child. I lay in the middle of a relentless hum, opening and closing my hand.

*

In *A Field Guide to Getting Lost* by Rebecca Solnit is a description of the chrysalis and the literal disintegration of the caterpillar. *The process of transformation consists almost entirely of decay.* Another book, *Gravity and Grace* by Simone Weil, offers up the concept of *decreation*, that is, when *something created pass[es] into the uncreated.* She distinguishes this from *destruction*, whereby something created passes into *nothingness*, a *blameworthy substitution.*

*

The mortality rate for women giving birth in the United States. The mortality rate for the most oppressed women giving birth in the US. The number of methods for monitoring the fetus during birth; the number of methods for monitoring the mother during birth. The number of days between birth and the infant's first required doctor visit; the number of months between birth and the mother's first required doctor visit. The number of doctor visits covered by insurance: baby or mother. The number of times you heard the word *birth* adjacent to the letters *PTSD* prior to giving birth yourself. The number of times you heard them together afterward. *A medication*, she says, *we are finally developing, based on how we treat veterans of war.*

*

There is no way to say it completely. I wished many times for her to have never existed. I wished for my own obliteration.

*

How each fragment initially began: with the question, *Who are you and whom do you love?*[2]

*

If the top of her head appeared and disappeared with my body's heaving, then I will remember her eyes wide open, an expression I cannot describe: half-animal, half-ancient. If it hadn't seemed like an unusual delivery, then it fractured open an abyss. If they wheeled me back to the birthing room from the operating room, then I saw how the floor was stained with blood. I didn't cry for forty-eight hours, and then I didn't stop crying. There are many others who fare much, much worse.

A friend had gently sent me a message with an article attached, containing the words *birth trauma*.

I remember being somewhat alarmed, somewhat relieved by the absurdity of a list of identifiers. Under what circumstances is something not *trauma*? One grows an entire human organism deep inside one's internal structures and then one day labors to expel it: another heartbeat, another mouth, another set of bones and limbs, the first look of wild alertness, wild vulnerability, a cry and a soul—one expels it out between one's own legs, along with blood, masses of tissue, excrement. Even when birth is over, it is often not; three weeks later, a large bulb of forgotten membrane began to fall out of my body like a planet—

*

In the Japanese art of *kintsugi*, one takes the broken shards of a ceramic vessel and reassembles it, mending the cracks with gold lacquer. The process of breakage and mending is not hidden away but becomes part of the object's beauty. One *creates and makes into the fissures*. The healing process, says artist Makoto Fujimura, consists of looking at the pieces of ruin until they are beautiful. One day, when she is nine months old, I take a pencil to the corner of a wall, and in small, almost imperceptible letters, I write the word *unfathomable*, a spell I cast onto the body of the house.

*

Later in the essay, Weil says, *We participate in the creation of the world by decreating ourselves . . . We must take the feeling of being at home into exile. We must be rooted in the absence of a place. To uproot oneself socially and vegetatively. To exile oneself from every earthly country.*

*

The Child was pushing aside my organs, making space for itself.

Eventually, I, too, would cut up an old boundary of textual sequences, in order to shake language loose: *scattered across my abandoned House sleepy with escarpment I am the span of the edge More and more my days terrains estrangement of your underbelly of skies that never end Some nights I dream where I have hidden water roots If ever they are waiting.*

*

Dear Isla: There is a rising cloud of watercolor smoke that travels up the spine of your back, reminding me of Chinese paintings. Secretly, it invokes a sense of awe in me, and I am not displeased when the doctor says it will probably stain your back forever. Still, whenever I see it, I am afraid to touch it, afraid that, somehow, you are my body's most tender bruise.

*

Dear Isla: This is my farthest prayerful state. I have been thinking about the function of suffering, not as in *purpose* but as in *depth, complexity*. When something breaks and we fill the fissures with what beautiful things we can find, what becomes of it? What becomes of the world?

*

Dear Isla: The day begins foggy, and I'm relieved by its lack of clarity—by the way the ocean comes into view, then disappears, the way the trees and hills are webbed in something dull and soft. Dear Child, when we speak of pregnancy, we speak of joy, we speak of wonder, a bewitching, and the miracle of maternal affection. Does it make me a bad mother to admit I wanted someone to speak of devastation? To say there has been much devastation, yet, and also—I continue moving toward you.

Wanting a Child Makes No Goddamn Sense

Tiphanie Yanique

Hi, baby.
I'm writing an essay on pregnancy and childbirth.
I need a single word or words that are antonym to "want."
    Hey, babe.
    Reject
    Disavow
    Repudiate
Maybe. But those words are active.
Want feels passive.
Want sits inside of a person and waits.
    Does it?

"I just killed my baby!" The woman was howling. She was the first thing I heard when I woke up. Actually, I was being woken up. People were shaking me and telling me it was time to wake up. And many other shes were crying. And we were all together in a room. The woman I'd heard shouting was just the loudest of us all. The women waking me were nurses or physician assistants. They were shaking my shoulders roughly and I wanted to elbow them. Hard. I was angry, but also confused enough that first I touched my face. And that was when I felt my tears. My baby was dead, too. And maybe I'd killed it. This is the end of the story.

The start of the story is me, on my knees praying. Me saying, Please dear God, please, if you give me this child, give me this baby, I will leave my womb open for another, dear God, I will leave myself open to another soul that you desire to pass through, dear God, if you grant me this child, this girl that I so desire, I will give you one; one for you, please, dear God. If you grant me my second child, I will give you, God, a third.

One thing to know about me, is that I was raised religious, and I am still religious. I am not a recovering religious person. I am not someone who thinks my childhood faith derailed my maturity or stifled my intelligence. I know my faith to be part of my maturity and part of my intelligence. When I think about why I exist, I think I do so for my man, my children, my best friends, and myself—and by those people I mean God. I mean God is in the people who love me and whom I love, and I exist for that love, which is God. I pray every day, two or three times a day. As with many women who say they are religious, I have never had an abortion. I am forty-two years old now, and so it doesn't seem unreasonable to say that I will never have an abortion.

Perhaps there is nothing passive about "not wanting."
Wanting is a state of being.
Not wanting is more active than wanting.

On the day I awoke to a woman confessing murder, my spouse and I already had a baby. Our son was a boy I'd named two decades before he even existed. I loved being a mother, instantly knew it was what I came to earth first and foremost to do. My writing? Yes, vital to me, but now and forever secondary to my child. I was so full of this miracle thing I had done—become a mother—that I felt sure that it really must be every woman's first and foremost thing to do. As a feminist, this feeling felt absurd. And yet, there was the feeling inside of me.

Two years after my firstborn, I was pregnant again. My mother-in-law, who thought it was her place, asked, "Are you just going to keep having children?" "Yes," I told her, which was spiteful, because she'd only managed to have the one, my husband, though she'd longed for a gaggle. This time, my husband and I didn't wait that three-month wait that is recommended. We just told people. We told everyone. I wore a T-shirt that said: It's not a beer belly, it's a baby.

So how did I kill my baby? Let me count the ways.

1. There was my yoga teacher. Hot yoga, to be exact. I walked down the block to that beautiful, addictive place daily. Nothing was better for my sanity than hot yoga. And when I was pregnant, my hormones were pretty much insanity inducing. I cried every other day, which everyone said meant the baby was a girl; all those extra hormones. My hot yoga instructor was a man, and when I asked him if it was okay to take hot yoga while pregnant, he said his partner never stopped hot yoga throughout both of her pregnancies. Then he walked out of the hot room. Sat on a bench. And his heart slowed until it stopped, and he died. The yoga studio emailed us all explaining that he had a heart condition, one unknown to himself.

2. Now let's consider a baby's heart. Which isn't fully formed until halfway through the second trimester. I was in hot yoga the day before I found out I'd killed my baby.

3. I was not taking care of my expectant body. For example, I drank wine whenever I wanted. Because how good had I been when pregnant with my son, my first? I'd been damn perfect. And how hard had that been? So hard. I walked my two-year-old to preschool two days a week, so I could do my full-time job in those not-enough hours. I watched him by myself three other days. My husband wanted sex, but I wanted sleep. I got neither. Had nothing left over to give, and so had killed my baby.

4. I'd flown on a plane. In fact, I'd just flown back from my childhood home in St. Thomas because I had a doctor's appointment, a prenatal check-in. Second pregnancy, so my husband didn't come to any of the doctor visits; he and our son were back on the island. My cousin, who was a nurse, cautioned never to fly while early in your pregnancy. "You go on the plane pregnant. You get off the plane not." Her exact words. Which I had ignored, and so had killed my baby.

5. Finally, and mostly, I had killed this baby by wanting this baby too much. I wanted it more than anything. I wanted the baby more than I wanted my job or to write another book. I'd wanted my boy, whom I already had. And I wanted my girl, who was in me—until

I woke up to another woman screaming. My want, my excessive, awful, deadly want, had killed my baby.

Is there a "not wanting" state of being?
    No.
    Not wanting inherently requires consideration of wanting, then acts in opposition.
    Not wanting is a rejection of wanting.

When I'd gone to the doctor for my prenatal checkup, she stared at the screen. Stared and started and stared. Her face carried the kind of frown you only see on cartoons. Her lips a hump on her face. "I can't find a heartbeat," she said. Then she turned the screen so I could see what could not be seen. "I will leave you here with the image. Stay as long as you need to." How long did I need to stay? I have no idea. I stayed for a long time. When I left the exam room, each staff member looked at me tenderly, but no one said a word. I felt like I was floating, which I understand now meant I was in a state of shock. My baby was dead inside of me. Nested and perfect and quiet. With fingernails and a heart but no heartbeat.

And I had to get the baby out.

The doctor had said so. I remembered this hours later. She'd said that if I didn't go and get the baby out that I may start bleeding in the middle of teaching my classes. Or I may bleed and bleed and not get to a hospital in time and just bleed out. "You have to go as soon as possible," she'd said. "If you want, it's okay to wait until your husband comes back. Go on Monday, or you can go tomorrow." The tomorrow place was an abortion clinic.

"It won't be nice there," she said. "But it's the same procedure, so they know what to do."

At home, I called my son's father, who was still my husband, and hollered into the phone. I wanted him to tell me, "Wait for me so I can be there with you." But I never asked. In fact, I felt it best that he stay away. If he came back early, I would have to take care of him and our son. It was going to take all of me to take care of myself.

And also, there was something stranger: I didn't believe my baby was dead. The baby could not be dead. Because I had heard her in my mind since I was fifteen years old—I'd named her then. I was sure the doctor was wrong; I still felt pregnant. I wondered if the doctor was inept or a cruel liar. If only that one doctor believed that the baby was dead, then maybe the baby wasn't dead.

None of this made sense, of course. And yet it was completely logical to me: I was going to an abortion clinic as soon as possible so that I could prove that my baby was alive.

Is there something human that makes this word want so particular? Or is there something grammatical about the word want that does this?
There are only three verbs: be, do, have.
Want is a variant of be.
Ah-ah. That means that want is being. A natural constant state.

Another thing to know about me is that I curse. A lot. My friends will tell you that I do this like a sailor. I give the middle finger to people I respect, as a sign of my respect. I curse when I am happy. I curse people out when I am angry. I have cursed out strangers. I use curse words you have never used and never should. Still, I think my body is holy, even when bleeding. I think your body is holy, too. Religious men do not think I am religious. Religious men think I am a threat to their faith—a few have even told me so. And then I have cursed them out.

Which brings me back to the abortion clinic. It had a very nice waiting room. The chairs were comfortable, more plush than any hospital or doctor's office. Most of the women were there with other women. There were no men in the waiting room at all. Some of the women, like me, were alone. Then there was the examination room, which was like the living rooms in hotel suites. All of us women were going through something we hadn't planned on going through; a thing we didn't want to go through. We were sad or scared or angry or confused. The designers of the clinic didn't want to make all this worse with uncomfortable furniture or discomforting decor. Many of us, I'm sure, were grateful. I was, in fact. Grateful that this place was open for me on a Saturday. Grateful I wouldn't bleed to death on Monday when I taught my night class. Grateful I didn't have to wait for my husband to get home. But gratitude is not happiness. No one was happy in that clinic.

Is it that language creates certain possibilities of being in the humans who speak it?
> **Humans exist in our senses.**
> **In order to consciously process those senses,**
> **there must be a sense of self.**
> **The sense of self is therefore unitary (I am).**

In the examination room at the abortion clinic a tech did a scan, as was the law in New York. I wanted to confirm the sex of the baby, but I didn't ask. The woman asked me when I had had my last period. I answered. "Seventeen weeks," she said to me. "Heartbeat, 140 beats per minute."

"Excuse me?"

She repeated: "Seventeen-week old fetus and heartbeat, 140 beats per minute."

"Heartbeat?"

"Yes," she said, dull and flat, like women came in and doubted her all the time.

"My baby is alive?"

"Seventeen-week old fetus and heartbeat, 140 beats per minute."

"What. The. Fuck. Are you saying? What are you motherfucking saying?" I was screaming this at the woman. Screaming it as I sat up from the examination table. Pulled my clothes on. "Get me the fuck out of here." My baby was not dead. This woman was about to kill my baby.

The woman backed slowly out of the room, then rushed back in with a doctor. A man. He looked at the screen and then looked at the woman. He asked me to lay back down. He took out an instrument, jellied it, and pushed it hard over my stomach.

Even now as I write this, I can feel the adrenaline crashing through me. I can feel my arms and shoulders and neck growing tight. My baby was still alive. My girl. The one I had named years before and was waiting for. Wanting so badly. The one I had thought I had lost. The one I had thought I had killed. Maybe she had died, but here she was, back. Back in me. With me. I was crying and hiccupping. I was breathing so hard, I was breaking.

"I want you to relax," the doctor said. "Your heart is beating so hard I can't hear anything else." He didn't say what he could see. He didn't say what he couldn't see. I took deep breaths. I calmed myself. I spoke to my girl in my mind, which I felt was the most true way to communicate with her, because she was, after all, inside of me. Was nothing apart from me. Was me. I spoke to her like I was praying. Which I was. I was praying to her.

So, then the opposite of want might be satiated.
The opposite of want might be simply being.

It is not so unusual to think that a fetus is the same thing as God. To a woman who wants that baby, an unborn baby is a divine thing. And so, praying to that baby is a way to talk to God. It is a way to talk to something that is not yet. Something that is not of this world and so is greater than this world. This is not about when life begins. What I am talking about is completely untied to life. This is before and beyond life. A pregnant woman knows that the not-life inside of her is actually still mostly spirit. And so is still mostly God. I know many pregnant women who talk to their enwombed babies with their minds. These women are praying.

Which is what I was doing.

Which is why when this second doctor said to me in the abortion clinic, "There is no heartbeat," I started cursing that motherfucking bitch mother's cunt asshole what kind of dumbass bitch mistake did you just make don't you fucking know I wanted that heartbeat you stupid fucking ass-licking pussy-face son of a whore.

I don't know when I calmed down. I don't know when I realized, as I do now, that the woman, just a tech, had just been saying what she was trained to say. She'd just done the math from the date of my last period and presented the numbers that added up. Seventeen weeks, 140 heartbeats per minute. She hadn't looked at the screen at all. Maybe she never looked. There was no heartbeat. This time the doctor made me look, didn't just suggest it. "Look," he said. And he made me listen: "Listen."

> **Gratitude is the cure for desire.**
> *Is desire a disease?*
> > ***Excessive. Excessive desire.***
> > **Gratitude is the cure for excessive desire.**

The next thing I remember is waking up to a woman screaming that her baby was dead and that she had killed it. And I could feel in my body that my body was empty. Which I had not expected. I felt cold at the base of me. Cold like that part of me was gaping open to a chill. Someone had put a pad in my panty. And now they were handling me roughly. Telling me to go home. They needed the bed for someone else. That was the end of that pregnancy. The end of that story.

I have no memory of how I got home that day. Subway? Taxi? Black car? Did I walk? No clue. But I remember that when I arrived to my empty Brooklyn apartment, I went to my knees and made a promise to God. God, if you let me have my baby girl back again. If you bring her back to my womb. I will leave my womb open for another, for a third. I didn't have a name for a third baby. I didn't have a want for a third baby. But I promised God, that if he gave me back my girl, that I would leave my womb open for whomever He needed to get through. Would make the pit of me a hallway.

And that is what happened. I got pregnant again, fast. Two months later, a new beginning. Pregnant with that girl. When I was pregnant again and showing big, I remember the head of my first child's preschool saying to me, "You have been pregnant longer than anyone I know." Which I gather meant she thought maybe I had been lying about being pregnant earlier because I'd cited my pregnancy months before as one reason I was applying for a scholarship for my first child. I had told her, as I had told everyone, about that second pregnancy. But I had never told her, or really anybody, about the miscarriage. And then I was pregnant again as soon as I could be. Most people didn't even realize I'd miscarried at all.

This new pregnancy was nothing like my first, or that second lost one, for that matter. I felt more exhausted than I knew a person could feel and still be awake. I felt scared, waiting for the baby to die inside of me. I broke my hips apart in delivery. And I don't mean this metaphorically. I mean the rupture in my hips showed up on X-rays and I couldn't walk for weeks. Couldn't run for years.

And my promise to God? My doctors said no. No, you should not get pregnant a fourth time, not again. And when I got pregnant that fourth time? My spouse, who was still my spouse, shrugged. "Whatever you want," he said. But I'd made a promise. And so we named the third baby Nazareth. And yes, Nazareth's first steps were taken in a church. And yes and yes, he is a miracle baby. But in that last point, it must be said that he is no different than any baby. All mothers are miracle makers.

Gratitude might be too active a word.
Gratitude might be active.
Gratitude might also be a state of being.

Do you understand that what I did to have a second child after my miscarriage, was make an agreement with God to have a third? Do you understand that I understand that bargaining is just a stage of grief? Can you tell that my children's father is no longer my spouse? You won't have known that the psychologist who assessed our custody agreement wrote that my desire for a third baby was cited by my ex-husband as a reason for the divorce. But I know this all. Understand all this. I do. There is nothing logical about wanting to have a baby. It makes no fucking sense to want a heart from your own body walking around outside of your body.

Truth is, I badly want this essay to be like all the essays I have written and hope to write. I want this essay to have meaning, because that is what I believe writing is for. And yet this essay is wanting of meaning. There is only me and my sisters crying about our dead babies. There is only this thing that only women and women alone know. There is only me and another person, who also had a surprise third child—texting back and forth, forth and back, about the word want. There is only that this person is also my partner, my day-to-day coparent, and we are also texting, of course, about being in want and in gratitude for each other. And there is communication that is love, which we call prayer; and praying is the active verb of hope, itself a derivative of want; and there is belief, the state of being prayerful; and there is a life, which is a prayer. And nothing else.

After Birth

Stories of Birthing and Grieving at the Same Time

Bhanu Kapil

My father, as he did each time, marched out of the Indira Gandhi airport and straight up to the first vendor of roasted, buttered corn on the cob, eating it then and there as we stood with the oversized suitcases next to the bus stand.

My son, though I wouldn't know his gender for another two hours, rested on my body like a wet swan before resuming his journey towards infancy, then childhood, and adolescence.

My father was a goatherd.

My son texted me, in awe: Mom, you'll never guess who I saw in the elevator. (Ilhan Omar.)

Braiding a memory of my father with a memory of my son, I'm preparing to return to the time following my son's birth, which was also the time that followed my father's passing from this earth.

My father lost his temper once, at Virginia Waters, where we'd met the Pannus for an outdoor picnic. *No*, he barked, slapping the side of my head, when I asked if we could have fish and chips instead. What an injustice it then seemed to watch him, from our patch of grass (parathas with mango pickle tucked inside, wrapped in tea towels, unfolded now upon our laps), drinking beer with Mr. Pannu, resplendent in his pink turban, in the garden of the country pub. A shout. A yelp. We looked up to observe the sight of my father leaping over a fence, pursued by a German shepherd. Did we clap?

"That was the quietest birth I attended in twenty years of doing this," said the midwife.

When we tell the story of my father's passing, we evoke, in turn, the sight, just before he took his last breath, which is to say, an in-breath, a large glistening tear that dropped onto his cheek like a dewdrop or diamond. I'm not an artist, but sometimes, I draw that tear in my notebook.

"No, it's not working. It's slowing everything down," said the midwife, helping me out of the water. To my dismay, I realized that the ice cubes I'd been encouraged to hold in my palm, a distraction, were doing nothing for me, and also that the contractions paled in comparison to the menstrual cramps I'd experienced since the age of ten. Breathing, I began to breathe toward what was happening instead of, as I'd been trained to do, away. I can still remember the moment when a switch in my brain turned off, or on, and the following, fully formed sentence appeared in my mind: "This is not pain, it's sensation."

I remember drinking coffee in the airport. Arriving in Paris in a sarong, at the end of a bitterly cold winter, I was searched head to toe. Home at last, I remember how nice it was to be there, in London, basking in the warmth, the hot shower, and my mother's chai. Why did I wait until morning to go to the hospital? Of all the things, I remember that, on the train, I saw the teacher I'd had at the age of ten, for the few months before he'd left, a rumored breakdown. With a shock, I saw that he was wearing the scarf we'd brought him as a gift from India, after the holiday. The scarf, fifteen years later, was threadbare, but recognizably tan, turquoise, and a darker brown, identical to the one my father owned. Feeling upbeat, buoyed by the coincidence, I walked into the cancer ward. My father burst into tears. "Why didn't you come? I waited all night for you."

The doula drew a bath, filling it with healing herbs and flowers. Then I slipped in. "Do you mind if I pee?" she asked, lifting up her skirt.

I breathed in the dark, cloudy smoke from his esophagus, breathing back light, as I'd been trained to do in the Buddhist tradition. In the morning, my father's brother called from the jungle, or the edge of the jungle, to ask: "What is happening there? Why is a line of black smoke leaving my brother's throat?" In that moment, I understood that this embodied way of praying was as real as my hand on the windowsill or my fingertip on the windowpane, drawing a line in the condensation.

And walked back out. I couldn't do it. (The hospital tour for expectant mothers and their partners.) The glimpse of the operating room, the implements lifted from the pan. It was too much.

The milk in my son's half-open mouth was luminous.

I remember the icy green or bright grass outside the window of the room where my father died, and the ravens bouncing and hopping on it, like a snapshot. "My father has died," I said to the nurse at the front desk. "Yes," she said, "we know," exchanging a look with her colleague. What is a colleague? That question doesn't belong in this essay, and yet here it is, waiting to be prized.

The midwives (there are two as my primary midwife is on probation) and doula leave. It takes me years to wonder why they didn't show me how to breastfeed. "You're a natural," said Midwife One. "We'll be back in two weeks," said Midwife Two. I saw the doula in a bar five years later on Pearl Street in Boulder, Colorado, and we hugged. In fact, my son couldn't latch on and was, in ways that make me ache to recall it, profoundly hungry for the next two weeks. "You need to go to the store right now and get some formula," said the doctor. In the International House of Pancakes next to a Safeway, I wept and wept and wept.

Two years later, my son's father banged the kettle down, then set the tea three feet away. I was nursing my son, home from a shift at the salon (facials and massage). "Oh," I said, "you don't want to be my husband anymore." "No," he said, with tears in his eyes: "I don't."

Writing these words, I have so much compassion for the young, exhausted parents we both were, low on funds, and trying to make it work in the delta of grieving and migrating that those years also were. Three questions: Do you share a grief practice with the one you love? Who left as your child arrived? Did you give birth in a country that was also your own birthplace, or did you give birth in a country you were still adjusting to?*

Last week, I proofread my son's essay on the political aftermath of Rihanna's tweet of solidarity with Indian farmers.

My father glanced up at the grazing buffalo, returning to Virginia Woolf's *To the Lighthouse*, the book he was reading in the shade. In an attempt to learn English, he had selected the most difficult book he could find. Where did he find it? Who brought it to India and left it there? That question doesn't belong in this essay, and yet, I prize it.

---

* And was the cost of that?

The Distance of a Sky

Lena Khalaf Tuffaha and Deema K. Shehabi

In the summer of a pandemic, as our young adult children launched into their own lives, the turbulence of borders, unbreachable distances, and relentless bombardments in our long-suffering homeland filled our skies. The world seemed poised for endings. I wrote to Deema K. Shehabi, poet, sister of my heart, asking her to ruminate on pregnancy and giving birth in diaspora, a way to return to beginnings. What follows is our correspondence, the thobe we embroidered together.

Dear Lena,

What is longing? A moist faith?

A sorrow, shaped like a sister?

An unadulterated wish to merge with the cosmos, like a giant redwood chuting into cobalt blue?

I am here, in a small town next to a mountain, in the Valley of the Moons.

I am the woman with the rising belly lifting herself onto the hammock and swinging low.

My eyes trace the silhouette of Mt. Saint Helen, recording her dents, her bubbling extremities, the paths of her pyroclastic flows.

The land here gestures toward the sky with no fence in sight.

It's the same way a certain cemetery, where my loved one lies, forces my eyes up, sequestering them in the air.

It's late October; the earth nets scents of Jeffrey pine, evening primrose, California wood strawberry, Cleveland sage.

I am swinging low.

I hear murmur in the grass.

* * *

Dear Deema,

At a dinner table, passing a plate of smoky eggplant, we spoke of our children, their fledgling language.

You likened it to music.

When I speak of longing, the fragrances of unreachable cities rise up in me.

So much of my American pregnancies are a study of imagined geographies. *Here is what you might be feeling. Here are the new networks of veins growing inside of you. Here is a template for your birth plan. Here are the milestones. Here are the crossings.*

During my first pregnancy, my mother-in-law sent a loaf of sesame bread from Jerusalem, swaddled like a newborn for its ocean passage.

And it is the one small as a sesame seed, the poet says of our homeland.

Where I live now, there will never be checkpoints on my way to the hospital.

In my plan, I write that our newborn must be placed in my arms for her father to whisper a first *athaan* in her ear. As I write, a new distance occurs to me: she was raised in a city of empty skies.

Years after my first daughter is born, I meet a man who confesses that in his childhood his parents never told him he was Palestinian. He is a newborn.

I think now of the years spent carrying, the body become home. Some mornings,

I am capable of singing.

* * *

Mornings, we hoist our homeland onto our chests, though it hangs on us like a precipice.

The news drapes over and annuls our joys, though certain conversations are buoyed by duality of being.

The part who you see that I am, in many ways, could not exist without you, someone said.

What we don't see is what comes to us. Once as a child, I heard screaming through a window and thought a woman was giving birth.

Later, I would find her dancing in a black dress embroidered with daisies, no evidence of labor. In a veranda swirling with tulip tiles, I danced with her, hoping the morning would never come.

When my child was born, I told myself not to count the long hours and prayed the tether would release in the water of my dreams.

In another story, I am the woman whose child arrives with no sound, leaving a whittled stone in my throat.

That I would rise after birth was sometimes in doubt.

* * *

When my great grandmother felt her first contractions, she was travelling with her husband, an Ottoman colonel. They were in Hebron when she delivered my grandmother Sara, namesake of her birthplace. They stayed for a month before returning to their home.

When my grandmother prepared to labor, she traveled home to Damascus. My mother carries the city of her birth, of her first month, in her American passport, relic of a world now inaccessible.

In my birth preparation class, there is only one other woman who is not white. She looks over at me and smiles quietly.

I am full of her silence.

The instructor, a white woman, wants us to practice vocalizing. She encourages us to get in touch with *the fierce animal of the self* as we labor. She tells us this is what women in *other cultures* do, they intone their way through pain.

I do not return her gaze. I am distracted by this anthropology; I cannot practice breathing with her voice in the room. The parts of me that are visible pass seamlessly from one estrangement to another.

My friends come to visit in the hospital after each of my daughters is born, each friend cradling her own pregnant belly. Among my heirlooms are a set of three pictures like this—curve of a tender skull visible in my arms, a ring of aunties around the hospital bed, their laughter softening the light. One friend's mother, eyes glittering mischievously, asks: *Fayn il shabara?* She reaches into her blouse and snaps off the tiny satin bow at the center of her bra. She pastes it onto my daughter's hair with a drop of shampoo.

To nurture in this stillness, this lushness, in the predictable. This is what all the journeying parents seek. And what do our safe-and-sound children become? Let them be shapeless, without wounds.

At the protests that thread the years together, we carry our children in our arms or on our bodies. We intone our way through pain.

In my third pregnancy I found myself wondering: Which war will be yours, little one? Her eldest sister nursed as children skirted bullets on the streets of Ramallah. The sister after her nestled inside me as the bombs fell on Baghdad.

When will the parts of the self, dodging shrapnel in ancestral cities, become visible to you?

Which rooms will you fill with silence? How old will you be when they come to think of your fierceness as animal?

* * *

Time's an estrangement we have no control over—

The hours unraveled from cities, women giving birth in a sudden blast, astrolabes without ships,

trees falling with no witnesses in the forest.

Who are we without grief?

Dry lightning erupts over bone-parched hills and ignites 560 fires all at once. Sempervirens swallow the flames; you have to peek into their cavities to catch a glimpse of the inferno.

We catch the ash on our fingertips and wait for the hours to desist.

When our cities go down in front of our eyes, we cling to motherhood; it becomes our flag.

When I cup my son's face into my palms, I renew my promise to the tether.

The Offering

Cynthia Dewi Oka

The night before was one of the few times she was home that entire fall. Because of this, the house must have been quiet. We hid the dog at T's house. Tossed bills that had piled up, unopened on the kitchen counter, into a drawer. Even the old, yellowing fridge ceased humming of its own volition, as though sensing the rockslide poised inside my mother. My younger sister, Gladys, could have been in her room or at a family friend's. When I ask her eighteen years later where she was that morning, she can't recall either. There is a saying in Indonesian, *maju terus*, which means keep moving forward. This orientation informs the development of a certain kind of character, who is comfortable with holes in the story and things crammed into those voids that don't necessarily belong there. For example, it was the last day of December. There must have been a diamantine cast on every surface. The world appeared solid as a ghost.

Immediately after she woke up, my mother would have knelt at her bedside and prayed. We had been taught that faith meant believing in the unimaginable outcome, which a.) reflected God's will and b.) meant there was no such thing as tragedy. For her, faith made sense of the streets outside being perpetually swept; water we could drink cold and clear straight out of the tap; churches standing tall, not thinking of fire; her own body's endurance through years of fourteen-hour factory shifts while her husband, a former dentist, remained unemployed. The list went on, but at the top was her daughters speaking English as though it were their first language with the eldest just half a year away from graduating high school. When she was done making the bed, she would have gone to my room, where I had just fallen asleep, wretched and nauseous. She would have resisted the impulse to tussle my hair and say, Wake up, little pig. Two weeks ago, I had sat across from her in the small waiting room down the hall from where a ventilator breathed for my father, and told her I was pregnant.

* * *

We were silent on the drive to the imaging lab. The trees, stripped and shaking in the wind, were as ugly as they were seven years ago when we first arrived. On the way from the airport to the pastor's house where we would spend our first month in Canada, my father had repeated over and over, what a beautiful country. I thought then that the devil must have been crouching in my eyes because my father couldn't be wrong. As long he was alive, my father did not permit my mother to drive. T, who raced cars and regularly drank gangsters twice his age under the table, whose knuckles were almost always scabbed from a fight, was careful to keep both hands on the wheel. Out of respect for my mother, he had insisted on sleeping on the couch last night. I thought it was a tacky display of chastity; she was sad, not stupid. Every bump on the road was torture; I had consumed a liter of water for the ultrasound as instructed by the doctor and my bladder felt ready to explode. In the back seat, my mother closed her eyes.

I don't remember it at all, but the lab must have been like any other lab. It had a pink counter in the lobby. Generic IKEA watercolors of beaches and oppressive pastel geometries intended to signal the absence of danger. I imagine a receptionist with dark lip liner and neon yellow nails tap-tapping on her clipboard a Top 40 song that was stuck in her head. Usher, probably. I avoided the gaze of the other expectant mothers in the room. They all looked old to me and anxiously proud, bulging through their yoga pants and flower-printed maternity blouses. My mother handed me my social insurance card from her wallet, then sat down by a leaning tower of magazines she couldn't read. T probably stayed outside for a smoke. I really resented his not quitting when I had to, even though he was the one who begged me not to get an abortion. I asked one of the nurses floating behind the counter if I could please relieve myself. She shook her head. I stared at the forms in my hands and pissed myself a little bit anyway.

By the time I was led to the changing room, my bladder had gone mostly numb. I took off all my clothes and put on a patient gown the shade of Pepto-Bismol. My stomach was still flat. No perceptible change except for the aching and itchiness of everything under my skin. I was told to stand and wait at the end of a narrow corridor with closed doors lining both sides until the technician came to get me. It was cold. My bladder began to pulse again. I was guided into one of the rooms. Lying down on the examining table eased the tension, but not by much.

I closed my eyes and saw gold water flecked with tiny motes. In a closeup view they were starfishes with a human face at the end of each arm. The water rose and rose.

The doctor must have noticed my age on the medical chart before she came in. In this story, she paused with her hand on the door handle, brow furrowed, while the nurse debriefed her on my vitals (okay heart rate, slightly low blood pressure). What a waste, she would have said, shaking her head. When there are holes, we fill it with whispers we have collected. Inside, she was a model of compassion and profession-alism. She lathered my stomach with warmed gel, then began to move the sensor across the surface of my belly. My bladder screamed under the pressure. Tears welled in my eyes. Oh, honey, she said. I know it's scary, but look, your baby is perfect.

Back in Indonesia, I was always at the top of my class. At the end of each academic year, students would gather in our school's pavil-ion, kneeling shoulder to shoulder on the dusty floor. The sun was an invisible detail scorching the west-facing sides of our bodies. With sweat salting my eyes, I would pray for the first rank award, the only achievement that would make my father smile and look away from me. I prayed like that again now, squinting at the black-and-white sound-blobs morphing in and out of each other on the screen in front of me. Please, please, let me see the beautiful country.

The doctor asked if I would like a picture.

We were submerged in the baby's zumph-zumph-zumph-zumph heartbeat. It must be what a rave sounded like. T used to go every other weekend, dressed in white from top to bottom, a drawstring bag stuffed with mini ziplocks of molly swinging from a gloved hand. A few months ago, I convinced him to let me try one. I waited for something to happen. Then I decided to make it happen. I flailed around, rambled in gibberish, laughed hysterically, fell down like I had been struck by the Holy Spirit. Every hour, T checked on me and made me drink half a glass of water. I thought I must have been invincible for the molly to had no effect. I asked him for another dose, and he confessed that he had given me an aspirin with the marking scratched off. In that dark room, being shown evidence of a life I couldn't feel or see, I was just as embarrassed.

I asked the doctor if I could go to the bathroom now.

Later, T stared at the picture for awhile then laughed. Looks like a bunch of meatballs, he said. Gladys would have agreed. We might have picked her up for lunch, and she and T both probably ordered the meatball pho. My mother might have given the picture a glance, though whether it was the answer from God she wanted I couldn't tell. More likely, my brain allowed the image to degrade: her slender finger pointing out which blob was my baby. She had been pregnant five times herself; only two of us survived. You are proof of God's grace, she would tell me and my sister. I tucked the picture in my back pocket.

* * *

The sky was black by the time T parked the Honda Civic in front of the consignment store, as though a giant squid had come to wring out the sun. Its ink spilled in loops around my neck like someone else's hair. The dirty glass door tinkled pathetically when my mother opened it. Inside was a narrow room crammed with so many dresses that one literally had to wade through waves of fabric to get from one end to the other. Christmas music played from a little PA box mounted in a corner of the ceiling. The two ladies who ran the store looked like sisters, and from their greeting, I guessed they were Russian. Their faces were heavily made up, and hairspray swirled thick in the electrically singed air. They must be heading to a party right after their last sale of the year. T loitered awkwardly around the sale counter while my mother, sister, and I plunged arm-deep into a hanging river of taffeta, satin, charmeuse, organza.

It had taken my mother less than twenty-four hours to formulate a plan after learning of my pregnancy. We would prepare for a wedding in March before I was showing too much, a family-only ceremony held in the Indonesian church that she and my father had founded in Vancouver. My father would be heartbroken, but he would learn to forgive me, especially since I would be purified by marriage even if I couldn't consent to it as a minor. Plans are better than stories because they minimize the holes where sin proliferates. I pulled out a shapeless chiffon gown from the rack and left my mother to explain why her size four daughter was selecting a size eight. It will fit her better later, she kept repeating over the objections of the shop owners, who had prepared several mermaid- and princess-style dresses for me try on. The dressing room was a dirty red velvet sheet hung from a circular rod. I stripped down to my underwear.

It's good to marry young, I thought I heard one of the storekeepers say. More time for more options. I am forty and already I have husband number four.

I looked like a collapsed tent, even after my sister zipped up the back of the dress. I had to pinch the shoulder straps with both hands to keep the whole thing from sliding off. The layers of chiffon pooled around my feet like froth. When Gladys and I were little, my parents used to bring us once a year to Yogyakarta in central Java to visit my mother's side of the family. We would travel in a caravan with aunties, uncles, and cousins to spend the day at the Southern Sea beaches where many people, especially young men, had been known to disappear. Despite her status as the divine consort of the sultan of Yogyakarta—the last remaining royal family in Indonesia—Nyai Loro Kidul, goddess of the Indian Ocean, remains dissatisfied, famished for love. "Loro" means pain in Javanese. Before we jumped in the waves, our mothers would check for traces of blue or green in our clothing because the Nyai is drawn to those colors. I looked at my reflection in the mirror: brown and white, the wrack line where my father's beautiful country and her kingdom met.

* * *

He had almost left us before. One day in late August, he bled out until nearly all his blood had been replaced by transfusion. I wasn't there. I had gone to T's after my shift at the local amusement park, ignoring my mother's pages. She frequently paged me "911" for random errands or because my father was having a moment of either lucidity or amnesia that made him want to talk to me. He and I had barely spoken for a year. Exchanging sentences felt like tiptoeing on broken glass around the mouth of an active volcano. Did you do your homework? Yes. Did you read the Bible? Yes. What did it say?

When T and I finally arrived at the hospital, my father had gone somewhere we couldn't reach. His eyes rolled back in his head, his skin clenched around emaciated limbs so that entire lengths of bone jutted out of him like teeth. He seemed to be arguing with someone, in a language eviscerated of syntax. We understood nothing. The doctors told us it was a matter of time. My grandmother stood up with her hands raised and shouted at him, Ask Jesus for forgiveness, my son! Ask for his forgiveness! I started toward her. I wasn't sure what I meant to do exactly, but I definitely meant harm. T dragged me out of the room.

Later, my uncle told me that my father had called for me. Doctors, nurses, friends, church elders. His brothers, his mother, my mother, my sister. He had looked at every face and said: Cynthia.

* * *

All blue and green.

A child appeared, though he was hard to find with the untrained eye. He swam among planets of sound.

Another child disappeared, who had grown mute in the architecture of a man. To find him, the man shed his speech, his flesh, his ideas, the labor of his hands, his loves.

It was almost midnight. The ventilator and other life support systems had been turned off. Air, emptied of their humming and beeping, threatened to suck the organs out of our bodies. I turned up the volume of his favorite song, which was playing on repeat from a portable CD player by the window. T pulled the drapes closed over a charcoal sky sprinkled with fireworks. While my mother busied herself with monitoring his vital signs, Gladys sat at my father's side, back straight, one hand holding his. At thirteen, she looked just like him. She even had his square fingernails. My sister had always seemed to know how to not be his enemy. How to soothe his rages. How to say no to him and survive. Seven months from now, she would walk me down the hall of the delivery ward of another hospital, tracking the minutes between contractions. Instead of "auntie," she would teach my son to call her "Kiki," after Julia Roberts's character in *American Sweethearts*—the overlooked sister (and personal assistant) of a vain, selfish movie star played by Catherine Zeta-Jones. At the end of the movie, Julia wins the love of John Cusack, while Catherine is humiliated for her treacheries. Kiki is what my son calls her to this day.

I'll be right back, she said suddenly and ran out of the room.

I may be lying.

When she came back a few minutes later, her hands were full of candy canes. I want to say that we laughed. Or that at least I ran out to get more. After my father went into coma a few weeks before, the first thing she, T, and I would do when we arrived was empty the bowl of candy the nurses put out at the front desk. We'd race from the elevators—one of us checking for nurses while the others threw the loot in our backpacks. Few things are shittier than stealing from late-stage cancer patients, but every time, the bowl was refilled, almost magically, within minutes. For months afterward, I'd find mint drops, gold-wrapped caramel suckers, licorice bits, and strawberry bon bons wedged in the seams of the car seat, my pockets, or melted onto my copy of *Hamlet* for lit class. Sometimes I'd think about this place, its disinfected walls where my story as I knew it ended, and remember the sweetness we took that was not meant for us.

My father's name is Paulus.

I want to say I kissed his forehead.

That I told him I would name the baby Paul.

His breathing grew more labored, iron grinding iron. My mother laid her head on his chest. Gladys made a pile of candy canes on the overbed table where no meal of gummy eggs, runny mashed potatoes, Jell-O in shades of Crayola, and soggy bread had been served in days. Either firework or lightning flashed. Somebody said, Let it rain.

Indian Condition

Excerpt from *Heart Berries*

Terese Marie Mailhot

My story was maltreated. The words were too wrong and ugly to speak. I tried to tell someone my story, but he thought it was a hustle. He marked it as solicitation. The man took me shopping with his pity. I was silenced by charity—like so many Indians. I kept my hand out. My story became the hustle.

Women asked me what my endgame was. I hadn't thought about it. I considered marrying one of the men and sitting with my winnings, but I was too smart to sit. I took their money and went to school. I was hungry and took more. When I gained the faculty to speak my story, I realized I had given men too much.

The thing about women from the river is that our currents are endless. We sometimes outrun ourselves. I stopped answering men's questions or their calls.

Women asked me for my story.

My grandmother told me about Jesus. We knelt to pray. She told me to close my eyes. It was the only thing she asked me to do properly. She had conviction, but she also taught me to be mindless. We started recipes and lost track. We forgot ingredients. Our cakes never rose. We started an applehead doll—the shrunken, carved head sat on a bookshelf years after she left.

When she died nobody noticed me. Indian girls can be forgotten so well they forget themselves.

My mother brought healers to our home, and I thought she was trying to exorcise me—a little ghost. Psychics came. Our house was still ruptured. I started to craft ideas. I wrapped myself in a Pendleton blanket and picked blueberries. I pretended I was ancient. A healer looked at me. He was tall and his jeans were dirty.

He knelt down. I thought I was in trouble, so I told him that I had been good. He said, "You don't need to be nice."

My mother said that was when I became trouble.

That's when my nightmares came. A spinning wheel, a white porcelain tooth, a snarling mouth, and lightning haunted me. My mother told me they were visions.

"Turn your shirt backward to confuse the ghosts," she said, and sent me to bed.

My mother insisted that I embrace my power. On my first day of school I bound myself a small book. The teacher complimented my vocabulary, and my mother told me school was *a choice.*

She fed me traditional food. I went to bed early every night, but I never slept well.

I fell ill with tuberculosis. Mother brought back the healers. I told them my grandmother was speaking to me.

Zohar, a white mystic, a tarot reader, told me she spoke to spirits, too. "Your grandmother says she misses you," she said.

"We could never make a cake," I said.

"She was just telling me that. What ingredient did you usually forget?"

I knew this was a test, but a strange one, because she didn't speak to my grandmother either. I remember my mother was watching us, holding her breath.

"Eggs," I said.

My spiritual fraud distanced my grandmother's spirit from me. It became harder to stomach myself, and harder to eat.

"Does that happen to you?" I asked.

"What?" Zohar asked.

"Did you ever want to stop eating?"

"No," she said.

Zohar asked my mother if she could sleep next to my bed, on the floor. She listened to me all night. Storytelling. What potential there was in being awful. My mindlessness became a gift. I didn't feel compelled to tell any moral tales or ancient ones. I learned how story was always meant to be for Indian women: immediate and necessary and fearless, like all good lies.

My story was maltreated. I was a teenager when I got married. I wanted a safe home. Despair isn't a conduit for love. We ruined each other, and then my mother died. I had to leave the reservation. I had to get my GED. I left my home because welfare made me choose between necessities. I used a check and some cash I saved for a ticket away—and I knew I would arrive with a deficit. That's when I started to illustrate my story and when it became a means for survival. The ugly truth is that I lost my son Isadore in court. The Hague Convention. The ugly of *that* truth is that I gave birth to my second son as I was losing my first. My court date and my delivery aligned. In the hospital, they told me that my first son would go with his father.

"What about this boy," I said, with Isaiah in my arms.

"They don't seem interested yet," my lawyer said.

I brough Isaiah home from the hospital, and then packed Isadore's bag. My ex-husband Vito took him, along with police escorts. Before they left, I asked Vito if he wanted to hold his new baby. I don't know why I offered, but he didn't kiss our baby or tell him goodbye. He didn't say he was sorry, or that it was unfortunate. Who wants one boy and not another?

It's too ugly—to speak this story. It sounds like a beggar. How could misfortune follow me so well, and why did I choose it every time?

I learned how to make a honey reduction of the ugly sentences. Still, my voice cracks.

I packed my baby and left my reservation. I came from the mountains to an infinite and flat brown to bury my grief. I left because I was hungry.

In my first writing classes, my professor told me that the human condition was misery. I'm a river widened by misery, and the potency of my language is more than human. It's an Indian condition to be proud of survival but reluctant to call it resilience. Resilience seems ascribed to a human conditioning in white people.

The Indian condition is my grandmother. She was a nursery teacher. There are stories that she brought children to our kitchen, gave them laxatives, and then put newspaper on the ground. She squatted before them and made faces to illustrate how hard they should push. She dewormed children this way, and she learned that in residential school—where parasites and nuns and priests contaminated generations of our people. Indians froze trying to run away, and many starved. Nuns and priests ran out of places to put bones, so they built us into the walls of new boarding schools.

I can see Grandmother's face in front of those children. Her hands felt like rose petals, and her eyes were soft and round like buttons. She liked carnations and canned milk. She transcended resilience and actualized what Indians weren't taught to know: We are unmovable. Time seems measured by grief and anticipatory grief. I don't think she even measured time.

A Conversation Between
Mother and Daughter

Shaina P. Jones and Jada S. Jones

Shaina P. Jones: There are some ways of knowing and being I've gathered and grown into over time. I'll say that I cannot confirm the origins or societally recognized validity of them, but they are. They come in the form of directives, recipes, gossip, old wives' tales, stories passed down, Bible passages, names, family photos, and unuttered truisms. They are the things with which I plan to build my home, for when I've become big with small bodies that share parts of my face, sounds, qualities, and quirks. Here are a few:

- My great-grandmother Jean and her tough reminder not to stand up and eat because it'd make your house poor.

- My mother saying, *We all we got*, again after my little brother and I fist fought for a hundredth time, to remind us that siblings fight but that no person on the planet could carry us, go to bat for us, dust us off like our sisters, like our brothers, like our mamas.

- Natalie, a once-advisor whom I hold close as kin, a mother whom I hope most to mother after, concentrates on the sound of her son's voice as he constructs a mosaic of sea creatures, their abilities, their fears, their food. She is prompt with further inquiry, to which the son brightens like a plant leaf in the sun, to which he searches his oceanic archive for answers to her questions to which her pride becomes perfume hanging all around her.

- Momma's, Jean's, Shirl's, Jada's Recipe for Frying Chicken: clean chicken with white vinegar and water, rinse well, season chicken with Lawry's seasoning salt, garlic powder, black pepper, Sazón, spicy brown mustard, and a few droplets of hot sauce. Pour flour into a grocery store bag, place chicken in, close bag into your fist, shake, until chicken is completely covered, place chicken into the oil. There are no measurements, you just know when it's done. There's a smell, a look, a certain crisp about it.

- aracelis hands me *The Collected Poems of Lucille Clifton 1965–2010* to borrow, then to keep, then I recite "won't you celebrate with me" in the same way I do my grandfather's protection prayer before leaving home each day. She lifts a small baby boy made of her and her love into my arms and we sit and talk and he sits and listens to us, small gargles as if at some point saying, *Me too or maybe or why?* or

- I am seven or so and my Nanna teaches me to make a yellow cake with chocolate frosting. Nanna trusts me with her secret ingredient meant to further fluff the dessert as it rises: 7 Up soda. We splash the soda into the cake mix and when served everyone begs to know who made it.

- My great-aunt Tammy tastes a slice of the cake after I proudly declare myself as its maker. That year and every year following, Tammy has asked for a yellow cake with chocolate frosting for her birthday. I am twenty-five now and some ten to twelve cakes behind.

- My grandma Ronny dancing as though nothing in the world can touch her up there—six foot, and on her jam like skin, tapping the grounds of her feet in a two-step, her gold and gleaming rings decorating the bark-brown of her fingers waving in the air like fall leaves.

Mama, how, if in any way, do you mother like your mother? Like your grandmother? Great-grandmother?

Jada S. Jones: Every Saturday, my mother Shirldina and I would go to 34th Street, where all the department stores were, and we would shop—Macy's, B. Altman's, the Gap! Mothering like my mother is green—which is also one of my favorite colors. The green represents the money my mother worked hard to earn, to use almost wholly on my well-being and jovial pleasures. Before my mother could afford a place for the two of us, we lived with Grandma Jean, and things were different. The house was a bit crowded, and there didn't seem to be enough money to go around for us all. I remember one weekend Jean was away in Atlantic City (Jean loved her penny slots) and the lights were turned off. My mother, her siblings, and I all used one lamp that got its power through an extension cord we ran through the hallway outside of the apartment.

When my mother got her own place, that sense of lack dissipated with the other people I once had to share space with. Shirldina was a telephone operator and made good money for a Black woman in the late '70s–early '80s in New York City. Of her stocks, bonds, fancy clothes, and gorgeous head of hair, I knew I was the most important thing that my mother had and she made sure that I knew.

Green is also vegetable—collard and turnip greens, broccoli and string beans—all life fuel, no matter the stage of growing, dying, uprooting, or planting. No matter her predicament, my mother never gave up and did her best up until her last breath.

Roma Jean's mothering was like a brain freeze from your favorite frozen drink gulped down too quickly. She was rough around the edges like me but had *her* way of letting you know she loved you. Like the time I came home drunk for the first time and she hooped and hollered loudly and with purpose. She scolded, *You think you're grown and that's what you get* and also went to the store for a Pepsi and BC Powder to make me feel better. Despite being a mom of seven, grandmother and great-grandmother of four, fun was a priority. Jean never lost her sense of self, because she made time to enjoy the life she'd been given, the one with kids, and the one before they existed. I, too, have patterned my parenting after Jean in the way that I have given my children hard truths, I help to dust them off after they've fallen, and I find the necessary dance floors where I gather with friends who know a party ain't a party till I walk in.

My great-grandmother, Sarah, whom I called Momma, and I shared moments together, laughing, watching *Matlock, Dynasty, Days of Our Lives*, our safety and momentary escape from our dramas. We cooked together, I eavesdropped while she'd talk junk to my Auntie J. Josephine was Momma's sistah. They didn't share blood, but they were connected. She had no biological children of her own but loved and provided for the many children she served at our home church. She'd ensure that every summer, every child of the congregation went on a week-long vacation to give them an opportunity to get out of the city. Momma, Auntie J, and me were pretty much a crew, even if I was the only one who thought so.

Speaking of crews, Momma would always invite my friends over. She fed them, gave them advice, checked up on their mamas. That's how I duplicate her mothering. I've made special moments with each of my children, individually and collectively. She is why I'm the *cool* mom, why all the kids love Ms. Jada. I learned from her that I have more than enough love, guidance, and wisdom to share with children even if they aren't directly connected to me. The Sarah in me is my understanding of young people, my ability to discipline and hold space, my role as auntie or second mama to kids outside of my family.

Shaina: Dear Spirit—God—Ancestors, thank you for my life, for all of the love and nurturing that I have had access to, for my many blessings, for your unconditional love. I come to this prayer and ask with a grateful and open heart. I pray for a future in which I have children both born to me and not, that they more than anything know love, that they feel seen and heard, that they know the alchemy of their skin in ways I didn't quite understand growing up, that they know freedom, that they know power. I pray that my children have access to the things that they need even when I don't even know they need them. I pray for a village of open, warm, whole people to cover my children—encircle them—with tools for living, growing, and loving. I pray that they never know my struggles, the struggles of my mother or her mother or her mother, firsthand, but that they know and honor our stories. I pray for patience and sweetness and resiliency and fight. I call these things already so. Amen.

What is your hope/are your hopes for me as a mother? For you? For mothers in general?

Jada: My prayer for you as a mother is that you won't have the hardship of a nonparticipating, unconcerned other parent and struggle with your children like I did. My prayer is that you will be strong and well-equipped emotionally, mentally, and financially to navigate your way and guide your children. I pray that you ground your family in God first, then through the challenges of life with love, guidance, and the patience of a snail.

Before my last breath escapes my body and Jesus guides me down the path toward the light, I, as a mother, pray to see each of my children happy, healthy, and successful. I pray for healing from our dark pasts.

My prayer for mothers in general is we be light and love to the blessings bestowed upon us in the form of babies that gurgle, children that get into mischief, teenagers that test you, and the adults that then care for you as you once cared for them.

Shaina: On April 16, 2019, I woke in a bed I had no business [being] in with the sun shouting through grayish linen curtains and an incessant hum from my phone underneath my pillow. My aunt Brandi, with whom I had been living throughout her pregnancy, called to tell me that she'd be heading to the hospital soon to give birth to her daughter. As her niece, her tenant, and her birth doula, I had promised that no matter when the moment came, I'd be no more than five minutes away and would miss nothing. Twenty-five minutes away by train, I dressed and sped through 116th Street like a hell bat, hopped on the 2 train to Prospect Avenue in the Bronx. In the house, I found my aunt dressed, just barely hunched over.

When we arrived, she was about three inches dilated, and the doctors sent us off into the streets of lower Manhattan to give my aunt, her cervix, my soon-to-be cousin Bailee, a push. The congregation of us assembled around the maternity unit waiting room—my play-aunties, my mother, my godmother, women of my childhood church ministerial staff—and left the hospital resembling a high school clique. I had always heard the women in my family talk about their prebirth stories where they'd done something physical to jumpstart labor—I have heard of jumping double Dutch, doing jumping jacks, squats, relay races, and dancing intensely. For my aunt, we began with food, sat around a long, narrow table, the six of us, burgers, waffle fries, Chick-fil-A sandwiches, and Arnold Palmers. After we walked to the pier where my aunts, my mother, and I all ran back and forth across this waterfront sitting area, we cackled at the facial expressions of white passersby confused at this very pregnant woman and her gang of girls squatting and running and jumping alongside her. We laughed and shared parts of my aunt's back to rub when her laughter morphed into a contraction.

In the birthing room, there are more of us than hospitals allow: me, my mother, Bralyn (Bailee's big sister), Inzzia (my play-aunty and Bailee's godmother), and Minister Lakisha. After I had run out of breathing patterns for her to mimic, once the pain had gotten too loud for making loops around the maternity ward hallway, I grabbed her headphones and turned on a gospel playlist I had made for her on this day. As Tasha Cobbs blared through the phone, the doctors began prepping her to push. With one of her feet in my hand and the other in her older daughter Bralyn's hand, my aunt began to push.

Birth is the closest thing to God I think I've ever seen.

Ma, can you tell me something about a birth?

Jada: Childbirth is the most wonderful feeling on earth at the end. The beginning is filled with hope and anticipation that the moment you have been waiting for has finally arrived. This life that you have been talking to, nursing, carrying is coming to meet you face to face. Then the pains begin to intensify oftentimes slowly, but they do progressively get harder to handle. When the pain is the most excruciating, when you are in tears because you think you can't take anymore, when you want to give up, then is the time to get ready for another big push. You weakly return to that excitement but just want to sleep from the process. Here you learn your first lesson as a mother, where you put your feelings to the side to make it happen for your baby. Determined and dedicated, you push and push with everything that you have, and there is an opening, a running of warm and goopy fluid, and a slimy small wailing person meets you on your bare chest. This is the part where you say, *Hi baby, I'm your mommy.*

Shaina: I've always wished that I could give you a different life. I've always wished that I could give you your mother back because I knew what luck I had to have you. I couldn't fathom my existence without you. From very young, I always felt that you were missing a big piece of yourself that we, your children (me, Justin, Josiah, Jaidyn), couldn't fill, that parties couldn't fill, that friends couldn't fill you, that lovers couldn't fill, and I hurt so badly on your behalf with this knowing. It made me feel the need to protect you at all costs because I felt that you were working with less than most people had to work with and I didn't want anyone to further exploit that disadvantage. I'd give anything to deal you a different hand.

What I've learned watching you, emulating you, trying to be everything you wanted for me, is that we are all working to fill our spaces that loss and pain have left us with. Mama, this work of building and filling and healing yourself that you've done these forty-three years of your life is gorgeous and perfect. People are so quick to point to our flaws, shortcomings, and mistakes; and slow to celebrate our work, transformations, and growth. And in case no one has celebrated you in this way, I want to. Ma, you are perfectly formed, perfectly breathing, perfectly becoming, perfectly *making it do what it does*. Here, and always, are your flowers for being while you worked, while you parented, while you hurt, while you lost, while you grew, while you mistaked, while you prayed your way through some of the heaviest of days.

Is there anything you have always wanted to tell me but never have?

Jada: I've always wanted to tell you that I'm SORRY!!!!!! Sorry for your trauma, sorry I didn't protect you, and I need you to forgive me. I wanted so much for your life to be better than mine and although it may have been hard, I KNOW you have become the woman God intended you to be. Similar to me, your childhood was full of hard stuff, and as I've aged, I've reaped so many harvests and so will you. I am so excited for your future.

A Conversation between Naima Green and Suhaly Bautista-Carolina

Naima Green: I feel really honored that you asked me to ask you about motherhood. I feel like we can't really talk about any of your work with herbal medicine, motherhood, museums, art education, all of the things and ways you show up in the world, without talking about the way you love. What does loving look and feel like for you?

Suhaly Bautista-Carolina: I love starting from love. Such a great point of departure. A lot of what I do is motivated by love. Everything I do is motivated by love—

Luna: I need to . . .

Suhaly: —I think fear too, connected to that. There's a lot of fear in love, for me. This fear that something that I love will not exist anymore or is not appreciated in the way that I want it to be. That has a lot to do with the way I move Moon Mother[1] or all my work in environmental justice or my work with artists and my work as an herbalist; it's rooted in a place of deep commitment and devotion to people and to this land, coupled with this fear that we're not treating those things right. And then this responsibility on top of it that I think really defines my purpose to intervene and model what it means to be in right relationship with people and communities and the land.

I was just having this conversation within the museum context about power versus agency. Power is bestowed upon you by systems or institutions or other people—it's something that you get. Whether you deserve it or not, right? And we can go down another avenue of self-power and what we allow ourselves, but I wasn't talking about that. We were talking about the power you have within an institution to make change. And someone used the word "agency" interchangeably with that and I thought, actually everyone has agency. We all have the ability to create change from wherever we are.

For me, I was saying that I wanted to model—

Luna: [*singing*]

Suhaly: —what it means to be in right relationship with people and with the land, from wherever I'm sitting, all these roles, in all these spaces that I enter into, that I remember that I have agency ... And so I try to do what I know is right, is what I mean. That's what I mean.

Naima: Tell me a little about your journey into motherhood. Did you always know you wanted to have a child?

Suhaly: No, not at all. I never really imagined my future beyond my own self. I think in my imagining of what it would be like to be an adult in this world it wasn't that I was always alone, I was with other people, but I wasn't bound to someone or married or with children. I didn't imagine my life this way for a long time, and I think it was because I really had this notion of liberty and freedom that was very—

Luna: I'm ...

Suhaly: —tied to being alone. I thought that being free meant that I had to be on my own to sort of not be bound. I was really committed to that idea of being free and doing what I wanted and traveling, and not being held back. That's what I thought a family would do.

I never really envisioned what a life for me could look like with kids and a partner. I didn't dream that. So I think it was really being with Naima and feeling like, "Oh, I'm still my whole self here." That made me feel like I could have whatever it is that we dream together because I didn't lose any of myself being with her, you know? Naima really also moved me into a place of imagining a life with children. It was always her dream. I think for her she didn't imagine a life without children. She just didn't know how that would play out.

So when we first got together, I think I was still on this like, "Let's see the world, let me show you what I value and what I cherish."

Luna: [*singing*]

Suhaly: That was what made my eyes glisten, just being out here and feeling free. And then I also was very afraid of childbirth. I wasn't afraid of being pregnant, thank goodness, but I really tried to avoid thinking about childbirth. I was so scared that something would go wrong, and I have too much information about Black mothers and the way this country treats or cares for Black mothers that I just couldn't enter into it without a huge fear that something would happen to me, and that I would be resentful towards Naiema for wanting this first.

There were all these thoughts swirling in my mind about never getting to meet my child, or . . . I couldn't divorce the idea of having a child from the idea of death.

* * *

Naima: What does it feel like to be a mother in your body?

Suhaly: We. Luna will be three on Sunday, and I, we just recently stopped nursing. Two weeks ago, three weeks ago. So, I think up until recently or for the last three years, four years, while I'm feeding this baby and nursing this baby and nourishing this baby with my body, I think I have felt both supremely fortunate and like a mystic, magical being that I can do what I have done. There will never be enough words to articulate what I think about women after being a mom.

And I've also felt extremely exhausted and disconnected from myself, belonging to a person. Needed. Required for someone's livelihood. There are a lot of different kinds of feelings when I think about what it feels like in my body. I'm at this really interesting point because I just stopped nursing, and we're in quarantine. How little I'm able to spend time with my own self at a time when I thought that ending our nursing journey would give me more liberty, would allow me to tap back into my body. It's like, actually . . . you're still in the same three-hundred-square-foot space, and people wanna be more carried and more cared for, and you just took away something that was her binky basically, and so now you have to supplement that with more hugs and more care, and more holding, more carrying, more... It's a lot. And I think it's beautiful. We're very close. She and Naiema are very close.

It's beautiful, and I think it's hard. It's too much to say, and I'm still stretching into new territory all the time. Even the very, very beginning was hard because so much of my body was required for everything. Luna was born very, very little.

Naima: I remember.

Suhaly: Yeah, she was so itty. So it's also like, the letting go and the independence that they start to show happens so early. It's always happening from the moment they're in your body, and then suddenly they're out of your body.

And then they're always in your hands, and then suddenly they're holding your hand. And then they wanna not hold your hand, so you're just *watching* them go. But the attachment of this person from within your body to outside of your body, to letting them slowly be themselves, it's the most beautifully sad and heartwarming and heartbreaking event that you're just watching your whole life.

You're witnessing that happen, and you're nourishing their independence while also feeling an absence of being needed. I don't know. It's so funny because this is what we make fun of our moms for. We just want to be needed. And I still watch the ways my mom cares for us, or these gestures of love and care that she demonstrates to us by buying us things that she knows that we need, or like bringing us foods that she knows that we like. And so I'm like, "Of course." It would never have made sense to me before that. There was a time when I needed you for *every thing*, everything. To live, to eat, to breathe, to be safe, to not fall, to be loved, to feel cared for and smart and important, and to read, and to do my homework, and then there comes a day when you're just like, "Bye ma, love you. Call you later." And then you call less, and I'm just like, "Oh my God." I'm already crying.

She's three, and I'm thinking about when she's eighteen. And I can protect her so much now. But where do mothers find their strength to let their kids go into this crazy, fucked-up place? I want to protect her forever. So I'm like, "Stay small so I can put you in the car seat. I can always make sure you're in your car seat if you're little. Stay in your car seat and do what I say."

And how do you just trust that what you're doing, what you're teaching her, is enough for her to make the right decisions that she needs to make when she has to make the decisions by herself?

For me, there's no motherhood without deep fear. The moment you birth your kid, you birth this fear over your head forever because there's no love like that. And then you live with that in the back of your mind every time that you have to relinquish control or not see your kid or drop them off at school or daycare, all the things where you're not there, you know?

Naima: Yeah. Thank you. For sharing all of that. And something that you said ... You talked about the way that your mom is helping you care for Luna and I would love to know if you want to share a little bit about your relationship to your own mother, and how it's changed.

Suhaly: I couldn't have imagined that we would be here, my mother and I. And Luna. But they are so close. I don't know if the word is "divinely" crafted. Of course, they're this close because them being this close heals some sort of wound between us. Because, through Luna, we have to be closer. And I never believed anyone when they said that Luna would be the glue to bring us back together, or "Oh, just watch what happens when you have children, they change everything."

I think things were so broken at one point between my mom and I, that I didn't think anything or anyone could fix that. I just thought I would go through my life motherless and just raise my child with my chosen fam and my wife and we would be happy and build from where we started.

Luna: [*Laughing a gurgling river of laughter in the far background!*]

Suhaly: When I finally made the decision to fight for my family and say, "You can't pick and choose which elements of my life you enjoy or accept and pick those and leave the rest behind. That's not how this is gonna work." I think it really forced my mother to make a decision about what she wanted or needed in her life.

Luna: [*Laughing so hard in the background*]

Suhaly: That was a real breaking point for us because it took her a long time to actually make a decision and say, "I wanna be in my granddaughter's life, and I'll do what is required of me to respect your relationship and your life and your family because I want to be part of her life."

*　*　*

Suhaly: One thing that is really interesting to me is that Luna looks so much like me and my mom is really taken with that. She can't believe that Luna looks so much like me. She's like, "It's like looking at you. She says everything like you did."

All she says is: "She's more beautiful than you and she's smarter than you." [*laughter*]

But that adds another layer of magic to this because the way she treats her, the way she loves her, the way she dotes on her and obsesses over her ... Every profile picture in her WhatsApp is just always the latest picture that I've sent her of Luna. I can't help but think that she must be looking at me, must be thinking of me when she's with her, you know? There's no way not to, she's just looking right at my face, so I'm certain that there's healing in the way that she treats her, and perhaps more acceptance of who Luna will become because I was not afforded all of those things. She just wasn't there for me in that way and so I foresee a future where she can be the things to Luna that she couldn't be for me.

We're not a very communication-based [*laughs*] family in general. I think we struggle with that; we struggle with addressing things or calling them out and trying to have a conversation about them, but I think our actions demonstrate where we have grown and our intentions and the newness and the growth. I've had to forgive her, for sure. I don't know that I've completely let go of everything that I need to, and that, of course, feels like my work. But I think I have kept the door open enough for her to enter back in.

There was a time where I could have shut the door completely. I definitely had my own reasons for doing that and I am proud of myself for making room for her to grow out of where she was and into who she's become because I get to witness a new person with my daughter.

The young me is still very much healing from her inability to accept who I was, but I think she sees Luna as a gift and as new life, for her. I think she's wrestling with where that comes from, what love could produce this love. And the way she is a reflection of not just me, but of Naiema and me, and our community that is raising her, and so I have faith that she understands that now.

* * *

Naima: But also, maybe she then is trying to forgive herself for how she raised you, or didn't raise you.

Suhaly: Absolutely. And these are my reflections on where she might be based on what I know and what I see. I do think that she really cherishes this opportunity to be in Luna's life and that she knows that based on her previous behavior—the way she approached my marriage and me at some points—I know that she knows that there was a chance that she wouldn't be part of Luna's life.

I know she recognizes that there was a choice that I had to make about whether I would open that door.

And I think a lot of this happened at a time when my mom was really sick. And so I think part of that was also her wrestling with her own existence in this world, and whether she wanted to leave this plane not knowing her only living granddaughter. I'm sure that the timing of everything really affected the way she ultimately decided to move.

Naima: I know that your ancestral connection is really important to you and lineage and land. And I wonder, what do you want Luna to have from you and your ancestral connection and lineage?

Suhaly: I am satisfied with what she already has and knows and holds and carries, and I think about the way that I build altars in my home a lot and how we honor our ancestors in my home. I bring her into ritual so often and she is such a natural participant in all of those things that I know that what we practice is part of her already.

You know, I worry about being forgotten, right? We worry about being forgotten when we leave this earth and I feel like I don't have to worry about that with her. She'll know how to talk to me and commune with me once I'm not here anymore. She'll know how to reach out to me for support, she'll know those things because we do those things and we do them together now, there's no waiting for a time when she can absorb it because it's a way we live our lives, and I think she's part of all of it.

She's always in my altar, she's always playing with my medicines, always having conversations. Maybe with herself. I mean, I don't know who else [*laughs*], but we're enamored by our children so there's a way you speak about them where they're everything, you know? They're everything, there's nothing more...

Luna: Yes, dear.

Suhaly: Yes, dear.

Naima: [*Laughter*]

Suhaly: Giving her a window into that and just trying to be better every opportunity that I can. I hope she takes that. I hope she learns to return to herself and that she has everything she needs with her, around her, you know?

* * *

Suhaly: A lot of our queer friends don't have children yet or are maybe just having children. That felt like a big responsibility to figure out what that meant, or how it could be, to not have many examples around me of what that was like. It didn't mean that community showed up any less for me. It just meant that there were points where I was, like, I wish I had someone to talk about these things. Queer parenting. You know?

I wish we had that. Sometimes I wish we had that, and then other times I think we did it. We did it, and we trusted our intuition and we mothered and we're still mothering and we made it our own and we did it.

Sometimes I feel really good to know that we mothered on our own tip. We defined what motherhood was for us. And I'm proud of what we're doing. Or I'm so proud of Luna and who she is in this world already.

And I hope we can be that. I hope that in in our queer community, that if people needed us that they could turn to us, you know, for that support because it was something that we felt was absent, but I don't want that to keep being the case, you know?

People could find community in us, I think, if they were looking for it.

2

Twenty-First-Century Fertility Support

Seven Years, No Baby Yet

Celeste Mendoza

from family, friends, and the others

"I had no problem getting pregnant. Sit by me."

"I'll do it for you. My uterus is perfect."

"We got it on our *first* try. I'm so fertile."

"Eat less and exercise less. Your body needs to regulate."

"You just need to relax. You're thinking too much."

"Eat more and exercise more. Your body is out of balance."

"Aren't there doctors for that?"

"At least he hasn't left you."

"You're Mexican, right? Weird."

"You waited too long. How old are you anyway?"

"Motherhood is overrated. I have three and hate each one."

"There's nothing like love from a child. They can't cheat on you."

"It's hard for you to understand since you're not a mother."

"You must be repressed."

"Do you pray?"

"God doesn't want you to have children."

"You have your writing, right?"

Till the Ground Fertile

LeConté Dill

January 30, 2018: My journey is more recent, but already physically and emotionally painful, complex, and isolating. Even with all of my wellness and selfcare practices, connection with intuition, connection to spirit, it's still so hard. Like, why me? Or rather, why not me? But I realize I can't "suffer" in silence or in my head or in my pillow.

I started heading to the DMs of Facebook Messenger to discuss my fertility woes in January 2018. I decided to hit up one of my college friends who had recently posted something about fertility on her page that was both a declaration and a cryptic code. She was speaking my language, talking outta both sides of her mouth, being both revealing and vague. So I wanted to thank her profusely, but privately. I didn't know then that we would create a whole sisterhood in the DMs. I didn't know then that we would create a living archive with our messages. I didn't know then that others would come to the DMs to find *me* once I posted my own cryptic declarations on Facebook. I didn't know then that there is a whole sisterhood of sistahs thinking about in vitro fertilization (IVF), going through IVF, surviving IVF, reeling from IVF, celebrating because of IVF, cussin' out IVF. And though we're not alone, we still find ourselves in the shadows, in cryptic posts, in memes and message boards, in texts and DMs where we vomit out prayers and incantations. This essay chronicles these DMs and my reflections as I prepared to become a #IVFWarrior.

February 6, 2018: I *do* think these things need to be written (*mama never told me there'd be days like this*), but I also think words might not do it justice.

The world's first IVF baby, Louise Brown, was born in the United Kingdom in 1978, the same year as me. Since then, more than eight million babies have been born around the world as a result of IVF and other assisted reproductive technologies. Still, besides my first home-girl in the DMs, I didn't really know of anyone else going through this. Especially not any other Black people. I felt odd, alone. I felt defective. I felt like I was a mad scientist, an astronaut, an alien embarking on a special mission "to boldly go where no one has gone before" in order to make a baby. To make myself a mommy.

April 26, 2018: I just sprinted to a hallway that was quiet, but with good reception, to take a call with the fertility nurse and schedule some thangs. Then, I sprinted down the hall to meet with a student.

I had been married for almost a year and hadn't been able to get pregnant on my own—well, on *our* own. Hoping, praying, chanting, reiki, acupuncture, raspberry tea, yoga, sexy lingerie, and, of course, lots of sex, but not too much sex, and then sex aligned with fertility calendars, clocks, and apps. I had been married almost a year when we finally got the IVF ball rolling. In between my work meetings, teaching classes, mentoring students, working on research, and writing papers, the first step was to schedule a consultation with a reproductive endocrinologist or RE for short.

May 16, 2018: I just started seeing a fertility specialist. Tests on tests on tests. In fact, I'm going for another blood draw this morning...

I have low AMH (Anti-Müllerian hormone) and high prolactin. Ugh! I guess I'm earning my ditched Biochemistry degree afterall. I have to redo the prolactin test while fasting. I was too tired (and hungry) to go this morning. Then I had to get the HSG (hysterosalpingography) test to see if my fallopian tubes were blocked. Then have a consult with my RE about my genetic results and all these other tests. I'm really tired of running around, testing, monitoring, pee sticks, waiting, stressed. I appreciate having more data, but kinda feeling like chillin and waiting on nature.

I developed a whole new vocabulary upon seeing the RE. Acronyms and new words to google. I developed a whole new understanding of and appreciation for my body. Hormones, cells, and organs, oh my! But I was really fatigued. And this was only just the beginning.

May 31, 2018: Sooooo, I wanna de-stress, chill, and conceive. That's my June through August plan.

I wasn't yet ready to do IVF. And neither was my hubby. My line sisters said I was just stressed. That I needed to chill out, not be type A. Stop measuring my basal body temperature every day. Throw my fertility window out the window. Maybe then I would finally get pregnant. Get pregnant by stop trying to get pregnant.

July 10, 2018: Meditating and praying are indeed survival skills. My weekly restorative yoga and reiki are a godsend. And I start "womb wellness" this week.

I got even more intentional about ritual. Or rituals plural. Prioritizing me and my healing.

The mind, body, soul connection. And thank the heavens for Black women healers. I've heard that Brooklyn is indeed a blessing. You mean other places don't have spaces and practitioners and workshops like this everywhere you turn? Black women who look like me, who sound like me, who are shaped like me, who move like me—giving me space to breathe, stretch, and just be. Who encourage me to booty shake, pop that coochie, that yoni love. But why am I crying so damn much? And I thought I already worked this out in therapy ten years ago. Tending to my womb. Tending to a wound. Or wounds plural. I'm getting a cramp in my hand from scribbling in my journal so much, vomiting out prayers and incantations.

August 16, 2018: "To wait" and "To hope" are the same word en español. Esperar. There's a message there, too.

I was waiting and hoping to become a mommy. I had been waiting and hoping for a while. It's estimated that one in eight couples experience infertility in the United States. We were that one in eight. Always a damn statistic. We made up our minds to officially commit to doing IVF. Talking to the clinic's billing department. Talking to our insurance. Funny how those are the first things to do. We are in America, after all. My fertility prospects were tied up in a complicated, non-patient-centered, medical-industrial complex, and that mighty dolla dolla bill, y'all.

September 23, 2018: "You shouldn't move into a building with a couple of flights of stairs if you're tryna get pregnant"—Mom

My biggest cheerleader. My first fan. The conjure woman who conjured me . . . is a catastrophizer. If the sky is always falling, which way is up, Mom? Mommy. Mama. Mother. Mámi. I was trying to start out this leg of the journey hopeful and positive, not fast forwarding to the stress I'm putting on my future fetus simply by going home to my third-floor walkup. Mama's gonna mama, I suppose. And Mama only wishes me well. That concern be care. That fear be love.

November 16, 2018: Why am I here?

What does the road ahead look like?

Why do these doctors talk so fast?

Why am I so anxious?

I undergo more appointments. More testing. I'm a ball of questions, of anxiety. After I leave the doctor's office, I head to the Macy's shoe department. Retail therapy. *Miracle on 34th Street*!

November 21, 2018: I've been thinking a lot about surrender and agency all year. And how there *is* agency in surrender.

As a control freak (proud, recovering, whatever . . .), I realized that in this IVF journey, I was not in control at all. My hormones, my body, my doctors, my spirit guides would actually be steering the ship.

In vitro is Latin for *in glass*. *In vitro fertilization* would start with rounds and rounds of hormone injections that I would give myself, hubby standing by with gauze and sharps containers, egging me on (no pun intended), cheering me on. Next, my eggs would be removed from my ovaries while I was under anesthesia, and then they would be mixed with hubby's sperm in a Petri dish in order to be fertilized. After fertilization, the embryo would be delivered into my uterus via a catheter. Louise Brown, and other early IVF babies like her, was called a "test-tube baby" in the media. In the late eighties, I remember comedian Robin Harris (RIP) famously joking in his stand-up routines that one of BéBé's Kids was a test-tube baby. He repeated this joke in the movie *House Party*. I laughed, we all did. *Bad-ass, knuckle-headed* kids were test-tube babies. *Phonies and frauds* were test-tube babies. If you wanted to diss someone, you called them a test-tube baby. Just a joke, we thought. I'm not a joke, I now have to remind myself. I'm not a bad-ass, knuckle-headed, phony, fraud. What an experiment. What an act of faith.

January 14, 2019: On a good note, my new health insurance (thanks to hubby's job) provides two months of free therapy *and* behavioral coaching through the infertility program.

I am no stranger to therapy. Kudos to Young Conté for bravely seeking out psychosocial support for the first time as a freshman in college. That set me on a path to regularly engage in it from then on. So I was ecstatic that I would be able to have therapy for $free.99 during my IVF journey. Trained professionals to hear my venting, let me process, cheer me on. To remind me of my surrender and my agency. My strength and my vulnerability. My humanity.

February 1, 2019: Interestingly, I feel the anxiety/butterflies in my womb, not my heart.

Research says that women forty-one to forty-two years of age have a 5 to 6 percent chance of having a full-term, healthy baby from IVF. On the day after my forty-first birthday, I found out that I was pregnant from my first egg retrieval and embryo transfer!

Two days later, I found out that I was having an early miscarriage. My human chorionic gonadotropin (hCG)—the hormone that surrounds the growing embryo, eventually becomes the placenta, and detects pregnancy—was drastically dropping. A wail loud and deep left my body. My hubby holding me was both smothering and not enough. He suggested that I lie down; I demanded to stay awake. I shouted. I screamed. I needed to cry out. I needed to find out. Why? Surely the doctor, the internet, medical archives, or my journal would tell me why I was pregnant one minute and not the next. Would tell me what went wrong. Would tell me why I was wronged. Would tell me why I was wrong.

March 4, 2019: Work has been challenging during this journey, because I usually want to sleep/cry/Google/watch TV/chill rather than actually do what I'm expected to do.

I called it a "loss." I called it my period. My therapist suggested that I name it grief. That I name this grief. That I grieve.

I began to grieve.

I also began to plan the next round of IVF. Planning, plotting, on to the next thang is my coping mechanism.

March 29, 2019: I hate that each time, I definitely felt womb energy... then I didn't...

I went through with another embryo transfer using two of my frozen embryos. Once again, I got pregnant. I took several at-home pregnancy tests. They all read POSITIVE. I took pictures of all the positive pregnancy tests. I had proof. I put all of the positive pregnancy tests on my fertility altar. I also took several blood tests at the clinic. My hCG was rising! I bought a onesie and put it in a gift bag for the little one to open one day. I put the gift bag near my fertility altar. And one day, early on in the revelry, I woke up bleeding. I wailed in the bathroom. I hyperventilated in the bathroom. I screamed for my hubby. My fingers shook, trying to find the doctor's number in my contacts list.

The nurse said my hCG was plummeting. The doctor said my womb was empty. I leaned into her arms. Then I threw on my clothes. Rushed past the doctor and the nurse. Rushed past my hubby in the waiting room. We had to go. I had to leave. That place was suffocating. And yet, I had to return . . . several times, per IVF protocol, until my hCG levels were less than one so that they could officially confirm it as a loss. I had to sit in the waiting room with other hopeful, expectant parents. I had to sit in the waiting room bleeding. I had to sit in the waiting room grieving. I had to sit in the waiting room of the fertility clinic for tests to remind me that I was not pregnant, no longer pregnant, not a mommy after all.

June 28, 2019: I feel some kinda way.

I can't just "get pregnant." I also seem not to be able to stay pregnant.

July 14, 2019: Text message to my Tribe: I'm asking you to be in ritual with me tomorrow morning around 11am EDT. May we commune with spirit, be in spirit, and manifest abundance! Many thanks in advance!

We decided to endure another egg retrieval and embryo transfer. Third time's the charm, right? More injections and ultrasounds. More waiting and hoping. Esperar. Offered honey to the East River right outside of the clinic for Oshun. Wore white to my appointments. Ate so many pineapples. Pineapples are said to be the symbol of the infertility community—strong on the outside, sweet on the inside. They are also said to help the embryo implant into the uterus. Open legs, open cervix, open heart. My acupuncturist said I needed to open my heart. That there is where my seed would be planted.

August 11, 2019: Had ultrasound—saw the little grain of rice and heard her heartbeat!

I actually heard my own heartbeat once I finally heard my baby's heartbeat. That little grain of rice was a budding, blooming embryo becoming a fetus. Me becoming a mommy, after all. After all of this. Third time *was* a charm. We named her Miracle Whip. Whipped up in labs. Whipped up in love. My RE gave me something like three hugs. I leaned into her arms.

For someone who was supposedly "infertile," I was pregnant three different times in 2019. Five embryos took root in my womb throughout 2019. Four departed. Departed early, before heartbeat, but after a cleaving to my own heart. Cleaved, burrowed deep down within my longing, within my loving. What is love but a longing?

January 2, 2020: In my most recent dream, I would take Miracle Whip out of my womb every day. We would play and talk, and I would tell her how good she was developing. Then, she would ball into the fetal position, and I would put her back inside.

Chiiiile! Pregnancy dreams are off the chain! Those good *good* messages and visions.

March 2, 2020: She's here!!!

I wanted, needed, knew she would be here. Her name is Worthy. She is worthy. She reminds me that I am indeed worthy, too.

March 10, 2020: It's been an intense year. We don't look like what we've been through.

It's not lost on me that our miracle arrived before the world began to endure and witness intersecting pandemics. As the world "shut down." As the world began to reckon with itself. As we sheltered-in-place, as I built my nest, I began to notice that my little Miracle Whip was not only a real-life miracle for me, my hubby, and our family but she also was a symbol of faith for my other homegirls going through IVF. Between Zooms, Verzuz, and Club Quarantine; underneath baked goods, house plants, and athleisure; amidst protests, demands, and fatigue, my homegirls found me in the DMs and text messages. And they began to send some of their homegirls and their homegirls' homegirls my way, too. And, just like my homegirl had done for me two years prior and during my whole IVF journey, I realized that I had some insight to impart, some advice to share, some languages to decode, some jargon to translate. I could listen, be a witness, hold space. I could remind them that I felt so alone on my journey, but that I actually wasn't, and neither are they. We be kin. We be builders. We be building our kin.

March 27, 2020: Take good care of yourself. Feel and name ALL of the feelings. Lean on your Village (virtually).

July 18, 2020: Think about small and big ways to honor yourself through this.

September 25, 2020: Try to say no to work things that are not required or don't bring you joy.

October 18, 2020: Thinking of you and rooting for your embryos!

October 27, 2020: Continue to feel your feelings. And even in the darkest moments, hold on to that hope you have now.

December 9, 2020: Be sure to nurture yourself.

My messages to the many mamas-in-the-making were brief affirmations. Small but big prayers and incantations. These homegirls taught me so much more about the science and art of fertility, the science and art of grief, the science and art of sisterhood. I learned that even though Worthy is already here, we're still on a longer IVF journey together—as *worthy* witnesses, going to the shadows and tending to the light there. Me, her, us, our homegirls, and the other folks watching, waiting, hoping.

My miracle child is a testament of longing. Of loss. Of conjuring. Of waiting and hoping. Of surrender and agency. Of burrowing, budding. Of blooming.

What We Don't Say

Mariahadessa Ekere Tallie

This story does not have an ending, I am unfolding as a mother, as a writer, as a friend, as a wife, as a daughter, and as an individual every moment.

There are things that no woman tells another about motherhood. I will tell you this: I died. It was not childbirth. My labors were long and hard and beautiful. I have given birth twice, once to a screaming soul who shattered my idealistic visions of motherhood and the second time to an infant so ancient she didn't utter a sound as she was lifted by the midwife from the water of the birthing tub, she just started at us. Both times my heart was cracked, shattered really, and there would be no repairing it. The love that stretched and tore and suckled and broke my sleep was one so profound that nothing could have prepared me for it.

The yellow from the canvas of day bled all over the black watercolor of night and time became nothing. There was a rhythm of waking, of feeding, and of sleeping. Of changing diapers and cuddling and eating again, of sleeping again, and I was lost in the curves of my children's wrists and in the folds of their necks and the freshly baked bread–smell of a new baby and the fragile, startling cries that made me gasp inaudibly and sent my heart flitting in my chest like a desperate butterfly.

Motherhood was all consuming.

There was nothing I wouldn't learn, nothing I wouldn't do to make the journey of my children from the realm of the unknown, the ether, the ancestors, to the harsh world I knew easier. I dove into homeopathy, herbs, and aromatherapy to soothe my first born, I carried her wrapped around my back in fabric, I was as close to her as her breath. I eliminated all my favorite spices from my diet lest they upset her belly. I devoured writings on mothering. I was too exhausted to write, but I knew that gift was mine and I knew that in time I would get back to it. This gift, this new life, had come through me and it was time to focus on her. I'd get back to me.

When I did get back to me, I was gone. This is the thing that women don't tell each other about motherhood. That you will never be who you were. That you will not see anything the way you used to see it, you will never hear language the way you used to hear it, music, color, photos, friends, family, career path—nothing or no one came through my transition from single woman to mother unexamined. Least of all myself.

I remember walking through the Lower East Side of Manhattan with a friend one evening. My husband pushed our first child down the chilled, narrow sidewalks in a gray stroller while I carried our second baby prominently in my belly, "My whole life had been about me. I was self-centered," I said to our friend. "Of course," my friend replied, and he urged me not to feel guilty about that. "This is so different. I am not the center of my universe anymore." It was not guilt I felt. It was as though I was walking between worlds. The old me who roamed this very neighborhood with a panther's grace. The me who wound in and out of bookstores and cafes and had nothing but time and her journal on her hands. The me at poetry readings, featured and popular. The me who would disappear for weeks or months: gone to a retreat in Spain or on an adventure in England, sitting rapt in classrooms as teacher or student. That me with her lovers and dramas and poems and phone calls at 3:00 A.M. And that other me, the one who barely reached for pen and paper. The me who cooked and did laundry and graded papers and shopped for groceries while pushing a stroller. The me with a husband who worked the night shift. I was on, always, no clocking in or out, always breastfeeding, cleaning, changing diapers, singing the alphabet, or something. Old friends with self-absorbed ways didn't make sense to me anymore. The city I loved seemed coarse and cold (particularly when no one would give me a seat on the subway.) Who was I then? Full of a quietly growing life, pushing a toddler in a stroller, doing yoga to maintain my equilibrium, living in a tense home dealing with disappointment at having to do so much alone despite being in a city of millions, some of whom I had called family, some of whom I had called friends.

I would look in the mirror back then and see a warrior. Glowing skin, quick smile, delicately muscled with tear-stained insides, and questions and faith. I did not know that beautiful woman in the mirror. I just knew what she had to do. Knew what she needed to do to help her family get through that day and the next. She was lonely sometimes. I surrendered. Let myself dance invisibly. Let my identity fall through the cracks. Waited for a new self to emerge.

A new self did emerge. This is what women do not tell each other. I want to say it here: You will die when you become a mother and it will hurt and it will be confusing and you will be someone you never imagined, and then you will be reborn. Truthfully, I have never wanted to be the woman I was before I had children. I loved that woman and I loved that life, but I don't want it again. My daughters have made me more daring, more human, more compassionate. Their births have brought me closer to the earth and they have helped me pare my life down to its essentials. Writing, quick prayers, good food, a few close friends, many deep breaths, love, plants, dancing, music, teaching— these are the ingredients of my/this new self. I waited for this new self in the dark, in the bittersweet water of letting go, in the heavy heartbeat of learning to be a mother, against the isolation, I grew and emerged laughing and crying and here I am, sisters and brothers.

Here I am.

A Dollar and a Dream

Keeonna Harris

I thought I was done having children after my first two kids, but in 2009, at twenty-nine, I am beyond excited to play with the idea of growing my family. This will be my first planned baby.

Planning a pregnancy sounds straightforward and easy—with my first two kids it just happened when I least expected it. But making a baby happen on my time is a bigger feat than I imagined. I have so much to learn about this process: knowing my schedule, when I'm ovulating, knowing how to *plan* for intercourse rather than just have sex. I have to learn about my body all over again.

My mom taught me the basics: menstruation, feminine products, and sex in the context of how babies are made. Conversations about sex in our family were not positive. Sex meant pregnancy, and pregnancy was not something we were happy about. Our family stories associated sex with being sneaky. Pregnancy was karma, punishment for having sex when you were supposed to be doing something else with your life. My granny loved to say, "Boys and books don't mix." She always talked about how she was supposed to be at the library, but she was at the "mosy rosy" and got pregnant with Anthony, her firstborn son. I was taught to fear my body, to repress my sexuality, and that sex was scary and shameful unless you were married. What I knew for certain was to not have sex until I got married, and to not get pregnant.

The second part of my sex education came from TV. I grew up during the eighties' crack epidemic when commercials and DARE campaigns played on a loop. Using Black women as the face of crack cocaine. Television taught me that Black women are dangerous, a danger to ourselves and society. We are *fast*, have way too many babies, don't work, always got our hand out, and can't keep a man. The distorted image of Black women is one of the many manifestations of the white people's obsession with Black women and attempts to control Black women's bodies.

I got pregnant at fifteen the first time I had sex. My mom cussed me the *fuck* out. I was traumatized but determined to keep my baby and raise him. We didn't talk for months even though we lived in the same house. My mom was at San Diego State, premed, ready to be a doctor when she accidently got pregnant with me. My dad isn't reliable, so she got her nursing license and worked double shifts my whole life. I was valedictorian of my kindergarten class. I got in trouble a couple times, but I still brought home As every report card. I loved to talk about how I was going to go to Spelman, premed, and become an ob-gyn, like on *The Cosby Show*. Instead, I was launched into being a teen mom. I was determined to do this on my own, even after my mom cussed me out, even after my son's father got incarcerated. I was going to be the first to make my family work.

Fast forward fourteen years later, two kids later, married to the father of my first son; and here I am, tackling sex education so we can have another baby. Our first baby happened all at once, so when it took multiple tries I was stressed. Five months of trying, I knew it should be easier. Once you decide to have a baby it should be simple. I had been on birth control since the first baby, and the second baby happened while I was on birth control. In my mind, any time you have sex you can get pregnant, and a period is a relief. Ovulation, scheduling, the windows for fertilization, all of this is new. Add in the fact that my husband is incarcerated. My body and my scheduling come secondary to the California Board of Prison's family visitation schedule. I'm only eligible for family visits every six weeks, so I have to pay close attention to my calendar and try to book as close to my ovulation as possible. I get to know the corrections officer in charge of family visits very well with all the calls I have to make to schedule visits. Planning a baby means constant communication, me and my body, me and my husband, me and the prison.

On a regular visiting weekend, my friend Nicole and I check in to our room at the Motel 6 in Blythe, California. It's Friday night and we're trying to relax after the three-and-half-hour drive from LA. We kick off our shoes, and she lies across her bed; I sit on the edge of mine and turn on the TV to see if anything good is on BET. We settle in for a few minutes, until she breaks up the silence.

"You look pregnant."

I laugh so loudly. The kind of laugh that comes from the core of your belly, I could feel it rippling from my chest out of my mouth. Nicole and I aren't even thirty, but she sounds like my granny. What's pregnant even look like when I don't have a stomach? She knows we been trying to have a baby. She's serious. I look at the calendar on my phone. I'm late.

We walk up and down every aisle in the Dollar Tree trying to find a pregnancy test. Dollar Tree is the only store around. Blythe is a drive-thru town, the only people who live here full time are retirees, correctional officers, and a few people who just want to be close to the prison. Dollar Tree is the only thing that's not a gas station—to go to a real store or even grocery store is at least a thirty-minute drive. Nicole put me up on game that Dollar Tree has pregnancy tests, but we can't find any. We give up on our scavenger hunt, ready to head home empty handed, until I spot the pregnancy test nestled between the batteries and gum at the register. I snatch the last one off the hook. PREGNANCY TEST. Big letters on a little cardboard box, looking hella bootleg. But it's here and it's a dollar.

I sit on the toilet back at the Motel 6, looking at the pregnancy test, waiting for two lines. It's a dollar-store pregnancy test. How good can it be? I chew my lip, staring at the test. Waiting.

"What it say!"

Nicole keeps yelling through the door. This test is so bootleg, how do I know it's gonna work? All I can do is stare and wait.

"What it say!"

What if it says yes? Is it a real yes? This shit cost a dollar.

"What it say!"

What if it says no? Imma be pissed.

"What it say!"

Five months is too long to wait. We been trying forever. I'm getting disappointed. How long is this dollar store test gonna take?

There it is.

Two faint lines.

My whole life, I relished the fact that I'm a tough girl. I grew up all over LA, Watts, Compton, Long Beach, Rosemead, Baldwin Park, Azusa, Glendora. I'm a hood girl, I can navigate anywhere I'm at. Nobody can punk me for nothing. I can manage in any space. I can survive and make it through. Obstacle? I overcome it. Anything they throw at me, *blaow*, I block it!!! I told myself I was the exception. I thought I was special because I hit all the stereotypes but with the opposite results. With a baby on my hip, I continued to be a honor student and graduated a year early.

I thought I was the exception to the rule, and when I grew up I realized that yes, I am special, but I wasn't the exception. I was in the company of many Black girls who raised kids on their own while defying the myths of the jezebel and the welfare queen. I was raised by a single mom, and her mom was a single mom. The racist, infamous 1965 Moynihan report on the Black family would brand me as part of the "matriarchal structure which, because it is so out of line with the rest of the American society, seriously retards the progress of the group as a whole, and imposes a crushing burden on the Negro male, and in consequence, on a great many Negro women as well." But there was no crushing me. No burden I couldn't handle. I was a teen mom, expected to drop out of high school, but I graduated, and here I am about to graduate with a bachelor's degree. I was supposed to get a minimum-wage job, but here I am working in an income bracket that my mom had never seen. I have a new car, I pay the rent for our whole family, I take care of two kids off my income alone, I provide for my family. On paper, I'm good!

A picture of me and my oldest son, Tre, for my high school graduation. In my family, the high school graduation photo is a milestone—each person takes their graduation photo with their big accomplishment. My cousin who graduated at the same time as me took hers with a basketball, because she was a star basketball player. For me, then and now, it is important to have the picture with my baby. He was my extracurricular activity, my pride and shame, and I wanted to have all of it together.

My first two pregnancies were so unexpected that I couldn't plan, only react. Pregnancy this time feels like sunshine. This is my third baby, but my first in so many ways:

- The first time I don't cry from uncertainty when I find out I am pregnant.

- The first time I'm not worried about how to provide for a new baby.

- The first time I am happy and unafraid to tell the father I am pregnant.

- The first time that I'm not ashamed to be pregnant.

- The first time I have a baby while married.

- The first time I'm not mad at my body for betraying me.

- Most important, the first time I'm not scared to tell my mom.

I am proud. I wear this new sense of warmth like a shiny badge.

The next morning, I get dressed with more care than usual. It's before 7:00 A.M., we have to get ready to go get in line. Nicole is in the shower, but I'm already up and getting ready. I'm double, triple checking everything like the first day of school. I'm taking the kind of care to stunt on all the other kids. I want to look beyond good. As I slowly rub lotion onto my legs, I glance over to my outfit lying on the bed. I look closely to make sure there are no wrinkles. I dress in front of the mirror to make sure that I look good from every angle. Today is our day. I get to tell my husband I'm pregnant, and we can share the moment together, in person.

As I wait in line, my head is on a swivel. I am anxious, looking around, checking the clock. What's the hold up? The COs are taking their time today. Me and Nicole are there with Rae. We are regulars. We call ourselves regulars to let the outsiders know we are frequent visitors at Ironwood State Prison. The regulars, these women, are my family, the one I chose. We are bonded by long drives from LA to the middle of nowhere, birthday celebrations, hotel barbeques, new babies, tears, break-ups, and weddings. These regular women are my normal. They are as vital to me as my own body, they are the connective tissue that has carried, supported, and held me in the best and worst of times. They are like breathing; I can't live without them and yet I don't always think about how necessary they are to my life. Their love helps me love me. Today I'm surrounded by my regular family and about forty other strangers in the visiting room.

I sit at the table fidgeting, chewing the inside of my cheek, sitting up high in my seat, trying to see if I catch a glimpse of my husband through the small glass window on the giant steel door that separates visitation and the prison. Once he is through the door, he moves to the table as quickly as he can, almost running, trying to be as quick as possible without moving so fast that the COs are going to check him.

He hugs me quickly and we sit down. He knew I had something to tell him because he called me the night before, but I told him I wanted to wait and talk to him in person. When I say I'm pregnant, we are both beaming, full-face smiles. He can't hug me, we already used our hug when he walked in the room, so we hold hands and smile. We get to enjoy the moment, the best we can.

I don't trust the Dollar Tree pregnancy test, so Monday morning I go to the doctor's office in Glendora. The waiting room is cold and brown, and I'm the only one in the room. Just me and the receptionist, waiting for the side door to open and hear the nurse call my name.

"Keeonna, come this way"

I follow close behind the nurse.

"Undress and put on this gown, the doctor will be in shortly"

I sit on the examination table, kicking my legs, waiting on the doctor, still a little giddy. The door swings open. As I sit naked under the gown, I'm fifteen again, and a happy doctor's visit turns into an interrogation.

"How many kids do you have, again?"

"I see . . ."

"And you're twenty-nine . . . so you started early . . ."

"Oh, you're married?

" . . . why isn't he here today?"

"Prison?"

"I see . . ."

"So he just went to prison?"

"Oh . . ."

"So how did you get pregnant?"

In under five minutes my doctor had ruined my day. I pictured a magical moment that would be the culmination of all my learning about my body. I had done what I was supposed to and made this baby the right way: planned, married, and on schedule. What I wanted to be an empowering confirmation of my hard work was confirmation of what the doctor thought of me and what others said about me. The questions took a sharp turn from my medical history and my pregnancy. I became spectacle, and questions turned into morbid curiosity masquerading as small talk. The audacity that he felt so comfortable asking me all these questions. A gynecologist is already invasive, he's all in my business with his questions, his eyes, his hands. It's uncomfortable enough when it's just about a medical procedure, but this was more. This was about surveillance of my Black body.

Enough, I need to get my happy back. I tell him directly and clearly, "No more questions. If it's not about my baby, it's not your business."

I needed the doctor to have a healthy baby, but the doctor and the prison had started to feel the same—watching me, policing me, stopping me from being me. This is how the state works. It creates a web of surveillance and control. It makes you question your own autonomy over your own body.

I start to focus instead on the baby. Everything that went into getting to this moment. I remember how happy I am to be pregnant. I sit up on the examination table. I am back. I worked too hard to get this baby, all the months, all the planning, working through my body, working through the prison. I'm not gonna let this doctor take anything from me. This baby being in my body right now is a *fuck you* to the prison and medical industries trying to keep me from being me. I had to take my happy back.

The Water Clock

Vanessa Angélica Villarreal

In late January, you will arrive on a blade of yellow, dividing tissues of light. How it will begin: enormous, I will again awaken to absence, rub oil on the pearled scarring low on my belly, veined and ragged as red cabbage. I will wrestle with gravity and pull at the sheets to hoist myself up off the bed, and then the rupture—before I can take a step, a pitcher of water will tip over inside me, and *splash*—I will think I'd spilled something, look for a drinking glass emptying itself onto the tiles. But instead I am the source of the water, myself a kind of hourglass, spilling time.

The space between the breaking of water and the first contraction is a time dilation, a hyperspace composed of many presents, many timelines—history imagining itself as the future. I collapse into my own birth, my mother's birth, her mother's birth, the first birth, a mystery so utterly mundane. *Who are you? Who will you be?* Every cell in my body knows what to do without me, bypassing my birth plan to work from a more ancient blueprint. I'd studied and read the accounts, knew the beats labor would take, prepared for the tearing universe in my body to produce a new life, a person who has not yet existed, emerging from the nothing. I'd done so much reading and preparation, I'd forgotten to prepare for nothing at all.

I want to apologize to you now, I was afraid. Not like most mothers facing their first birth, but a deeper fear, stored imperceptibly in the medulla. That's why my body shut down. I already knew I'd lose your father, could sense his disgust for my body, afraid of how labor would bare my naked animal truth. Days after the positive on the pregnancy test, he would drive me to your first ultrasound, and on the way would say we wanted different things, to live in different cities, suggested I abort. Your father could not admit then that he no longer loved me or thought me beautiful. Throughout the pregnancy, I could feel him planning to leave, to be with other women, repeating the decision his own father made at his birth to leave him and his mother for other women. The bigger I grew, the further he drifted away, like an opposite moon repelling its planet. Unconscious of it, my body registered his every unspoken signal, every unmet smile, the widening distance. That is the truth I knew but could not name. And so, when my water broke, my body shut down, protecting itself from its hunter.

I called him at work, and he performed compulsory excitement at the news of my water breaking, a prescribed role he played through dread. I felt the kind of virginal peace I'd seen in Catholic imagery all my life, the way I'd learned to be feminine, passive and calm. Not hysterical with panic and fear. So I dressed, put on light makeup, and once at the hospital, the nurses sent me back home. No contractions yet, no pain. I could wait for the contractions at home and come back when labor had started, but if nothing happened in twelve hours then they'd take me in.

This is where I begin to lose time.

* * *

The week before your father ended our marriage, I'd come back from a trip to Chetumal to visit my tia-abuela Mela for research about my grandmother, your great-grandmother Angelica. I want to tell you the stories I recovered from silence—the stories my tias y tios tell of what their sister survived. We come from indentured farm laborers who lived and worked on a cotton rancho owned by a Spaniard in Torreon. She was a child bride, married off at fourteen to a castizo twenty-one years her senior, and gave birth to my mother at home at fifteen, nine months after her wedding day, and then a baby boy ten months after that. These are stories you will never find in state records, documents, or archives, where our family doesn't exist. In documents, our family begins in Texas as adults, ghosts emerging from the nothing of crisis and escape.

Despite her otherworldly beauty, my grandmother's body was a site of colonial invasion, a map of intimate and medical violence. She was battered and raped as a teenager by her first husband and had to escape him with her brother's help. She would remarry a Chinese doctor in Tampico who was even more violent and cruel, who beat her so badly while pregnant that she lost every child, forced to deliver each one as a stillborn via an older version of C-section, cut from sternum to womb—a traumatically invasive early version of the now-routine procedure that made you possible. How she fled from him in the middle of the night and had to put her children in a taxi alone. How vulnerable her body was to men's deceptions, the illnesses they brought into her bed. How she would get cervical cancer from what we know now as common HPV, and how it would grip her body like a gnarled root, unchecked over the years. How the results of her tests were withheld from her. How in her thirties, her body would be ravaged with flowering scars where her womb should be. The puncturing of her bladder and an open wound in her side, angry and red as a raspberry, through which the catheter line was threaded. How I saw, firsthand, the deformations doctors made on her body in their experiments, how in exchange for pro bono treatment, she was not a cancer patient but a subject of study. How those structural violences would eventually kill her in the form of preventable cervical cancer, an accumulation of trauma at the door between world and womb.

You will not believe me when I tell you my body carries the nerve ghost[1] of her pain. But know this: my first IUD took three separate appointments to insert with the doctor citing my "unusually clenched cervix" as the barrier. Inexplicably, I still ended up pregnant two years later—the IUD I thought in place was expelled into thin air, never to be found again, not even by an ultrasound wand. How we conceived you.

Shortly after you came into the world, I got a second IUD. You are five years old now, and it is still in my body, expired, two years overdue to be removed. Four separate doctors have tried and failed to remove it, citing an involuntary clenching in my unusually constricted cervix. The door to this world that was locked on the day of your birth, would not let you out into this world were it not for the knife and the light.

It has to be her. Perhaps it's magical thinking to say that it's her making a fist out of my body, guarding its entrances from breach, invasion, conquest. Or maybe I dishonor the brutality she had to survive, abstracted into language for my art. But this isn't abstract—I feel it now. The clenching, the brace. Whatever it is has agency, is felt both as a presence and also an absence in my center; grief and its retribution. What she went through and inherited, doesn't die with one person. Every scar, every wound, every hurt in her is a rip in the universe I carry in my bloodmemory.

§

I could not contract for you. My body would not start labor. They hooked me up to a Pitocin IV, gradually increasing the dosage. Nothing. The nurses remarked, *You should be screaming your head off right now*, remarked how they had never seen a patient withstand so much Pitocin in their bloodstream and not start contracting within hours. They took me off for a few hours to give my body a break, told me to walk, then restarted the Pitocin. And still, nothing. After eighteen hours, I had not dilated even one millimeter.

Later, I would do research on failed labor, unable to find a single article under the search term "no contractions." Then hours later, my research would branch out into dozens of case studies, where I would finally find something: a study done on pregnant women in war zones, and how in the midst of armed conflict, the body would delay labor in response to the extreme stress caused by the presence of mortal danger. I remember saving this article on my computer, favoriting the site. To this day I cannot find it—the one piece of language that made sense of my body at the time of your birth.

I do not want to overstate my quiet life in a Boulder suburb. Your father never hit me. My wounds are interior, psychic, permanent, caused by heavy blows of neglect, silence, resentment, criticism, disgust, his desire for others, desire for freedom from me. I could never hold him—he too was sand, slipping through my fingers. And eventually, he came to despise me.

You have to know I was ready for you, no stranger to pregnancy, labor, or birth. At thirteen, I was my mother's birth partner while she labored to deliver my brother. The night her water broke, unstressed, I hung a stopwatch from my neck and roused my uncle from a thick, drunken sleep to drive us to the hospital in his Chevy S-10 as I coached her through contractions, gave information to doctors and nurses, filled out forms, witnessed her body in labor, told her to breathe as my brother's head slightly emerged breached, only to be pushed back in for an emergency C-section. In surgical scrubs, I held her hand on the operating table as they shot anesthesia through her trunk, her head bobbing back and forth as the surgeon lifted my brother into the world. The staff commented on how mature I was, how resilient to the gory scene of birth, failing to understand my role as the eldest daughter of immigrants—parent to my parents, mother to my brother, stranger to myself—a role I, myself, could not yet name and did not yet understand. I wanted to tell them how I had already witnessed dying through a child's eyes, the body in pain, the presence of death. But instead I smiled, gracious and obedient in Docs, a shaved undercut, and ripped jeans, slept in the hospital bathtub, changed and fed my infant brother, while our mother recovered in the hospital bed.

* * *

We must have gotten to the hospital at night, eleven o'clock or so. A gown. The IV. The fetal monitoring strap. Your father looking bored and tired on the couch. A lavender bath. The insult of a quinoa bowl on the hospital tray. No pain, no *whoo whoo hee hee*, no dilation, no attending nurses monitoring my progress. The birth plan I'd copy/pasted from a website that was immediately disregarded and ignored. I don't remember much but the sense that everyone was waiting on me while I lay in bed, not laboring, and the guilt of wasting everyone's time and not being able to control it, not being able to accommodate the doctors and nurses or your father by *just starting contractions goddammit*, being good and working as hard as I should be. The blame so heavy in the air, every second counted against me, still not laboring.

If I could have started labor, I would have. Did they think I was lazy? And after hours of nothing, the doctor, a blonde, white woman, Boulder, Colorado–thin and brisk, came in the next morning to ask how I was doing. She wasn't my doctor so, trying to build rapport, I joked, *Great! Hungry, could really use a cheeseburger,* and she did not laugh but frowned, said in front of your father, *Are you serious? A cheeseburger? This is why we've had to do fetal monitoring, this is why you have gestational diabetes and have to take insulin, you cannot eat right now, it delays labor, especially not a cheeseburger, was this your diet the whole time? Do you know how much saturated—* and I had to assure her that no, no, no I hadn't eaten anything since coming to the hospital, that I was just joking and had been good. I cannot fully describe the shame of that moment: my exposed belly, legs open under a flimsy gown, her gloved fingers in my fat, disgusting brown body, my purple organ bare under bright lights, the scene of my animal. I felt the comparison to her own ideal body, chiseled by wealth and whiteness, all witnessed by your father, handsome, blond, and long-haired, feeling like he could do better in a wife than what I had let myself become. I've hidden this away from myself, from you.

There is so much to be said about my relationship to labor, to feminized labor, to domestic labor, to emotional labor. The United Farm and Commercial Workers union meetings I went to with my mother as a toddler; my uncles, driving eighteen-wheelers across the country; my indentured great-grandparents picking cotton in Torreon; my tios and cousins, picking apples in Washington, spinach and strawberries in California; the cooking and cleaning I did at twelve, the bleach I poured into sinks to earn outings to the mall; the midnight feedings so my mom could sleep; the free childcare that bound me to the house on weekends; the full-time jobs I held at sixteen; being hired as a maid for my white high school boyfriend's rich family, me cleaning his toilet in front of him for seven dollars an hour; the two eight-hour shifts I worked on my feet five days a week throughout my twenties, food service from 4:45 A.M. to 1:30 P.M., then retail from 3:30 P.M. to midnight; my repossessed car when I lost my job, and the fifty-dollar Wal-Mart bike I bought to replace it; the worker's comp claims; the promotions I got for working twice as hard, for being deferential and excellent, but always at the lowest pay grade; the cooking and cleaning I did to earn your father's commitment, a new recipe every night; the miles I ran and sit-ups I did and weights I lifted and lingerie I bought to earn his desire; everything I said yes to, offered, did for free to prove I deserved kindness, love, to prove I belonged.

I have always been in labor. I am still in labor.

* * *

Vanessa Angélica Villarreal and Jesse Walter Johnson
Birth Wishes for Joaquín Johnson, due 2/4/2015

Thank you for taking care of us during this wonderful time! These are our birth wishes; we understand that you are the medical professionals and will defer to your expertise on all decisions.

Major points:

- Please do not suggest Pitocin or pain medication unless I ask for it, including to deliver the placenta.

- Please do not comment on time limits, apparent pain, or length of labor.

- Please do not suggest invasive baby monitoring unless medically urgent.

- As long as the baby and I are healthy, I prefer to have no time limits on labor or pushing.

- I prefer to have no episiotomy and risk tearing unless I'm having a medical emergency. [N/A]

- We will only consider a C-Section if it becomes urgently medically necessary.

- As long as my baby is healthy, I would like my baby placed immediately skin-to-skin on my abdomen.

- Please do not separate me and my baby until after my baby has successfully breastfed.

- Please wait for the umbilical cord to stop pulsating before it is clamped.

- Please do not circumcise my baby.
- My doula, Kerry Stokes, will take my placenta.

* * *

The doctor finally gets me to sign the consent form for a C-section, each paper a tangle of clauses that free the hospital from liability in the event of any accident, harm, or death. A metal table and a long, silver needle in my spine. A sheet barrier between my head and the rest of my body, surrounded by masked faces. Your father next to me. You deserve to know the story of your birth as a swell of joy, of miracle, of the small tendernesses your father and I found for each other in you, amid all the conflict. Stay here a moment and know the overwhelming love we felt for you.

* * *

Later, I will see a text from his friend asking if I was okay, happy, healthy. *I don't know, she seems kinda out of it*, he replies. I cannot keep my head up. I feel like vomiting. I hold you, your little swollen face clenched like a pink fist, and cannot place you on my breast. I am too weak.

In the family suite, I will be cathetered and bound to the bed, unable to move from the waist down, and I will want you to lay on me, sweet baby, robbed of our first moments of bonding. And your father, sitting in a chair in the far corner of the room, will say no, I can't, that I am still drugged, that I shouldn't fall asleep with you, that you could suffocate, insists on putting you in the hospital bassinet. And I quote the baby books back to him, tell him I'm awake, it's okay, I feel better, ask him if he can keep an eye on us so that I can hold you for a while, do skin-to-skin. And he will raise his voice and rage, *That's bullshit, you're not some magic mother that can just sense where the baby is, you're going to roll over him*, at me in front of my mother, trying to sleep on the sofa.

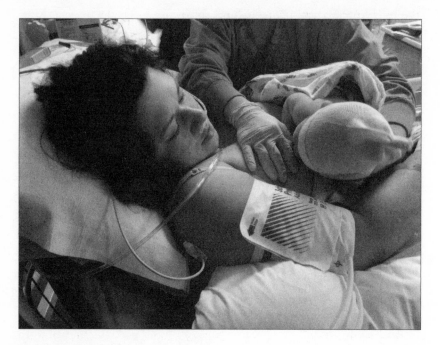

Vanessa Villarreal and newborn.

This will push him over the edge. He will storm out of our hospital room and report me to the nurses at the desk, like a coworker filing a complaint. *My wife is trying to sleep with the baby, can you please come take him from her and explain that it's against the rules?* And a nurse will come in, take a look at us, ask me if I'm okay. She will explain to your father that this is perfectly healthy, bonding is preferred, that he could just watch for signs of me falling asleep and move him to the bassinet then. Later, when your father goes home to take a shower and change, another nurse will check in on me, ask me if I'm okay, if I'm safe. She has two domestic violence pamphlets in her hand, one about the increase of intimate partner violence during pregnancy and early parenthood. I will be too dazed to respond, to assure her that I'm okay, that your father was just stressed and underslept.

And so the first interaction you hear between your parents is this: me, trying to hold you, bond with you, be with you, cut in half, pissing blood through a tube; and your father screaming at me for trying to do so, reporting me to authorities who might discipline me, enforce the rules and separate us, punish me for trying to sleep with you. Even tonight, you will roll out of bed at 4:00 A.M., find me asleep, laptop still on my chest, on the couch and tell me to come sleep with you. And I will. I always will.

You will lose nearly two pounds waiting for me to lactate, suckling at my breast's dry source, wailing in hunger and pain; another way my body shut down and failed you. The lactation consultant is a white woman who will grip the flesh of my breast and flatten it like a hamburger, growing ever more exasperated with each attempt. I am visibly overwhelmed, underslept, stressed, my hair a nest of uncombable knots. My mother, dressed in an elegant red blazer, will try to ask questions on my behalf, and the woman will scoff, say *Chill abuela, why don't you make yourself useful and wash the bottles in the sink*. Being a Mexican woman with a heavy accent demotes her to domestic labor in the institutional space of the hospital, unworthy of speech, even in the interest of her daughter and grandson.

And again, it is I who is not working hard enough, this time to breastfeed you. Had I just contracted like every other mother, the labor hormones would have triggered milk production, but since I never labored, there was nothing telling my body to produce. You did not eat for two or three days; breast milk had to be sourced from other mothers. And I felt judged, deemed unfit, irredeemably and fundamentally incompetent. I raged against myself for not lactating, for being unable to control an involuntary process—a vital one that would keep you alive. I think about how if I had lived in an earlier time, my grandmother's time, neither of us would have survived. I could not even birth you, could not even feed you.

And so motherhood becomes a site of failure, my body a site of blame.

* * *

The first day home, your father suggests we go for a walk to get me in the habit of exercising again. He and I agree that I will handle all of the night wakings and feedings so that he can sleep—he is the breadwinner and needs rest to be able to work. Every day I am supposed to pump every twenty minutes for two hours, then once an hour for two hours, then every twenty minutes every two hours again in a cycle, even through the night, to stimulate lactation. Mere teaspoons will come out, not even enough to reach the first tick on the bottle. I will want to cosleep, and your father will grow angrier every time you wake.

Within the first few weeks, one night I will become feverish, sweating through chills, trembling uncontrollably in bed as if in a blizzard, unable to get warm. My tongue will taste electric, alkaline. I tell your father *I think something's wrong*, and he will say I am being dramatic. On the phone the next morning, the doctor will ask me to come in for an emergency visit because my C-section incision could be infected. And once I arrive, she finds that it is. My bloodwork shows toxicity, a depressed thyroid, elevated stress hormones. She asks me if I'm okay, if I'm safe. She asks me how things are at home, if your father is handling the transition well. I tell her about how irritable he's become, about his response to the chills and fever the night before. She gives me the same pamphlet the nurse did about pregnancy, early motherhood, and domestic abuse. I tell her that I'm not in that situation. She hands me a heavily photocopied sheet that lists types of domestic violence and abuse that are not physical. She schedules an IUD appointment in three months and reiterates, no sex for at least eight weeks minimum, preferably twelve considering my birth experience. When I come home, he asks if I'm okay, asks when we can have sex again.

I don't have many memories of the first few weeks other than the kitchen table, the pump, the television, my life lived on Facebook in the absence of companionship. The sink under moon and sun. The constant laundry and dishes. The silence of the darkened living room. The loneliness of the kitchen. Sometimes tenderness, or laughter between the three of us. But mostly, the deep love blooming between you and me, the coos and smiles you give me, a balm on my wounds. Your father loved you so much too, your relationship to each of us rich with affection, but as a family, strained. Your father and I had become disconnected, and fight we did; I felt invisible and exhausted and unwanted, while he felt overwhelmed and responsible for everything. Neither of us could do right in the other's eyes.

Please, stop reading here. Begin at the next section.

The day before the eight-week mark is a Sunday, and around noon you fall asleep in my arms to the white plastic owl spinning stars on your ceiling. I lay you in your crib to its gentle white noise. Your father suggests we take a shower—the one place we don't fight. We embrace, stand facing each other under the stream of hot water and he begins to kiss me, touch me between my legs. I say, *I want to, but I don't feel ready, it hasn't been eight weeks yet—tomorrow is eight weeks,* unable to tell him I probably need twelve like the doctor recommended. And he says *Yes it has, one day won't matter*—he needs me, he's missed me; don't I miss him, don't I miss it, us making love whenever we wanted, like before. And he is stroking me, puts my hand on him, slips his fingers inside me. And I can feel I'm not ready, surprised at how quickly we got here, how unusually forward he's being, and smile in a way that says *I'm sorry,* step out of the shower, and go to the bedroom to get dressed and give him privacy. But instead he follows, puts his hands on my hips and suddenly I am on my back at the foot of the bed and he's inside me, interlacing his fingers with mine, pinning my hands above my head as he tells me how much he's missed me, how good I feel after so long. It hurts, a hot tearing. So many feelings surface, entangled together—shock, arousal and refusal, yearning and revulsion, a sense of obligation and duty to fulfill my husband's needs, my own deep need to be desired by him, to please him, anger at how undesirable he's made me feel, fear, powerlessness to stop, a strange knowing that his need was not for me but for any body. But it is my husband and I have missed him so and I am so grateful to be wanted again, wanted like this. He finishes, sighs, says *Thank you,* and goes back to the shower, still running. I sit in a daze on the edge of the bed, wet as a used rag, flooded with shame and arousal. I finish alone. Then the disgust. I didn't say no—had I said yes?

* * *

I don't want to make him a monster. I was a monster of insecurity, neediness, accusation. Neither of us was ready. We never got a babysitter or went on dates after you were born. He comments on my lower abdomen, asks me if I should join a gym. So I joined a gym, took HIIT classes, fat blasters, bikini-body-after-baby classes every day that I could, meal-planned 250-calorie lunches every Sunday for the week. Nothing worked—my body held on to its two-hundred-plus-pound post-baby weight, my abdomen deflated and scarred, a failure to become fit and beautiful again, each day feeling uglier, fatter, browner than the last. And somehow, I found myself in a life I had no say in, a life that felt fragile and tense with the unsaid. And so he'd begin to buy companionship, eat frozen meals, replace every aspect of what I could give him with something he could buy to put in its place. You know the rest.

* * *

I write this with the hope that you'll never find it, while also needing to document what happened. I have searched every archive, every record, every census, every border crossing—none of our family before me exists in Mexican state records. Maybe I don't know their real names. They were born on ranches, baptized in little churches, their crossing also an erasing, their names swallowed into the whiteness beyond the line. Institutional memory will say our family begins with my grandmother's death certificate, her inaccessible hospital records as an experimental patient, my mother and father's green cards, my birth certificate. My mother's birth, my grandmother's birth, my great-grandparents, ancestors—all unrecorded, bodies gone undocumented, unaccounted for, stranded in time. Your grandfather says with a kind of pride, *el arbol empieza aqui*, the tree starts here, happy to leave them behind. I am desperate to recover them.

And when I am gone, what you will find of my life is a paper trail of precarity—of perfect report cards that steeply decline after my grandmother's death, of write-ups, an expulsion, alternative school, truancy, suspensions, psychiatric hospitalization, repossession and debt and somehow, miraculously, degrees. A book. And then, the divorce papers, discovery documents, settlement proposals, financial statements that shatter the life I thought I had to reconstruct, a much uglier reality beneath—truths your father hid and will never admit, questions he will meet with only silence, even in the face of evidence. The papers I leave behind will show a troubled woman, framed by a language of losses.

But I'm not done yet. I will make something of all this.

It is a special kind of cruelty that I cannot find or access any records to prove the existence of my family, of the people who loved me, but am surrounded by the record of the man who didn't. Years from now, all that might survive of me is the trouble, the leaving. And so I write to your future self, having taken note of your imaginative inner world, your sophisticated language at five, and especially of your defiant and lonely nature—a distant specter of me as a child, remade in you. I want to spare you the future and its silences, tell you all the names I know that made you possible, place your birth in a timeline that doesn't begin with you.

Tonight, I am somewhere in time when the world feels uncertain, turned upside down. A reaping of what we have sowed. Much strife to come. The world may look very different from where you stand when you read this; already, there is not much I can leave you to inherit. So in a way, this is my gift: a document that will give you access to answers I never had, reconstruct a timeline that would be lost without my testimony. A point of your many origins. A record of something repeating in me, repeating in you.

It's not your fault.

I Am in a Room. I Am on a Rock.

Ruth Irupé Sanabria

I was in the second grade, it was 3:00 P.M., and for reasons I can't remember, I was roaming the halls of Phoebe Hearst Elementary School when I heard a classmate pounding on the school's front entrance yelling to be let in. Her voice felt urgent; she needed to use the school phone to call her mother. I flew into a hot, dizzying panic. If I could squeeze my fingers between the doors and push in the bolt, then the doors would swing open, and I could save my comrade's life. I yelled for her to push on the door just a little to give my finger a bit of wiggle room. She pushed with her whole body and I managed to wedge my finger between the steel doors. Then she yelled, *Never mind! My mom is here! Thanks!* and pulled the door shut. I snatched my hand out just in time, or so I thought. My left hand instinctively gripped my right. I turned and started walking down the hallway, fixated on the exquisite golden details of the old floors of Phoebe Hearst Elementary.

When I reached Mrs. Melvin's first-grade classroom, I felt a wetness in my hand. Looking down, I saw blood. Behind me, a trail of blood. My left hand softened. The tip of my right pointer finger was ripped right down to the bone. Then and only then, did I feel pain. The teachers, the cab driver, my mother, the nurses, and the ER doctors dutifully sprung into action at respective stages of the incident. The next day at recess, classmates gathered round for the gruesome details and teachers laid off me until my right hand had regained its ability to hold a pencil. No one called me stupid or said that *this* is what I deserved. No one joked, no one minimized. No one made fun of my English for those few weeks. Best of all, I didn't get in trouble with the authorities; they did not interrogate my mother. My nail fell off and to this day, I respect doors.

Because my injury was addressed, it gave me the headspace to repurpose the scar into my body's compass; I can discern left from right with 100 percent certitude without feeling pangs of ugliness, stupidity, and worthlessness. Though I am to blame for the finger incident, I am not to blame for the underlying condition that triggered my panicked response to the sound of someone banging on a door—an early indicator that I had post-traumatic stress disorder (PTSD), a condition I didn't know I had until I was in my late twenties, when I landed in therapy after a botched abortion nearly took me out.

Born under the boot of a military dictatorship in Argentina, by the time I was seven years old my childhood had already been defined by the slow burn of complex trauma. Any meaningful discussion regarding motherhood will invariably take me back to 1975, when my own mother, then a young college student, balanced her studies with work, pregnancy, and an underground revolutionary activism that risked her life and mine. I don't resent my mother for this (I probably would have done the same), but I was born hopped-up on cortisol and adrenaline. That is, I developed PTSD in utero. Unable to be consoled and having to be fed through a tube because my body rejected milk, the doctors questioned what my mother had done during her pregnancy to make me such an unusually high-strung baby. She played it off. The day the Fifth Army Corp surrounded our neighborhood with military trucks and helicopters to break down the door to our apartment, she had a fraction of a second to decide whether to run for her life or fight. She ran, leaving me behind on the bed in the apartment. She heard gunshots, then me crying, and, not knowing if I had been killed, she kept going. By the end of the day, the soldiers had disappeared both of my parents.

Millions of children like me end up in the United States already having learned how to navigate myriad states of chaos and terror by decentering ourselves and prioritizing the emotional needs of soldiers, prison guards, paper pushers, captors—essentially all authority figures, including teachers, doctors, social workers, and even our own parents. Doing so means survival. We learn to repress and to use coded language for pain, fear, and despair so as to decrease the chances that a slip of the tongue separates or kills us. We learn to not take up space and to not ask for what we need. In a classroom, this might look like a random and unexpected display of apathy, disengagement, or attitude from the student who is always on top of her academic game. At an ob-gyn office, it might look like skittishness, reticence, or a sudden barrage of defensive and/or offensive questions. The criminalized body of the refugee child has become the body of the pregnant woman feeling the hot shame of having forgotten her password to the self-care club; all of her failed attempts at entering have essentially locked her out. Words and phrases like "forgiveness," "calm," "boundary setting," and "the past is in the past," "you're an adult now," "get over it," and "manifest your best life" are grenade launchers aimed at her psyche.

That I know of, I have been pregnant five times. One ended in miscarriage and three resulted in live births. My second pregnancy occurred in 2003. The years following the turn of the millennium were a notably brutal time in the United States. Not only were most people still processing the traumatic loss of lives from September 11, 2001, and confronting the same social justice issues and human rights violations of today but also hundreds of Muslim, Arab, Middle Eastern, and South East Asian people were being detained, their whereabouts unknown, on the pretext that their surnames or country of origin made them potential terrorists. In gross violation of constitutional and international human rights law, the US illegally imprisoned and tortured hundreds of men in Guantanamo Bay. The Patriot Act sanctioned spying, wiretapping, and tracking by, among other things, secretly accessing the credit card, internet, and cellphone activity of anyone who criticized or questioned why the government was doing this to its citizens. I had lived through this before. In fact, I had been born into it—not exactly the same situation but eerily similar in some aspects. The cellular memory in my body struggled to differentiate the New York and New Jersey of 2003 from 1970s and 1980s CIA-backed Operation Condor in Argentina, Bolivia, Brazil, Chile, Paraguay, and Uruguay. And as luck would have it, I got pregnant.

I was not excited about my pregnancy and cringed when friends congratulated me. At that point, I did not know what PTSD was or that its myriad manifestations had shaped the quality of my life and almost every decision I had ever made. I didn't realize I had been slipping into a constant state of paranoia and flashback. Not even the people close to me realized it. They were so accustomed to my being critical of repressive regimes and institutions that, given the obvious political climate, it would make sense that I would be more amped up than usual.

Gradually, I retreated into myself as I struggled to brush off intrusive thoughts that my child would be born in a concentration camp. I didn't share this with anyone because I had been conditioned neither to take up space nor burden people with my fears; after all, who wasn't afraid? I figured I could handle it on my own. Plus, I was certain that the National Guard soldiers at Penn Station were watching me a little more closely than they watched the other commuters. Sharing my fears with others might endanger them. When President George W. Bush declared, "You are either with us or against us," across all the news channels, I was certain that someone had already entered my name into the dissident database, checking "pregnant" in the notes. Though I knew it was irrational, I couldn't stop feeling that if we didn't get away now, I would be killed. I feared that, should my baby survive, her adopters would indoctrinate her to believe she was genetically diabolical—a message that was repeated to me over and over again when I'd visit my parents in the prisons for subversives. Or that the police would stage a standoff in which I supposedly fired the first shot; my baby dying with me. My daydreams became so vivid that I'd find myself spending hours stuck in imagined dialogues and confrontations with any number of enemies. These daydreams felt like pressure-relief valves and often I'd "wake" from them at the sound of my own voice or the taste of my tears, not knowing why I was in said room.

On the surface, I held "normal conversations" with people and did "normal things." I was a graduate student in New York City pursuing an MFA. I'd bought a fixer-upper in a working-class community in New Jersey with my partner, who played guitar and worked as a public school teacher. I walked my dogs every day. Maybe I didn't need help. Maybe everyone else needed to wake up. I stopped using the house phone, didn't trust cell phones, secretly called my dad from the corner payphone, never letting on that I was calling to hear his voice one last time before they came for me. In the parking deck of the train station, I sat in my car, keeping it together: *Those are not screams. I am not being followed.*

Then it occurred to me. The only way to save myself and my baby was to have an abortion.

In 2003 you couldn't google "abortions near me" and get thirteen million results. I procrastinated. The pro-life protestors who mobilized around the nearest open abortion provider scared me. Fortunately, one of my friends had a contact and I finally found a provider who agreed; I was entering my second trimester.

As the anesthesiologist at Robert Wood Johnson University Hospital prepped me, I am told that my doctor is a no-show. Another doctor whom I have never met has agreed to take her place, and he has brought along a resident who would like to observe how an abortion is performed. Though I'm not comfortable with the new doctor and resident, I am already in my gown on the operating bed, IV in my arm, so what else is there to do but nod okay and soon the room goes black.

The abortion was botched.

For over four weeks, the initial medium-to-heavy bleeding did not taper or stop. I was still going to work. Exhausted and anemic, I'd drive over the Outerbridge Crossing into Staten Island, teach a poetry workshop, come back home, take a nap, then head back over the Outerbridge Crossing to teach another workshop.

Though my mind was still not fully mended, the abortion had provided significant relief to my PTSD by removing a major stressor and reducing the hormonal fluctuations that had been dysregulating my brain chemistry. I was beginning to accept that I would need therapy, but first, my body. Despite my anemia, I now had enough emotional wherewithal to reach out to Dr. No-show with my concerns about the never-ending bleeding. She listened. Then simply said, *What did you expect? You got an abortion not a haircut. You are supposed to bleed.* She gave me a script for antibiotics and sent me home.

A few weeks later, I am in the ICU at Raritan Bay, feet elevated and strapped to fluids and oxygen. My body has cracked open. My body is draining itself of itself at a velocity that they cannot stop. I am air. Everywhere is the white light. Though English is my dominant language, the ICU doctor made a split-second decision to yell to my dying brain in Spanish, calling me to come back home in the language I first knew. I felt a faint tug on my soul.

Once I was stabilized and in the recovery room, another doctor came in and explained that instead of a D&C he recommended a complete hysterectomy. I didn't understand anything he was saying to me. All I knew is that I wanted to have children one day, just not now. I declined the hysterectomy, and the following day, they gave me a couple of scripts, including iron and more antibiotics, and sent me home.

By the end of the week, my bleeding resumed. Although it was a light flow, I was terrified. I didn't know where to turn. Within three weeks, I would end up in another emergency room, this time at Riverview Medical with a hemorrhage that started in the bathroom of a restaurant where I was celebrating my birthday. This hemorrhage was not nearly as dramatic as the first one, but still.

Again I received medicine to reduce the bleeding and more antibiotics. A few hours passed, and I was sent home with instructions to make an appointment with the doctor who performed the abortion. Problem is, I didn't know his name and I didn't know how to go about getting this information. You should know, I save all important medical information in neatly organized binders. I should have saved the abortion discharge papers, but at the time, I was sure the government would use that piece of information against me, so I got rid of all the evidence.

It felt like I was dying. In a last-ditch effort to save myself, I typed up a timeline of my abortion, printed it out and, without an appointment, walked into the ob-gyn suite at Robert Wood Johnson. I'd gone there after college for pap smears and birth control. It had been several years, but I was desperate. Dr. A agreed to see me even though she was overbooked. I could not look at her as she read my timeline. She asked me a few questions then told me that I should call my partner because I would not be leaving the hospital that day. Bloodwork showed that I needed a blood transfusion but there was no time for that, I needed an emergency D&C. Later, the doctor who performed it said that what he had removed from me was *pretty gross.*

I am encouraged and relieved when I read articles describing the ways in which health-care practitioners are moving toward trauma-informed care. Hopefully one day, knowledge of a patient's trauma won't just be an asterisk in her medical file but rather a means to better understand the layers of protective silence, distortion, and noise that might be playing out in that seemingly "unremarkable" pregnant woman who just completed her intake. Hopefully one day, doctors will be better able to determine with whom to discuss, even months before it is medically necessary, what it means to perform a cervical check for ripeness. I am in a room. I am on a rock. I walked to the edge of the ocean, I sat on barnacles. The rock was black with waves and moon. The moon sat in silence with me; the sea pulsed against me. It was night and I found a person, I found someone to crawl up into, myself. And maybe I am high and drunk, and when I'm not, I am getting high or drunk.

By no means do I digress. That my list of unreported and untreated traumas and microaggressions is longer than the scope of this essay; that after each traumatic event, I behaved normally or thought I did; that for me, physical and psychological pain was normalized; that when I sought therapy or medical help, I left the offices feeling more helpless, ashamed, and further estranged from my own body than when I walked in is not a unique story. One day, addressing the effects of complex and generational trauma on the body will be considered as important to prenatal or abortion care as is tracking fundal height and weeks since your last period. Until then, millions of us continue to arrive here—or have lived here for centuries—at a loss for words when asked in a routine visit, "How do you feel?

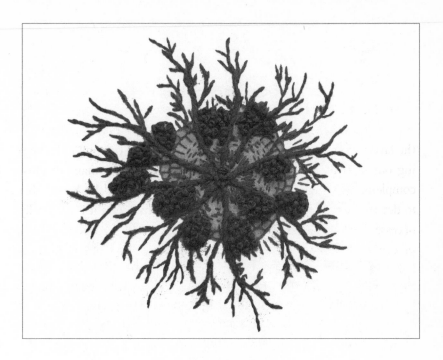

"Anatomy of the Breast"
Laurie Ann Guerrero

Note: This embroidered poem is part of a series of embroideries, REDWORK, created by the poet and artist Laurie Ann Guerrero. In color, the embroidery thread is cochineal red sewn into unbleached cotton.

Artist Statement I

Laurie Ann Guerrero

Thread—red—divisible by six strands and unraveled for the needle, then sewn: tool for and product of a magic contained within the (unvalued) body and the (unvalued) body of work. Body as its own institution, world unto itself: both creator and destroyer, both perpetrator and victim. Vessel of both dream and lung. Its ability to act, fortify itself in situations meant to destroy it, heal, perpetuate life. A carnival of response: fever, triggers, expulsion. But also, compassion, and the making of milk and insulin and empathy. Where both the flesh's orgasm and the soul's grief are experienced simultaneously.

Excerpt from "Your Black Eye and My Birth"

from *Heart Berries*

Terese Marie Mailhot

After the residency, when we got home, I drove to a parking lot and called an abortion clinic. They immediately allowed me to speak with a doctor. I explained the situation: I am violent, I have hit myself in the face to cope with worthlessness, I hit you, and I wanted to die. I wanted to take pills I still had from before I was pregnant. Also, I want to live.

The doctor said she was confident that, given my circumstance, a late-term abortion would be considered necessary. I asked her for the price, and she directed me to the receptionist. It was roughly four hundred dollars, if, after consultation, it was approved.

I called you to ask for the money, and, instead, you pled for the baby's life. I hung up. I was familiar with the baby's life, but I couldn't think of that. I made more calls to foundations for women, clinics, groups, and then called back the same doctor. I was willing to sell my car or anything to have sanity again.

"When does my baby have bones?" I asked.

"This is something we should talk about in the consultation," the woman said.

I knew immediately that the Thunder Being inside of me had good bones. I thought of the bones from my lineage, which had been cemented inside the walls of residential buildings. I thought of my ancestors. I hung up and drove home.

In the next weeks, our baby in my womb reminded me of my brother Guyweeyo: willful and scared.

He kicked before the doctors predicted he would. He hiccupped each night at eleven.

I believed my mother spoke to our baby in my sleep. I think they devised a way to punish me for even thinking that a Thunder Being inside of me could be bad.

For a hundred days, it felt like Baby Guy was crawling out of my throat. I heaved until my face became blotchy. We believed it was an allergic reaction, but our doctor said it was the blood vessels bursting from the strain of puking so often and so hard. No pill worked against the nausea.

I realized, after looking at my silhouette, seeing our small person expanding my reflection, that pain didn't burden me. Trying to forget damaged me the most.

Your eye has long since healed. I chose to be lethargic instead of angry in the last months of our pregnancy. Each night, I rested my head in your lap, and you placed your hand on my stomach. He kicked you, and I felt my mother raising her hands to me in the way Salish women do in ceremony, to say "thank you."

When the day came, I wasn't sure I was in pain enough, because the baby had conditioned me so well. We went into the hospital anyway, and Casey Guyweeyo was cut out from me, larger than he should have been. His skin is milk, and his body feels electric and unforgiving. He seems like the child my brothers, my sister, and I—could have been.

I Chose to Stay Awake

Maria Hamilton Abegunde

This is my story.[1] You ~~may or may not~~ You will find it difficult to read, unbearable, unfathomable, unconscionable. Truth untethered to pretense or what is deemed palatable is like that. Truth told with the unapologetic clarity of a child or an adult who has healed at the cost of everything—it is a diamond-studded blade attached to an obsidian machete. Oya, mother of change/transformation, wields it. But, because Osun, mother of love/compassion crafted it from the stones of Sango, the blade destroys pain and illusion, and restores justice. This story is a mirror into me/you/us/them/we. Look. See. Do not turn away.[1]

PART 1

1993: The first and only other time I have publicly told part of this story. *Mother's Underground Magazine*, issue 13: "The Womb." A one-page essay titled "Reflections of a Lost Child(hood)."[2] Gwendolyn Brooks's poem "The Mother" opens that issue with this first line: "Abortions will not let you forget."[3] This is true. I have also learned that *what* you remember/do not forget will always surprise you.

Remembering China Town, 1980[4]

> After each bout of nausea
> I thought only
> of shrimp in lobster sauce[5]

---

1   Readers are invited to enrich their reading of this text by reviewing the endnotes.

clinging to rice
on a plate with small
peeled shrimp floating
in the sauce
that stewed them.
The day I ended
the morning sickness
I craved a dish to myself
and eggrolls
and chow mein
and . . .
aromas drifted through my body to fill
the hollow
with promises
of the once again familiar
and welcomed
experience of food.
I devoured it all
ignoring cramps that gnawed
at me foreshadowing
the forever intrusive
memories of May
days teeming and fecund.
Sweet and sour
sauce dripped into my lap
from the delicate
fried vegetables
in my egg roll.
I ate my fortune
cookie
without reading its message.

PART 2

learning to eat
my voice was
easy . . .

I chose to stay awake. Not because I was afraid of dying. At fifteen, that was always a possibility, or worse. No, I was certain that the
sucking and scraping out of my womb would be nothing compared to
the sound of my father's breaking heart and shattered dreams. Cliché.
But true. The sudden death of every hope he had of ending bad family
cycles without juju would cause fear to propel his fists on top of my
head and into my body.

My mother was dead. We had buried her just months before. I knew
she would die the afternoon she left home. I kissed her as we stood in
the driveway, both of us silent; the way teenage girls and their mothers
ignore each other because they won't recognize each other for another
twenty years. A whisper in my ear, *the kiss of death.* She looked at me
knowingly. She would never see us again.

After the funeral, I said to someone: It is good she died, she no
longer needs to suffer. Though it will be decades before I understand
the spiritual meaning of my words, at fifteen I understand that my
mother's death from a painful illness ends the violence in her/my/
our life. I know without a doubt that my choice, my ability to choose,
assures that I will never repeat what my parents cannot fix with rosa-
ries, raised voices, and rum.

I stay awake because I want the memory. All of it. Not just the
one my uterus will remind me of in the following days as it reshapes
itself into the uterus a fifteen year old should have had to begin with.
Or the one I will have thirty years later when I finally find someone
with whom I want a family but cannot conceive because I am too old.
Should haves. Would haves. Might have beens. Doesn't matter. I want
the memory of what I did to save my own life. Again. I want the memory of what it means to choose to live.

Denial is checking the crotch of my cotton panties every day for
months waiting for what will not arrive. It is lying in bed every night

without moving so I don't get sick. It is ignoring what I know to be true: the day one of my childhood rapists and groomers pushed me face down on the bed and ejaculated without pulling out, that it was in that moment I conceived. It is knowing that the fertility calendar I've kept for at least four years has never been wrong and has kept me from getting pregnant since age ten.

Denial is the dial tone in my ear when I call his house and the woman who is his guardian hangs up the phone like it is all my ~~fast-assed, damn~~ fault and none of his. It is knowing that I can't pray my way out from under his brothers and friends who stalk me on the way to and from school, pull me down on floors, push me against walls, inside closets; pass me between them despite my wailing. Or the sisters and girlfriends who watch.

Denial is ~~knowing believing~~ trusting that in eighth grade Ms. [fill in the blank] will protect me when I run to her and stand nearly under her arm because [I know] she saw the boys pull up my shirt and grab my breasts. She does not. She pretends I am not there. Or perhaps she is pretending she is someplace else. She stacks and restacks her papers, never once turning her head to look at me or to look into the room. I am silent. She is silent. Finally, I return to my desk.

~~Denial Shame~~ Courage is pushing through the laughter and whispers of other girls as you walk down the aisle to your desk and they point at your size-B breasts. They know how even the teacher has abandoned me. They are glad it is not them. In high school, not one will be my friend.

But by then, ~~denial success surviving~~ acting "normal" is getting As, being on the honor roll, and being on student government anyway, so no one knows that anything is wrong or that every day you fight to keep your body covered and safe.

The first time I cannot eat. The first time I almost vomit in bed. The smell of salt fish and fried plantain at 4:00 A.M. I hide in my bedroom, place my back against the cold wall. I am grateful that my father has closed my door to not disturb me as he cooks. In bed, hand over mouth, hand over belly, swallowing bile and a rising moan. I strategize. Telling my father that I am pregnant is not an option.[6]

I tell whoever is growing in me that now and forever, I am the one who must, who will, live. A small, quiet voice agrees with me. Each night, we weep. Like with my mother and me, we know that we will never see/feel/hear each other again. Our time together is precious, and we do not waste it telling each other lies.

At fifteen, I am rational, deliberate, cold, having had to perfect a life of lies and performances of ~~perfect lovely ideal normal~~ an imagined Black girlhood. No one sees my father sit by my mother's bedside for a week before she dies. Or hears him crying before sunrise months after she does. No one sees us laugh with one another or dance in the street when the music is good. No one sees my mother's black eye. Or hears my father's yelling after he drinks too much. No one hears him tell me how beautiful I am. Or knows how afraid he is. How afraid we all are of everything. All the time.[7]

Though I do not yet know how I will do it, I am certain I will survive this as I have survived everything else. Who does a fifteen year old call to help her live? Only one person comes to mind: a college exchange student I met two years before, the same year the boys pull up my shirt. I still have his number, and when I call and tell him what has happened and what I am thinking, he does not judge me. He says he will help me. He will give me the two-hundred dollars I do not have for the procedure, pick me up, wait for me, and bring me home.

He gives me his mother's number. Call her, he says. And I do, this Black woman I will never speak to again or meet. She tells me about her own abortion, why she did it, and what to expect. She does not condemn me. She does not ask me if I go to church. She does not tell me to pray. She knows I am frightened; she was. She listens to my determination to be free.

You want to know, don't you, how a "~~good~~ girl" from good West Indian parents, who both work full-time jobs to send her to ~~good~~ Catholic schools for the best education they can afford, ends up making phone calls from her friend's house and sneaking out to Planned Parenthood only to have them tell her that they can't do it because she is suffering from gestational diabetes? How she cried walking down the street wondering how a piece of toast and jelly could deny her what she needs most?

Admit it: You want to know how that ~~good~~ girl walks home from Planned Parenthood crying because she is three months pregnant and terrified that she will have to kill herself. You want to ask that girl *Why you get yourself in that situation? After all your parents do for you? Ungrateful child. (suck teeth) Why you don't keep your legs closed? Didn't they teach you better? Didn't you know what you did at three months could have killed you? And the baby? You don't regret it, yet, nuh? Why you can't keep this to yourself?*

It's okay. I'm not mad at you. Let me ask you: What do you know about the need to own yourself? What do you know of the summons to rebirth that demands you tell your story so you don't forget, even if everyone else will?

I'm breathing calmly. Listening to Earth, Wind, & Fire and the Commodores as I write this. Not thinking about what people who do/don't know me will think or say when they read this. Black women who've never been girls and who want to stay alive can't afford to fill their heads with the expectations of others.

I've never cared. I don't regret it, not from the moment I made the decision, not after I entered the building of CRASH. I told you, I wanted the memory. All of it. The full weight of it. Lights and comfortable chairs and all. The clean smell. The fear of the other women as they talked quietly to each other or themselves. The person who took me, sitting in the waiting room with me until it was my turn.

I chose to stay awake so I would never doubt myself. Or what I did to be free.[8]

The doctor says something about my age, how young "they" tend to be. He is white and under his comment is a sigh of ~~disappointment~~ judgment.

The nurse is West Indian, like me. Nose like a hawk's beak. Skin the color of burnt brown sugar. Silver bracelets. Gold rings. Fuchsia nails. She looks at me and says: "Don't squeeze m'hand so, child. You go scratch me." She pulls her hand from mine. My palm is chafed.

In this room, I am alone with sterilized steel. I am ashamed to be frightened, so when the cramps begin, I do not cry. My hands grab the edges of the table. I clench my teeth. And I keep my eyes open.

I notice everything:

How the steel opens my uterus, probing to find what I need to give up to have more. How the suction is so strong, and I begin to wonder if my insides will be pulled out and if I will bleed to death. How the deeper the entry, the harder the cramps.

How the last sounds of life leaving a body is like water rushing through a cavern. When the water stops, it is the sound a body makes when it hits earth after falling from the sky breathless and without grace.

The doctor is patient, or maybe he is already tired at the beginning of his day.

The nurse does not look at me. I am not her daughter. I have no mother.

The doctor scrapes. Leaves no trace of life. No sediment of cells. No remnants of any self.

The nurse guides me off the table, into panties and pad, and to a room to outlive complications. Only when I leave do I breathe fully again.

PART 3

>   . . . how long it has taken
>   to perfect
>   the release
>   of my long
>   swallowed
>   scream

I take a chance and tell a teacher what I did. I can trust her, she does not teach at my school. She is brown like me, and from Egypt—the only brown woman I will see in four years. She is a scientist. She will know the truth.

I tell her: My baby was alive. I saw the nurse and doctor hold it before putting it in a glass jar. I cry, but she does not comfort me. Instead, she quietly tells me that what I saw was not real. She is a biologist: Even at three months, the fetus is so tiny you can barely see it. She tells me she, too, had an abortion once and this is how she knows. We stand apart from each other until my cries subside into whimpers. I wipe my eyes and face as I go to my next class.

I tell myself what I saw. Who else does a fifteen year old tell her secrets to?

I write poetry as I always have; poems I won't publish for decades or ever—journals that will be published after my death. I write because my life depends on it. I am the one to remember: the day on the bed and the day on the table, both times my body pulled apart.

Writing is choosing to never be silent on paper so even if no one will listen to me speak, even if no one believes me, one day someone will listen to me read and will read what I wrote for themselves. That person, she will recognize herself in my words and she will create her future by choosing her own life.

I chose to stay awake I chose to stay awake I chose to stay awake I chose to stay awake I chose to stay awake I chose to stay awake I chose to stay awake I chose to stay awake I chose—

I do not require your forgiveness.

What you should be asking me is this: *Daughter, you were how old? Daughter, who raped you? Was there more than one? For how long they force you to do this? What happened when you told someone? Eh-eh, how come no one see? (suck teeth, shake head) How long this was happening? Daughter, how come no one believe you? Daughter, can we hold you? Tell you how sorry we are? How ashamed we are that we abandoned you? Daughter, can we tell you that we love you? That we believe you now?*

PART 4

Because
only blood sacrifice
rights
some wrongs
frees
some souls
(like mine)

It will be years before I understand pain breaches dimensions between worlds.

I am grateful that neither memory nor matter demand retribution for my choice.

Gratitude to the ancestor who knew my life was full payment for what I suffered.

I bow down to the ancestor for bearing the sacrifice I refused to make.

Honor to my fifteen-year-old self for gifting me the life I have lived and continue to live.

Years later, my mother and grandmother come to me in a vision. They open my back with their hands and remove the grief I have carried since I was a child. Deep in my spine, they embed a symbol that connects me to them forever.

The year before the sacrifices—my mother dying and the ancestor choosing not to be born—was the year a tornado hovered over the Atlantic Ocean then spoke to me on my grandmother's veranda. This is the last year my mother is alive, and we are together on the island of her birth.

My grandmother and my mother remind me of what I cannot remember.

They say, the tornado said:

Daughter, blood offered for your past, present, and future is accepted.

Ibae baen tonu!

PART 5

learning to eat
my voice was
easy

but, oh, how long it has taken
to perfect
the release
of my long
swallowed
scream
only blood
rights
some wrongs
frees souls
from pain
and memory

know
the sacrifice was not in vain

I am free.
I remain free.
This is what I do
with my freedom.

I tell the story.
I tell the story so we can stay free.

Ase-O!

The Beginning and End of It

Patricia Smith

The first time the it kicked, and every time after, you were nauseated at the sight of its rhythmically pummeling foot/fist idly hunting for a way out of its sloshing shelter, its dark soup. If not for those ill-timed little rhumbas—which always seemed to happen when you were stupefied and bare-bellied in a mirror or stumbling into cavernous clothing while your mother screeched weep—you could almost forget it was there.

Well no, you couldn't forget, because your scrawny little self had swallowed a moon and then another moon, because you were always starving, because you ritually crammed peppermint sticks down the center of sour pickles and crunched the cool hurt, because more than a few times you found yourself sprawled on the kitchen floor in front of a gaping Frigidaire, scooping vinegary pigs' feet out of their cloudy liquid straight from the jar, slurping the skin and scraping the hock with your teeth until the bone shone white in the icy-blue light. Black folks insisted on their January 1 pigs' feet because, they said, pigs' feet were always rooted in the ground and pushing forward, which is the same direction you should want to go every year. But you and the it couldn't wait for a holiday. Not enough forward left for the two of you.

Come to think of it, folks who came up to Chicago from Alabama or Mississippi had a story for everything a pig had to offer, for every vile plop of innard, for every weary foot and unplucked snout. You actually even looked forward to your mother's Saturday morning chitlin' assembly line—the vinegar, the scrubbing, the vinegar, the scrubbing, the rinsing, the scrubbing, the rinsing, the three endless cycles of hot water. You saw no real reason for the sanitary ritual. You were convinced that the it would probably fancy a little dirt.

Your stomach lurched at the vampish stench while the church sisters hissed and sniffed at your dainty retching and babbled about the Lord Jesus and His reasons for things. Eventually they'd come to the conclusion that there was even a reason for *you*, sneaky gal, definitely up to sumthin', up from college for no reason, hiding evidence of the it under a series of beflowered shifts, your sadiddy mother skittish and sweaty with deception. Because it would never do for the child she'd bragged and bragged about to be—*Jesus Christ, Lawd no*—with burden, like those nasty gals in the projects, the ones who asked for it with their practiced swivels and the whole of their mouths.

As long as the it was merely suspected but never verified or outright asked about, your mother could keep her standing in the flimsy hierarchy of the reverent and bountifully blessed. She could slouch saintly in the front pew of Pilgrims Rest Missionary Baptist Church every Sunday, drowning in her choir robe, then rise to lend her creaking alto to the mix:

> *When peace, like a river, attendeth my waaaay*
> *When sorrows like sea billows roooooll*
> *Whatever my lot, Thou has taught me to say*
> *It is well, it is well with my soooouuulll . . .*

She could keep right on singing, and you could keep right on cramming your mouth with all the improbable parts of swine—jellied slabs of hogshead cheese, pork rinds plunged into bowls of tabasco, bacon slathered with mayonnaise or mustard, and pig's ear, fried deep and crackling. The it brusquely insisted upon itself, and the it had to feed. The it wanted stink, lard, some slither, and maybe even a little dirt. And you were the it's fat shuffling harbor, the it's one vein, the it's mouth and tongue. You were all the it needed, and you were everything in its way. Sorrows like sea billows were rolling. There was one comfort: After every huge filthy meal, the it, sated, grew quiet.

You were often alone, free to give the it whatever it demanded. You were an only child. Your father could not live with your brittle, spewing mother. Your father, who you loved with a ferocity that terrified and confounded everyone but the two of you, could not live with your mother and her monstrous Bible, her closets of pious couture, her hallelujahing over everything, her staunch refusal to wear pants (because God, for some reason, told her not to), and her holier than thou and thou too—even though he still remembered the flash of gold at the front of her mouth, how she swerved to brown liquor music, the way her hips used to spill over the edges of barstools. She found God, God found her, and God smushed her flat, siphoning her of everything but her rampant pride.

Daddy was your boozy blues crooner, your storyteller, all your laughter. He told horrible jokes and took you on field trips—to a field alongside O'Hare Airport to watch planes take off, to the candy factory where he worked, where he'd give you your own hardhat and let you taste all the sweets before they took their final shape. He was a snuggler, a griot, a confidante. The one time your mother charged him with the task of spanking you for some infraction, you screamed bloody murder behind a closed door while he wept quietly. He never touched you.

Daddy did not know about the it. There was no need to tell him. He loved you past seeing.

Because your mother was no longer the spunky Alabama gal he married, your father had moved into his own place nearby, but elsewhere. You and your mother mapped out your respective corners in the apartment and existed in them. Occasionally she'd rouse herself to spew accusations and double negatives and Lord have mercies in your general direction, alternately screeching and keening, calling into question your character and common sense, which oddly always seemed to sound like *just couldn't keep your damned legs closed*.

Then she would lower her voice to speak directly to the Lord her God, because the two of them had to reckon with a few delicate matters, while you tiptoed into the kitchen and opened the refrigerator, swigging directly from the milk carton, gnawing the fried skin from chicken legs before rewrapping them in foil, stuffing your mouth with feet and ears and tongue, maybe even a little dirt, just trying to fill the bowl of your body with anything other than.

Neither of you said anything about the future, about the looming specter of the it curling all its adorable into the family, maybe even healing the fracture, you didn't talk about pink or blue, breast or bottle, or pushing aside the particle board furnishings to craft an altar for a newborn. You didn't cycle through a list of possible names—no James or Adam or Richard, no Otis like your father, no Marilyn or Debra or Linda, no tangle of syllable and sound like Chevellanay or Taranishia. You saw no reason to page excitedly through the massive Sears Roebuck catalog, cooing at bassinets, changing tables, knit booties, onesies, and crib mobiles dripping with jesters and giraffes.

Sometimes your mother would simply stand in a doorway and stare at you and stare at you before collapsing in a well-orchestrated heap of crocodile tears, gospel verses, and the writhe of the Holy Ghost. You could only watch, well aware that her greatest concern was how the it would ruin her.

You both knew that the it was there, growing, feeding gleefully on filth, and that soon it would be alive in a very real way, writhing and wailing and asking and asking.

* * *

It made perfect sense that the two of you didn't talk. You never did. Throughout your life, your mother always seemed to be surprised at the fact of you. After what you always assumed was a businesslike bit of sex, she conceived as a way to cement her new life as a Northern woman and to keep her husband home.

But after said husband had reached his limit of spewing, you stuck around. Gradually your mother realized that you weren't leaving with him, and that you might actually turn to her for occasional guidance.

You, the bitty hindrance, kept her away from what she craved most in life—first, her fair share of West-Side nightlife (which your father, nevertheless, duly enjoyed), and second, her quest to be some sort of fashion-forward, petition-wielding, jet-setting Baptist princess, ready for Sunday service seven days a week. And she was not actually married anymore, not in any real way, just in case some God-fearing man needed something more formidable to fear.

You just never "presented well."

From the moment you were born, your mother decided that you were too dark (your father was only a shade lighter, but she'd had her fingers crossed) and that your nose was too wide. She spent hours pinching your nostrils together, while you read or watched television. You grew up gangly and shy around company, ashamed of your blue-blackness. The prospect of talking about things, especially woman things, with you just reminded your mother that she had a daughter to build. Not surprisingly, she decided to leave it to the Lord.

So you never talked about periods, what they meant or that they even existed. At twelve, when you discovered your lace-edged panties doused red and your favorite pants ruined, you stashed the soiled clothes inside a record cabinet. You were convinced that you were dying, and you wished to do so dramatically. You didn't tell your mother because you didn't think you loved her. You didn't tell your father because you loved him too much.

When your mother found the bloody stash, she held you in her arms and made something akin to mother noises. Then she gave you a big white pad, a huge pair of panties with hooks to hold the pad, and a huge can of a gaseous, cloying spray called FDS to spritz on yourself and in any room you had soiled with your bloody presence.

"This is gonna happen every month," she announced. And that was that. That not-knowing-about-sex or not-knowing-the-blood-had-any-thing-to-do-with-sex was all you knew about sex until you left for college.

And she never mentioned that you weren't dying.

All your life, you'd had been hammered upside the head by stars, which turned you stupid in the widest way. Suddenly after high school, you were on your own sans rudder or religion, just gone because it was time to be gone, your mother seduced by all the dull glitter you kicked up as you walked away. Nobody knew nothing, and you knew less than that. You were an only child with no visible scars anywhere. You often fell asleep with the earbud of a transistor radio feeding you a scrubbed reality. You'd grown up with Paul McCartney in one ear and Smokey

Robinson in the other, and all you knew about romantic love, or any-thing akin to it, was that misty in-between. You trusted every syllable of every word of every line of every song on every record you'd listened to, and every syllable of every line of every book you'd ever read. Worst of all, you'd trusted all the adverbs.

Usually. Patiently. Smoothly. Meaningfully. Happily. Thankfully. Joyously. Blissfully. Wonderfully. Sweetly. Innocently. Those long-winded words were all you needed to tell the story of the you who waltzed into college, that next phase of your life, armed with a head full of mawkish song lyrics and cheesy teenage triumph novels, and a determination to live them.

Silently. Sleepily. Gratefully. Deeply. Fast. Madly. Quickly. Really. Stu-pidly. Excitedly. Blindly. Wetly. Briefly. Fatally. Wildly. Suddenly. Easily. Afterward.

Those words were all you needed to tell the story of the you who opened the door of her dorm room, again and again, to an irretrievably erect frat boy who knew all the lyrics too. He'd memorized them just for you. Whoever you were.

* * *

So much utter ugliness and naivete in the interim—fervent letters, screaming matches, one-sided declarations of love, a tense meeting with a fraternity chapter head, all-night Greyhound rides, and finally—curt dismissal. In all truth, you had become brittle and spewing.

By the time you went home to a mother who would simply glance at your barely poofed stomach and wail, you were almost four months pregnant.

True to form, you and your mother never talked about it. She didn't ask the frat boy's name, didn't sit down with you to review your cher-ished sugary song lyrics for loopholes. You didn't talk about how ter-rified and flailing you had been. Her comfort, caution, and curse all sounded the same—some version of *just couldn't keep your damn legs closed.*

You didn't talk about how sex felt or was supposed to feel, and that's what you had the most questions about. Was it meant to howl for weeks after, like a bruise? When did the glow begin?

What was it called, that dead that dropped down over the face of the loved one? What did "Hey, you were just some good pussy" mean in the context of true love? What possible reason did Smokey Robinson have to lie to you? Why did you go into battle unarmed? Why had you been so hungry?

No answers were forthcoming, and the it was quickly becoming much more than a notion. It would soon be writhing and wailing and asking and asking. And there were no answers anywhere. There could be no love out of no love.

You didn't talk with your mother about how it felt to harbor such a ravenous stranger, although you suspected that she knew.

And even though it was damned close to being in the world already, you kept thinking of the it as the it because somehow—during the insipid silences between you and the woman who gave birth to you—you decided never to curse it with name.

Excerpt from "Better Parts"

from *Heart Berries*

Terese Marie Mailhot

Mom, I won't speak to you the way we spoke before. We tried to be explicit with each other. Some knowledge can only be a song or a symbol. Language fails you and me. Some things are too large.

What of the body, Wahzinak? What of your skin—that pine, and then the winter willow beneath.

What of the hair, Wahzinak? When you cut it, was it because he touched it? That is a type of mourning, too. Or was it the manner of the touch? How much of your movements do I contribute to a lack of love or the manner of it?

There is the sentiment that love is radical, from the very radicals you walked with. They say, now, that hate is the absence of love. It's poster fodder. I follow the logic to death.

What of death, Wahzinak? It's not the absence of something, but a new thing. I would never resurrect you, but I know your sons, my sister, and I often will you in our sleep. You told us it was dangerous to travel in our dreams. I know.

What of *your* death, Wahzinak? Was exacting hunger a type of satiation? The waist and hollow stomach in your soil—is that what you wanted? I died hungry that day. Everyone's stomachs were thrown into your cedar box—all your children, still your responsibility.

I hold my baby's head to my chest. The skin is the same as kissing a narrow stream, and even his hair feels perennial, without roots, just moving. Life is a running thing without roots for me. I'll take his stomach when I die, and throat, and he'll spend his life receiving better parts that I have not split.

Catalyst for a Daughter-in-Law

Laurie Ann Guerrero

> When you reap your harvest in your field, and forget a sheaf
> in the field, you shall not go back to get it; it shall be for
> the stranger, the fatherless, and the widow, that the Lord
> your God may bless you in all the work of your hands.
>
> —Naomi to her daughter-in-law Ruth (Deuteronomy 24:19)

There were parts I never
wanted to speak of. The child

widening me from the inside
made of me a stage. My breasts,

two mounds of clay, and you spoke
on his behalf and for every mother—

once and future, holy, my own, yours.
I took the washcloths

to my nipples, each bath,
in the weeks before he came—

toughening them up as you said
I should, that they would not be too soft,

too weak for the ravenous mouth
of a boy whose face I'd never seen.

I tried. I tried to love the natural
thing. Leading a would-be-man

to my breast. I do not blame you,
mother of the one I loved: all of us

children. And god himself—
fucking you at the pulpit.

Think of the Children

Kimiko Hahn

What are you?

Why am I writing this? Honestly, who cares about *slights* compared to injury and death? Who wants to hear about a body that is middle class and past middle age? (Already a grandmother!) Well, a younger woman asked me and so I'll tell my story.

In thinking about my body—a woman of color's body—a few strange partum and postpartum recollections occur to me:

My fiancé's mother telling him, "Think of the children." I was in the next room, and she didn't know (or did she?) that I was already a few months pregnant. We were not about to be discouraged by anyone—especially not by someone priding herself on some kind of pedigree.

A man shoves me aside to get to the cab door first. Can't he see I'm pregnant? If I were not Asian looking—

We arrive at the hospital, November 26, 1985, a vintage cashmere coat wrapped around my contraction-wracked belly. Alone while he parked the borrowed car, one of the nurses on duty tells me, "Clock in; you're late for your shift." I think, She takes me for a nurse. Yes, an Asian or Pacific Islander nurse. I didn't know what to say so just opened my coat. Breathe in, pause. Exhale.

On vacation, I am mistaken for the babysitter. Especially after the second daughter is born and she is surprisingly blonde.

What are you?

I am mixed. My father, German American from Milwaukee. My mother, Japanese American from the then territory of Hawai'i. They met after the war at the Y on Wabash, down the street from the Chicago Art Institute where my father was studying. My mother was at the Gregg Secretarial School and taking art classes on weekends. I was born in 1955 and mostly grew up in Pleasantville, NY. With my younger sister, we were a peculiar family in that white suburb.

I am what used to be called "the product of a mixed marriage." And here is something I've never told anyone: even before having my own mixed-race children, there were times I wondered why I was alive. *Should I be alive?* Should something with such dissimilar halves be alive?

Breathe in, pause. Exhale.

I was in the next room—

I've only dwelled on this self-erasing thought a few times and usually when I was judged by those belonging to a "pure" nationality or ethnic group (their self-description, by the way). *Judged*—that is, informed that I didn't belong. In fact, I have never belonged in any place or to any peoples. I have never felt I had any models by which to think about my own body.

Think of the children.

I did not resemble my mother or my father, but I do look more Asian than anything else.

Is it relevant that until I was eight, I didn't realize the man had anything to do with babies? I remember thinking that the woman just became pregnant (spontaneous generation!) and that any man could be the father. I recall feeling sad that my father could have been anyone my mother had chosen to marry. I felt a real sorrow. I looked more like my mother, Japanese, in a blurry sort of way. And I was treated as such (exotic or "Jap").

We were not about to be discouraged—

Who did I look like? What did I look like? Where was I from?

Unlike in 1945, when Americans of even 1/16th Japanese descent, were rounded up for mass incarceration, in the sixties it was cool to be part-Japanese. Eurasian. Exotic. Other. Then again, it most definitely was not cool. At certain times and places in the movement, it was not cool to be half white.

Judged—that is, informed that I didn't belong. Or in another version, if I converted, then I might belong.

Who did I look like? What did I look like? Where was I from? What would my children look like?

Clock in—

What to make of my own confusion? What to make of it in the context of being a mother and now a grandmother?

I was not mistaken—

If I am not comfortable with the body others judged an aberration, how could I mother children who would be mixed? How to be a mother? How to mother? Would one side be more of a mother? (And did my mother *mother me*?) (And did her mother *mother her*?) (Or was that the movies, the television shows—*mothering*?)

I still don't feel myself. Happily, I don't wonder if my daughters are okay—they are. They are brilliant beings, not Asian American, but not white. And they both love to tell me, à la Donald Winnecott's famous coinage, "You're *a good-enough mother*!" How did that happen?

I look at my granddaughter. She is a spirited three-year-old who calls me Baba for *Baa-chan* (although *baba*, strictly speaking, means "old hag" and not "grandma"). "Hey Baba!" she calls out to me. I don't know if she realizes how different we look—why would she think so? Moreover, what would it matter that she is blonde and her skin bright as milk? What matters is that she knows the sound of a peach floating down the river, *dombura-kokko-dombura-kokko*. That there are different ways to say stuff. Different ways to be. To be comfortable in one's skin.

Today, on my campus in Queens, there are so many immigrants and children of immigrants that I feel like I'm revisiting those years when it was wrong to mix, but young people did so anyway. There are so many students of color; I am surrounded, happily, by color.

Today, I think it is not what I think of myself, moreso *how* do I think of myself? There was a day in the recent past, before the granddaughter was born, that I felt like that aberration. But, over the years the fierceness of being an Other—even an Other to the Others—has overridden any fragility. Any fatigue. Any hesitation.

I do not hesitate to be this body.

I just opened my coat. I am having labor contractions. Let me in—

Tits and Ass

Deborah Paredez

> Tits and ass
> Can change your life
> They sure changed mine
> —"Dance: Ten, Looks: Three," *A Chorus Line*

BEYOND RECOGNITION

After the delivery but before the declaration of her name, after *What to Expect When You're Expecting* but before *What To Expect the First Year*, after the shitting and the screaming and the stalling at nine centimeters for several hours but before the stitching up of the vaginal tear, after the Commodores touched down with the lyric, *She's mighty-mighty/just lettin' it all hang out* on the playlist we'd made but before the earthbound dailiness of it all, the iconic gesture: the laying of the umbilical-tethered, vernix-glazed, tunnel-headed baby on my breast. The tableau of first contact in the realm of air and light, the transformation of the fetus into the person.

It's a moment that some (Many? A few? A select chorus played on repeat?) mothers recall with the awestruck language of Romeo—an irrevocable, destiny-driven, at-first-sight falling in love—or with the declarations of the once-wayward-now-saved soul—a deep and sudden sense of connection with something greater than the self, a confirmation of heretofore elusive truths. A consummation, an epiphanic transcendence.

What I thought as I gazed down at her blossoming face was, *Huh. I thought somehow I'd recognize you.* My elusive truth: the reckoning with so much unknowing.

What made me think I should already know her? Why did I feel like such a failure because I didn't?

TITS

Before becoming a mother, I never thought much about my breasts. By which I mean I took them for granted. Neither too small nor too large nor too burdened by a family history of cancer to shake or summon my confidence. And after I stopped dating white guys, my breasts became increasingly an afterthought as the men of color I encountered—my eventual husband among them—seemed more preoccupied with, well, ass.

Before becoming a mother, I had thought, *Sure, I'll breastfeed. Or I won't. Or I'll do both. Sure, I'll pump. Or I won't. Or maybe sometimes. And whatever I choose, I won't apologize for it.* As if personal choice was an act as singular and empowering and unburdened from racism and classism and misogyny as prevailing neoliberal values have led us to believe.

> *In the United States, public discourse on breastfeeding reveals the neoliberal cultural emphasis on personal responsibility.*[1]

Before becoming a mother, I scoffed at women around me who, as new mothers, appeared to be shackled by a commitment to the performance of self-abnegation in the service of their babies' slightest whims. (Can babies even have whims?) I recall myself taking a stance not unlike Samantha in *Sex in the City*—that paragon of postfeminist, girl-as-skinny-white-heterosexual-consumer power—when she declares to Carrie about Miranda's newborn son: *That baby's an asshole!* I felt actual disgust at what I perceived to be the choice among many (Most? Some? Middle-class?) mothers I knew and the practiced routines that seemed to mark their days and reshape our relationships: the strict bodily monitoring, the foreclosure of fulfilled desires not related to motherhood, the adoption of sole responsibility for meeting the child's needs even when a reliable partner was on hand and eager to help. I looked down at what I saw as their unnecessary suffering and their act of wearing that suffering as a badge of successful mothering.

By which I mean I was sometimes a shitty friend and a shoddy feminist. By which I mean that despite all those years I had spent reading and underlining passages penned by so many brilliant feminist thinkers and others, I remained deeply naive about the insidious forces of ideologies surrounding motherhood.

> *From the last decades of the twentieth century to the present, the notion of "good enough" mothering has been replaced by "exclusive motherhood," "intensive mothering," and "the new momism," or what I have termed "total motherhood" [which] requires mothers to be experts in everything their children might encounter, to become lay pediatricians, psychologists, consumer products safety inspectors, toxicologists, and educators. . . . Total motherhood is a moral code in which mothers are exhorted to optimize every aspect of children's lives, beginning with the womb. . . . Good mothering is defined as behavior that reduces even infinitesimal or poorly understood risks to offspring regardless of the potential cost to the mother.[2]*

By which I mean I was focusing on the wrong thing, pushing against the wrong source.

ASS

Before I bore down on the right place, I spent a good deal of time and energy bearing down on the wrong one. When it came time for me to push the baby out, I wasn't pushing through the vaginal canal at first. I was pushing through my ass. Apparently, this is a story that many (and this time I mean many) first-time mothers who've had vaginal births recount about their time in the trenches. Like them, I was focused on the wrong opening. And why shouldn't I have been? Until that moment, I'd only ever regularly practiced pushing through the one I defaulted to pushing through first. I had to learn, or rather, unlearn the gesture.

Come to think of it, I don't actually remember the moment I finally "got the hang of it." It's not like I was struck by an illuminating moment of awareness or that I consciously unlocked some deep interior room of knowing within me. Just that, eventually, I must have gotten it right because the baby arrived without any other medical intervention. I think I was just "pushing in the dark" or, more precisely, against the dark until by chance I pushed through and into the proverbial light. There was nothing "natural" about it.

For the record, I am known among those who know me as someone generally and easily committed to natural remedies and holistic care and alternative medicine and the occasional "woo-woo" form of bodywork, and to being attuned to my bodily needs, to its fluctuations and capacities and limitations. I had done the Kegels. I had hired the acupuncturist doula. I had considered my chakras and relaxed my jaw and moaned in a long low note. I had achieved the drug-free vaginal birth. And still, the (re)focused pushing was something that didn't come naturally to me.

By the time I got it right, I had managed to push out more than a small amount of my insides. The fallout from my steep learning curve combined with the delicate particularities of my own GI system meant that I left the hospital with and spent the next few months plagued by hemorrhoids the size of apricots.

TITS AND ASS

More than a few women agree with Elizabeth Stone's assertion that to have a child *is to decide forever to have your heart go walking around outside your body*. For me, it was more like having my guts hanging so far outside of my body that I couldn't sit or concentrate or shit easily for weeks on end. Which made it especially difficult to manage the other, more emotional pain I was facing: my milk was not coming in.

I'm no stranger to pain. The blessing and curse of my life as a regular migraine sufferer is that I have become intimately acquainted with the vicissitudes of chronic pain. (In fact, one of the few ways in which I have no qualms about deviating from my natural path is when I'm reaching for my latest prescription of pharmaceutical migraine meds). On my best days I believe my frequent encounter with pain has expanded my capacity for empathy and for enduring certain kinds of struggle. I have often said that my decision to plan for a drug-free delivery and to manage my pain throughout it was informed by the knowledge gained from years-long practice at inhabiting and moving through debilitating pain for hours, and sometimes days, on end. Of course, on the days I'm cowering in a dark room caught in its vice, I come to grips with the fact that there is no redemptive reason or higher purpose or precious value or nobility to be found in experiencing pain. As someone once brilliantly said: *It is what it is.* While the only thing that bearing pain may expand for sure is your capacity for bearing more pain, it does not make you morally weak or psychically flawed or romantically luminous or spiritually transcendent. It just means that sometimes you have the bad luck of getting the wrong strand in the crapshoot of genetics.

So I tried not to fear the pain caused by my tits and my ass. I tried, like many middle-class women committed to "natural" mothering and caught in the undertow of total or intensive mothering, to treat it by consulting all the experts and by consuming all the products. I scheduled appointments with the pediatric nurse who ended our session by giving me a onesie promoting breastfeeding that I tossed in the dumpster on the way to my car and private sessions with the pricey (but best!) lactation consultant who insisted I wake up every forty-five minutes throughout the night to pump when I wasn't trying with the actual baby. I paid for the herbal supplements and the stacks of breastfeeding manuals and the industrial-grade breast pump and the gentle yoga and the acupuncture and—

> *Class-privileged women construct breastfeeding as a consumer undertaking and as a project to be managed and accomplished.*[3]

During one of her house calls, my dear friend and acupuncturist, Claudia, gingerly and with great compassion and a complete lack of judgment, tried to explain that in Chinese medicine the treatment for the hemorrhoids would be to encourage the chi to draw upward, while the treatment for my stoppered breasts would be to bring the chi flowing down.

In other words, my ass was at odds with my tits. My body a battleground between my needs and my child's.

So of course, I chose to tend to my tits. By which I mean my baby and what I perceived to be her needs. I had come to believe that this was not just the right option but the only option. One breastfeeding manual exclaimed: *When you believe in your breasts, they will work for you. If you don't believe you can breastfeed, you set yourself up for all the problems that lead to failure. A doubt can be a self-fulfilling prophecy.*[4]

Meanwhile, my own mother and husband were lovingly and eagerly feeding the baby bottles of formula while I insisted on sitting on the donut pillow and plugging my breasts into the godforsaken sucking machine or while I pored over the books or swallowed the herbs or woke at the insisted-upon intervals or lay sprawled on the couch sprouting needles across the length of my body or bent over a sitz bath sobbing into my unwashed hair.

The milk never came.

I cried and cried and cried, flooded by the deluded certainty that on an ontological level I was not fit to be a mother. I was filled with so much despair over my perceived failures and, when I wasn't sad, I was consumed with rage that I'd been so easily and thoroughly engulfed by the misogynist ideologies I had tried my whole adult life to denaturalize and reject. What kind of fucked-up feminist was I? What kind of fucked-up mother was I destined to be? How had it come down to this?

I hardly recognized myself. Sleep-deprived, my mind as blank as the emptied sky save for the daily hormonal fireworks display obscuring the stars, I was beyond recognition in every sense.

Like the milk, neither a reason nor a sense of resolution ever came.

Meanwhile, the baby drank from her bottles. The baby slept. The baby grew.

MEANWHILE / WEANMILE

There are times even now when I see a baby nursing, or as I write these words, that I feel a dull flush in my breasts, a phantom ache or echo of the feeling of "let down" though technically I never experienced its full force. But then, there are other forces that dwell there. The body keeps the score, they say.

> Shame is the consequence of not breastfeeding after having internalized the imperative of total motherhood. This sense of shame is revealed in the acrimonious accounts of formula-feeding mothers who simultaneously express regret and defend their decision.[5]

What if, even now, I'm still focusing on the wrong opening? What if this is a story of the ways my body didn't just fail to "let down" or didn't just let me down but delivered to me insight about my true desires in the face of nefarious forces that insist that my or any mother's desires are not just wrong or selfish but unrecognizable because they are, in fact, not permitted to exist?

What if it wasn't even that deep? What if *it is what it is*? What if the body in pain is not a moral lesson or a badge or a ballad? What if, as my pain over the years has reminded me, sometimes the body just doesn't work in the ways we'd hoped it would?

What if I widen the aperture? What if I pan out beyond the self-punishing, middle class, brown, American mother's body to include the forces that are bearing down on her and the forces that are sustaining her? What if the frame expands to include the meanwhile or the *weanmile*, that stretch of time and distance in which both my girl and I were learning to seek out other sources of nourishment. A space in which we—all of us—are learning to discern between sources that seek to feed us and those that seek to devour us. In the weanmile, a glimpse of the bodies and the structures that must actually be present to raise the child. In the weanmile, the baby's extended family or kinfolk or all the tías participate in nightly feedings and leave casseroles on the doorstep. In the weanmile: healthcare for all and paid parental leave. In the weanmile, scientific studies posit research questions that don't reify gendered divisions of labor. In the weanmile: no shame, no regret. In the weanmile, we are fed. In the weanmile: tits and ass shaking with nothing but pleasure across the toy-littered room.

3

Death to Breath

A Mother/Daughter Doula Story

Emma L. Morgan-Bennett and Jennifer L. Morgan

We write as mother and daughter. As a woman who has given birth and a woman who has not done so. As a mother who has informally attended more than a dozen births, and a daughter who has recently trained as a full-spectrum doula. We share a belief in the transformative power of joyous births. Our birth work is pivotal for understanding our dedication to reproductive justice. Jennifer teaches the history of slavery, race, and reproduction. Emma has just graduated from college after finishing her medical anthropology thesis examining doulas who enact birth justice in the climate of the Black maternal health crisis. In other words, we come to the work of reproductive justice together, from a place of joy and struggle and political commitments.

We do so because of our own individual stories and the way those stories intertwine with the history of race, racism, and medicine in this country. Our histories demand that we grapple with the way that the past lives on in our present. In the history of medicine, there are countless acts of exploitation and violence meted out upon the bodies of Black women, especially in relation to reproduction. When enslaved, Black women faced rape and exploitation as the logics of hereditary racial slavery were most brutally carried out in their own bodies, transforming their children into commodities on the balance sheets of slaveowners. After emancipation, Black women were subjected to the devaluing of their reproductive capacity, the horrors of medical experimentation, and the effort to destroy their ties of kinship and community. The history of Black women's bodies is a history of pain.

In this world, the act of giving birth has become increasingly fraught. Hospitals all too often reflects a society that discounts Black and Brown people from the moment we are conceived. Black women have real and tangible reasons for their distrust. For far too long, Black women have faced an escalated risk of death as they give birth. Pregnant and birthing Black mothers have died at rates disproportionately higher than their white counterparts. Today in the United States, Black maternal mortality means that Black mothers perish and leave their families behind at three to four times the rate of white mothers. The Center for Disease Control's graph of pregnancy-related mortality reveals an alarming upward climb since 1987 of the number of Black women dying per 100,000 live births. Unless something changes, Emma is terrified that she will face a more deadly delivery than her mother, a morbidity rate comparable to what her grandmother faced three years after the passage of the Civil Rights Act.[1] This unwelcomed intimacy between Black birth and death prevails even as Black lives are defined by surveillance and policing. We are gutted by the routine death of Black mothers not only in labor and delivery rooms but also at the hands of the police, we are devastated by Black men calling for their mothers with their dying breath, and as we write, we are both, at times, overwhelmed by despair.[2]

* * *

And yet. Black women have always acted to frame their own lives, especially in relation to their capacity to bring life to others. From attempting to protect their children from enslavement through the courts, to avoiding pregnancies or surreptitiously carrying out abortion and feticide while enslaved themselves, to raising children despite the onslaught of captivity and forced labor, the centuries-long history of slavery in the Americas is replete with examples of African women and their descendants wresting their reproductive bodies out of the symbolic grip of the slave market and into the sheltering context of Black kin.[3] In the aftermath of enslavement, as women's reproductive capacity became devalued by a white-supremacist society intent on devaluing Black life, women worked to refuse the use of their bodies and communities as the experimental sites of American social science and anti-Black eugenic public health campaigns. For decades now, Black women have defined reproductive justice so as to include the right to have as many or as few children as desired, and have been on the frontline of the fight for justice and equity.[4] Now, as doulas, as community members, as scholars and students, we see the way that Black women are working to create space to both call attention to the systemic dangers of birthing while Black and also to develop strategies and practices to counter death with breath and to channel birth's potentials through the curation of our bodies as a site of pleasure, joy, and futurity.

* * *

Our bodies are, indeed, a source of profound pleasure and joy. And the possibilities that exist as a woman bringing a life into this world have become touchstones for both of us as we confront systems that so profoundly devalue who and what we are. Pregnant with Emma while writing a book about reproduction and slavery, Jennifer felt a powerful urge to think carefully about her pregnancy as shaped by history. She committed to birth with a midwife and to be fully present during her unmedicated labor and delivery. She did not understand the risks she faced in a New York City hospital, but was blissfully delivered of her daughter with only a modicum of postnatal physiological trauma. As a new mother and a scholar, she sought to understand the urge to demedicalize birth and to support others who made that choice. As she watched women birth their babies, she began to see all that was at stake. Emma then grew up familiar with the dance of her mama rushing out the door after a hasty goodbye kiss, only to return with stories of babies that were slow to arrive and others who rushed into their mother's arms. Emma does not remember a time before she understood pregnancy and birth. She became "official" with her first boyfriend at the ripe age of six by exploring a birthing exhibition together in Boston, and then demanding first access to the warm and waiting car on the basis of all the work she would have to do to push a baby out—he graciously conceded her point! Then, in high school, Emma's comprehension of the joys and pains of her reproductive body deepened when she accompanied a dear friend to the abortion clinic after a morning of quiet companionship while listening to that friend navigate the crossroads of her own life. These moments add up, for both of us, to a commitment to thinking through the ravages of racial and corporeal violence facing women of color in this country in order to access the realm of transformative possibilities that we associate with women seizing control of our bodies and our futures.

As mother and daughter, we have crafted an intergenerational response to the histories that we confront and to the question of what it means to recoup birth as a space of trust and happiness. For many women of color, having children while poor or unmarried has been seen as evidence of their pathology. And yet, Black women continue to create families, become mothers (if they so choose), and to reshape the medical interventions that have enacted such violence. We have seen moments of possibility and power that compel us to ask, again and again, "How do Black mothers and birthworkers press forward to reshape and counter anti-Black reproductive violence in both the acts of birth and the demands for safe and joyful birthing experiences?" There is a space of connection between a mama and birthworker that can counter the afterlife of slavery—the legacy of dispossession and violence that all too often lodges in the body of a woman trying to give birth—one that we have both encountered and want to enable. By the very nature of the work they do, we hold witness that Black birth and birthworkers oppose the assumptions that Blackness can only signify morbidity. Instead, radical doula work asserts, both in theory and praxis, that Black liberation can be delivered, in part, by the reclamation of birth and medical spaces as spheres of trust, community, and love.[5] We have both staked a claim in the ground of Black birth, a place where radical doulas are positioned as guides and curators of trust- and care-filled birthing experiences for Black families. For us, it is through a reconfiguration of Black birth as a radically joyful act that the racial justice will grow.

* * *

From different vantage points, we both found ourselves drawn to doula work. Perhaps this is because we belong to a family that has held countless conversations about the reproductive afterlife of slavery around our kitchen table. We are descendent from women who made seemingly mundane choices about their reproductive lives in contexts that transformed them. Emma's great-grandmother divorced in the 1940s, confident that her parents and siblings would help to raise her daughter when she moved from Durham to Brooklyn to join them. Emma's grandmother, Jennifer's mother, created an interracial family in the 1960s, confident that Jennifer and her brother would understand themselves to be rooted in a Black family even as she pushed against the boundaries of what that meant. We understood, and understand, birth to be a site of vulnerability and generation. A place that calls us to define ourselves against the edifices that claim to do so for us. As doulas and as scholars we are invested in reproductive health and gender as a vital platform for Black liberation. We believe that birth can become a space of vibrancy and peace. We come to that through a particular dynamic—that of a mother in her fifties looking back over time from the place of her own menopausal postchildbearing body; and a twenty-four-year-old daughter just entering the age of fertility and motherhood, who as a trained doula has assisted a number of births herself, but who does not yet know what her own childbearing body will do. Our conversations about birth justice are inseparable from our own positions as a mother invested in the historical and a daughter assessing the future.

As Emma entered her twenties, she began sensing the stultifying fear of birth that constricted both her and her friends. They shied away from its associated pain and bodily transformation. Emma was struck by what increasingly felt like an assumption that pregnancy and childbirth were exclusively the site of loss and disempowerment. She recognized a vocabulary and narrative woven into much of the social media, movies, and conversations surrounding her that pregnancy promised a kind of social death—a shocking echo of Orlando Patterson's characterization of what defined slavery.[6] Motherhood seemingly threatened

the loss of one's youth, beauty, and sensuality, the end of one's autonomy and carefree attitude, the conclusion of the magic promised with
phrases of "independent women." But there was something more, the
weight of the world seemed to bear down on the choice of whether or
not to consider motherhood. How could one ethically justify conceiving
a child given the reality of racial inequity? How does one balance the
futurity of birth with the ends implied by the climate crisis and global
warfare on top of the systemic racism that could leave her baby dead
at the hands of the police or as the result of the neglect of a physician?
All signs in the narrative pointed to the conclusion that childbirth, as
an action invested in future life and creation, felt both interperson-
ally and systemically morbid. This feeling that Emma quickly began to
recognize as a generational one raises the question: What do we risk
losing if pregnancy and childbirth become moments in which women
are deprived of agency? What happens when we young adults become
disillusioned by the future into which we are supposed to surrender
our newborns? How do we recoup trust, and thus investment and
accountability, in a world which is saturated with white supremacy?
Reproduction, and specifically the birth workers and doulas assisting
this journey, then becomes a pivotal educational, political, and social
site we must turn toward as instrumental to generational healing and
community formation.

For Jennifer, the birth of Emma was a pivotal moment. Deep in the
throes of writing a book on the history of enslaved women and the ways
in which their reproductive capacity was used against them, Jennifer
faced her pregnancy with a determination to wrench it free from the
histories that would collude to devalue it. She felt a deep commitment
to experiencing the pregnancy and the birth as a nonmedical event.
She refused, for example, to "meet" her infant through the televised
image of an ultrasound, and traveled the entire length of Manhattan
to give birth in a hospital where a midwifery practice had a longstand-
ing presence. Despite the hospital environment, Jennifer gave birth to
Emma in a room surrounded by family, a best friend who acted as
an unofficial doula, and a midwife who respected her desire to shape
the experience even if she didn't understand the full weight of all that

Jennifer was pushing back against. Ultimately, it was in response to her own experience of birth that led Jennifer into informal doula work for the next twenty years. The astonishing possibility of the birthing room, the ability of some women to keep history at bay, even if only for the hours it took to push a baby out into the world—to Jennifer, this was a lesson as important as the ones she has learned in the archives. We are not only the products of our histories—there are moments of possibility that can be harnessed, that produce bonds of caring and radical love that she believes have the power to transform.

* * *

Harnessing the transformative possibilities of birth is a political necessity. Doing so is mandatory if the United States hopes to become the global healthcare leader it pretends to be. We write from the midst of the Covid-19 pandemic. From the reality that Black and brown communities have, yet again, been disproportionately affected by Covid-related deaths and the disparities rendered crystal clear by this public health disaster.[7] We are reminded that our call for fundamental transformations in reproductive health is situated in the midst of a broader understanding of public health. Care-centered and consensual health care is good health care. When medical staff do not mock or dismiss their patients' claims of pain, the dangerous history of distrust between providers and clients is interrupted. When patients are treated as legitimate arbiters of their own bodies, all manner of futurity is unleashed. Hospitals must establish themselves as police-free and truly confidential environments that abstain from the incarceration or policing of their patients. This encourages truthful communication about issues such as drug use or domestic violence as well as circumventing the horrific mistreatment of incarcerated pregnant people and their families at the hands of the police.[8] When antiracism and informed-consent training is institutionalized within medical curriculums, our emerging providers will be better prepared and better equipped physicians. We see glimpses of this with New York's recent decision to beta test a system of providing doula support to low-income women. But this is only a start. Given how systemic racism foreshadows the formation of nearly every American institution, policy and governmental support to financially and institutionally protect birthworkers (while protecting their complete autonomy) is nonnegotiable. At the same time, we cannot limit ourselves to pursuing reproductive transformation from within the confines of medical or governmental institutions. Radical community—the belief in, the commitment to, and the mutual support of—is the fiber that birthwork builds upon to defend the lives and joy that every Black mama deserves. And lest we forget, by adapting a reproductive justice and antiracism framework, medical communities will encourage the health and well-being of not only Black women but also the LGBTQ community, Latinx folx, Indigenous people, working-class whites, and all who have been historically marginalized and maltreated through medical neglect.

* * *

We have long recognized birthworkers as caretakers for individuals. We have both done that kind of care work and have been, in turn, transformed by providing it. To assist a woman in labor is a profound experience for the doula. After each and every birth we have witnessed, we have been astonished by the connective tissue that envelops the birthing room, by the threads of past and present and future held together in that instantaneous and irrevocable moment of crowning. We believe that such moments anchor us, in particular, in a history of race and reproduction that speaks to both the afterlives of slavery and the roots of Black radicalism.[9] But we also see birthworkers as caretakers of broader communities, indeed of humankind. As midwives and physicians deliver the future through infants, doulas partner with birthing people to reposition birth as is inextricable from community. As the historian Robin D. G. Kelly argues, imagination precedes construction.[10] As we fight for recouping Black birthing spaces as ones of trust and liberation, we envision births in which laboring mothers are listened to. Where, rather than considering birth only in terms of a potential health crisis, medical staff collaborate with and affirm mothers' birthing plans and desires. Where Blackness and Black families are embraced as they are, without judgment or expectations, and where birthing rooms are police-free environments where health, not politics or surveillance, is prioritized. These would be spaces from which every woman returns to their families healthy and alive—maternal morbidity and mortality disparities must not continue to cause needless death. Only then would the medical community begin to be able to reconcile and address its role in the facilitation of white supremacy. These demands echo those of countless Black women organizers within the Reproductive Justice movement, including the SisterSong Women of Color Reproductive Justice Collective and Ancient Song Doula Services. These visions are doable and in fact necessary for equitable healthcare. Through the prioritization of the above tenets, birthing centers and hospitals can retransform from sites of Black death to affirmations of Black life.

The Beginning and the End

Shannon Gibney and Kao Kalia Yang

It was early spring. We sat opposite each other at the small table on the second floor of a coffee shop on the east side of St. Paul. It was morning, still. There were conversations lingering around us, colleagues unwilling to part for the day's work; old friends savoring a shared memory from years gone by. In between us, there were books, mugs, crumbs on a plate, crumbled napkins, a laptop, a calendar, and an ocean to cross.

We, an Asian American woman and an African American woman, sat looking at each other. Despite the cool temperatures outside, there was a shine to both of us. We had agreed to team up to write our stories of miscarriage and infant loss and to collect those of other women of color and Native women. Our bodies were registering the beat of our hearts, the heat of the undertaking.

In the photograph that Shannon took to commemorate the beginning of our journey, we are smiling, our heads pushed close, our eyes staring toward the same place: a vision of a book, one whose title would speak to the magnitude of loss that we knew had been largely unwritten and unexplored in literary America, *What God Is Honored Here? Writings on Miscarriage and Infant Loss by and for Native Women and Women of Color.* Our goal was to pool our energies and stories together to call for a gathering of voices so we might sing our songs of grief, of hope, of hurt, and deliver to the world a truth, elemental and raw, of what it is like to inhabit our bodies and carry our losses.

That day, neither of us knew that we were setting out to create a community—a place where women who had never found a space to talk about, mourn, and honor their dead babies could finally do so. We did not yet know of the women who were waiting for our call, of that ancient sisterhood beckoning us across space and time.

We began first by writing our stories for each other. Kalia had known of Shannon's talents in writing complicated young adult books about race and identity, about the conditions of families, communities, and countries. Shannon had known of Kalia's work detailing the stories of her Hmong American family and community, the forces of war, the promise of peace. Kalia had lost a pregnancy at nineteen weeks. Shannon had delivered a stillborn baby at forty-one weeks. In the process of writing our individual stories, we wept for ourselves and each other. In the sharing of our stories, we crossed a threshold of pain; we felt not only our own but each other's.

The call for submissions to the book was carried out quickly across the nation. Our inbox filled with responses from both men and women, experienced writers and novices, people living in this country and others. While ours was a call for women of color and Native women's experiences of loss, white people submitted. We read each submission individually. We made comments. We gathered thoughts. We felt our way through each piece.

In a different coffee shop and in a different season, we sat, once again opposite each other. The big windows were full of green plants reaching for the sun. Cars passed by on the busy avenue dirty with snow. Their images blurred as the light of the day shifted around us. The shadows of the leaves grew long and touched the backs of chairs, reached across the tables. Together, we sifted through the submissions, our hands at our hearts at times, our hands at our throats at other times, as we discussed each piece. The piles of tear-soaked napkins grew at the edge of our table. We chose some twenty submissions from women of color and Native women. Each piece of writing connected with the deep well of loneliness inside each of us and filled it up bit by bit with an understanding that our losses, while intimate, belonged together.

The topic of our book was devastating, raw, and filled with unrelenting grief. It was an indictment of systems past and the present. We knew we lived, as many therapists, psychologists, and mental health professionals have observed, in a profoundly grief-averse culture. Here, it was better to move on to the next thing. There, it was better to pretend it never happened. Everywhere, it was better to tend to everyone else's feelings around death and dying than our own, that of a beloved baby or baby-to-be. But each and every woman in the collection knew that grief demands attention in order to move into and beyond itself. We knew that if we forgot our babies, it would be as if they were never here. All of us, in writing our stories and our poems, had made a decision to honor them and our journeys with them, however short.

The editing process brought us much closer to each writer. We asked contributors to linger over moments they had written through quickly. Those moments were often the hardest: the body of a would-be baby slipping into a toilet bowl, falling through the shaking hands of its mother, a scream of pain choking a throat, cleaving the air we breathed. These moments had made us who we were as writers and women, had forced each and every single one of us to reckon with our cultures, our religions, our spiritual beliefs, and sometimes the people closest to us.

When the book was finally done, and it was time for us to gather with each other and readers for its launch events, we found that often the spaces were quiet. Bookstores became silent as chapels. University rooms lined by windows were shrouded in the shadows of our grief. It was then that we wept openly. It was then that we talked through our tears and found words of comfort for our hearts and others. It was at those first events, where the initial heat we had felt in our bodies on that very first day when we met to speak of the book, that sheen on our skin, found its place in the world we shared.

The numbers at our events were always smaller than we anticipated, different from other events for other books we've written and been part of. The people who came were the people who needed to be there. One thing we had not expected were the older white women in the audience, some of whom approached us afterward to tell us what they had lost, how they had lost it, and how the culture at the time had made it worse. "When you read what happened to you, the line where you just said *The baby died*," one woman said, "I realized that I never said that. I mean, I never could say it. No one wanted me to. I just had to move around it, like, *She's gone.* Or *She's in heaven*, or something. I never felt like I could just say that my baby died."

It is now once again springtime. Outside, the tulips are peeking out of the grass still not yet brave enough to green. It has been two years since the publication of *What God Is Honored Here?* The book is making its way, slowly but surely, into the places where there are others waiting. Women not only eager to see a reflection of their experiences of loss but also in search of a community. Women who understand what it means *to be* in a world where so much of what and who we love cannot.

"The Evanesced: The Retrieval #99"
Kenyatta A. C. Hinkle

4

Born Ibeji

Cheryl Boyce-Taylor

I grew up as part of an extended family in a Christian Caribbean home. My mother became a Seventh-day Adventist when I was two years old. This was a strict fanatical religion. What saved me was my Baptist grandmother and the strong will I developed as an early adolescent.

I knew my mother loved me just by the way she worked so hard to take care of me and my brother. During the daytime, my mother worked as an assistant teacher in a daycare setting. She also made hats that she put on consignment at a friend's little shop and taught swimming at the YMCA in our little town of Arima. My parents were not married, but my father lived in the center of town about two miles away from my mother's family. In those years I spent very happy times both with my father and his family and with my mother and her family.

In those years, money was scarce, and things of luxury were hard to come by, yet I believed that I had a very good life. In 1962, my mother's eldest sister came to Trinidad to visit us. We were overjoyed. During her visit, she invited my mother on a family trip to New York. By the time she left Trinidad two months later, it had been decided that my mother, brother, and I would move to New York for better educational opportunities and a chance to live a fuller life.

For the next year and a half, my mother worked with the immigration system to get us passports and visas to travel to New York. Finally, everything seemed to be set for our travels. That week, my mother went to immigration services for her last visit, and they informed her that, as a teacher, they could not release her from her job because there was a shortage of nursery school and daycare teachers. She was devastated. They did offer a visa for me and promised that later, when things were better, they would offer visas to my mother and brother. This was a difficult decision for my mother. I was only thirteen, and she had never been away from me. After much prayer and fasting, she decided to send me to her sister. On a cold November morning in 1964, I arrived alone in New York City to live with my aunt Ena and her husband Lacy.

My aunt and uncle were kind people, but they were a bit cold and not at all affectionate. And I really did not know them. They were certainly not ready to parent a young, chatty teenage girl. For the next two years, I did my best to get along, I did very well in school, but the loneliness of missing my parents, close friends, and family weighed very heavily on me. As I look back, I can see that maybe I was struggling with some type of depression. I longed for some type of intimate connection with another person my age, so when, at sixteen, Anthony offered me his hand to hold, I was giddy. Our romance was on the fast track.

My life seemed to be blossoming wildly. The next year flew by happily, and then my mother arrived in New York City. By then, I was in my last year of high school, I had a sweetheart, and I was graduating with honors. And that fall, I would be going to Alabama for college. My mother was so proud of me. I was a butterfly... Life was a dream. And then I found out, three months before my graduation, that I was pregnant. I was ashamed and disappointed. I tried to hide my pregnancy from my mother, but I was seventeen and she knew everything about my life. She knew I was pregnant before I even told her.

This news broke my mother's heart, and even though she was super religious, she decided that I would have an abortion. The way she put it was that there was no room in the cards for a baby; my college education was what was most important.

So, two months before my graduation, on the warmest spring day, my mother's friend Lily took us to Brooklyn so I could have an abortion. I felt shameful and helpless, I had messed up my mother's dream, and, truthfully, I believed I did not have any say in this decision. I had watched my mother slave and work just to give me an education and a better life. I knew how much we had given up, leaving Trinidad and our family. I thought about my father; I was not going to spoil their dream.

Nurse Tully was a trained midwife; she birthed babies but also did illegal abortions. She lived in a dingy part of Brooklyn in one of those real old-fashioned buildings with a huge lobby that you could almost fit three apartments into. We had to walk up about four flights of stairs to get to her tiny apartment. I would never forget that narrow, dark railroad place. She took us back to the tiniest bedroom. In the room was a small bed and a table covered in white cloth. I remember long brown tubes and shiny silver instruments, and a stack of white towels on the table. On a second table with no cloth, there were a basin and two jugs. The room was eerily quiet except for the sound of a bird that continuously whistled and made irritating cackling noises.

She gave me a short, white gown and pointed us to the bathroom across the hall, where she instructed me to get undressed and come back and lie on the bed. When we took too long, she gruffly told us to hurry up. I tried not to look at my mother, but at times I could hear her sobbing softly. My mother gave me the quickest hug and helped me onto the bed. I remember quite a bit of pain but I made myself disappear, and after what seemed like ages, it was over. She gave us a long sheet of handwritten instructions and told my mother that she was to take me straight home and put me to bed until the action started. That is what she said: "Until the action starts."

We took a train and two buses back to Queens; all the while my mother held my hand tightly. I tried to block it out, but there was no denying that our lives were forever changed. Once we arrived home, my mother washed me up and put me to bed. At times I could hear her praying and crying while we waited to expel the fetus. It was the worst night of my life. Mom took care of me in silence and no one in our household ever knew what went on between us that night. Whenever my body would fall into painful spasms, my mother wiped me down with warm washcloths and tended to me wordlessly. Finally, it was over. We never spoke about that night again.

Two months later I graduated from high school with honors and went on to a local city college. I never heard from Anthony again, who said it was not his baby. That fall he left for a college in Michigan where he had a full soccer scholarship.

Mom was not good at speaking about love, sex, relationships, or birth control. She was strictly a God-fearing woman who was raising her daughter not for the world but for heaven and the earth made new. She spoke about the Bible, sang hymns, and prayed in earnest for us to go to heaven. After the abortion, my mother became stricter with me. Most of our weekends were spent in church, I tried to keep up with her plans for me, but her religiosity got harder and harder for me to manage. The year I turned eighteen, I met Walt, the man I would marry. Marriage seemed like the best way to get out of my mother's house. The best part was that we loved each other dearly. I found my prince, and he, his princess.

* * *

In 1950, my mother Elma gave birth to a set of twins, a boy and a girl. The boy was stillborn. The girl was one pound eighteen ounces. That little darling was me. Twenty years later almost to the day, I would give birth to twins, two boys, Malik and Mikal. My family was overjoyed. They believed we had gotten our twin baby back. Both boys were born prematurely at seven months. Our joy was short-lived, because within eight hours Mikal passed away. What a devastating blow for us and our family.

I managed to hold myself together, putting all my energies into the surviving baby, I held down my fears and my emotions, afraid that I would lose Malik, the two-pound fifteen-ounce baby who was struggling for his survival in an incubator. Malik remained in the hospital for three and a half months. Each day my fear escalated, and by the time I brought him home, I had decided I would never have another child. My husband, Walt, and I brought our baby home from the hospital on one of the coldest days of March 1971. We'd had less than three days of training on how to take care of a newborn. Luckily, Malik turned out to be an unbelievably sweet-natured baby. He was cuddly and well behaved, and the only time he cried was when he was hungry. We quickly learned to have his bottle ready for the next feeding. While I was excited to take care of him, fear grew in my body, and my husband

and I worked very hard not to become pregnant again. We must have gotten very careless, because the next year we were pregnant again.

We were terrified of losing another baby and had not gotten any counseling for the huge loss we both endured. We never bothered to discuss our fears openly and a few weeks later we decided to have an abortion. My husband seemed to bounce back pretty quickly, focusing new energy on the young toddler in our home. Inside, I felt guilty. I had deprived my son of a sibling and a child of its life. I mourned that baby in private, keeping my fears and tears from my family. Loss and guilt overshadowed my every waking moment.

After the abortion, I went to the Planned Parenthood in my neighborhood to obtain some method of birth control. I decided on the diaphragm, which took expertise and information on using it effectively. In 1971, there were not a lot of opportunities to speak openly about birth control because there was so much shame involved. I was offered birth control pills. I gained thirty pounds in about four months. I went back for counseling in a real undercover operation; I snuck back in the Planned Parenthood center, got a diaphragm, and used it without much direction. I did not know what the hell I was doing.

By the summer of 1972, I discovered that I was pregnant again. My heart sank. I knew I had to tell my family what was going on and, honestly, there was a part of me that was a little happy that I was going to make up for the abortion. Telling my mother was especially difficult. By then, I was in my second year of college and that was the only thing my mother wanted for me, a college education. I knew I would be letting her down again. This time her response was surprising and unexpected, she wanted me to have this baby as a companion for Malik, and as the Caribbeans say, "One child eh no child."

She promised that she would help us with our two babies as long as we stayed in college. We finally felt at ease and began planning for the new baby. I was overjoyed, but somewhere deep inside I was afraid to lose another baby. It seemed like stillborns and dead babies had become a part of my family's DNA. Once again, I didn't tell anyone my fears. I just pretended that everything was okay even though, up to that point, I had never mourned the death of my baby Mikal.

In my fourth month of pregnancy, I began to feel a lot of cramping. Immediately, my fears kicked in. Somehow I knew something was wrong with the baby. After an overnight stay in the hospital, I lost the baby. Shortly after that, I had a tubal ligation. I was twenty-five. I could not bear to be pregnant again. It has taken me fifty years to finally come to terms with those heavy losses. When my adult child died four years ago, I finally decided it was time to forgive myself. I am learning to be grateful for the beautiful child God gave me. My healing process has been slow, and I have finally learned contentment. I've been given many blessings. For that, I am happy and thankful.

i held a dream…

marcie r. rendon

i held a dream
and felt it slip away
from me into
eternity

i cried for a lifetime
echoes of childhood laughter
filled my ears
sunlit tears
of a lifetime
eased my pain
i cried for lost moments

i held a dream
and felt it slip away
from me
into eternity

Pity

Seema Reza

The first time I decided to have a second child, I was following convention. Our older son would be five by the time the new baby was born. It was time. My husband, Karim, was ready, and so I agreed. I was ready to buy a new house, decorate a new room—maybe in pink. I was ready to be pregnant and eat more cake. But I was reluctant to introduce myself as the mother of two.

One child is okay. One child will fold himself into the backseat of a two-door coupe. But *two* children? Two children require more car, less living room, a big backyard. Two children suggest you're in it for good. It is harder to find babysitting, harder to have sex, harder to be you with two children. So I wasn't 100 percent thrilled. Though I knew it was the right thing for my life. A decision Karim and I would not regret.

I was pregnant before we really tried. Before I had even laid all these thoughts out.

I was so *charmed* that he wanted another baby. And flattered, validated as a mother. He wanted another baby with *me*. So I was pregnant. And determined to take pregnancy in stride. I was twenty-four. Healthy. *Pregnancy is not a medical condition.*

We went on hikes and long bike rides. I drank tea (caffeinated), gave piggyback rides, went to concerts and the pumpkin patch. I didn't throw up. I didn't feel too tired. I hardly felt pregnant at all. I went to prenatal appointments, prepared four-year-old Sam for the new baby. *A baby is great*, I told him. *A baby will make you laugh and be your friend. A baby will be the best thing that ever happens to you.*

He was sometimes skeptical but mostly uninterested. I took him to hear the heartbeat for the first time. He held my hand and cringed when my blood was drawn and smiled shyly at the attention from the doctor and nurses.

Sam was at school when the first call came. Karim was at the kitchen table, repairing his glasses with a tiny screwdriver. I was flipping through a catalog.

The nurse said my AFP test numbers came out too high for my eighteen weeks. There was too much alpha-fetoprotein from the baby's liver in my blood. Something about a possible neurological defect.

Or maybe twins, I countered. *I read the pamphlet.*

She scheduled me for an ultrasound with a specialist forty-five minutes away. I researched AFP. Called my sister. Cried. Hyperventilated. Felt melodramatic for overreacting.

I didn't tell my parents—they had a vacation planned at the time of the test, and I hated to worry them for what would surely turn out to be nothing. Karim was starting his month-long end-of-year use-or-lose-leave-time vacation on the Friday of the appointment. It made sense to start the vacation by getting this cleared up. Everyone assured me everything would be okay. I agreed.

The doctor's waiting room was a bare rectangle. Walls lined with chairs upholstered in mauve. I was tempted to leap from chair to chair while I waited.

I was having twins! Or maybe my due date was earlier than the thus-far predicted May. I filled out the form. A genetic *Cosmo* quiz.

Are you Jewish, Hispanic, over thirty-five? Are you and your spouse related? Do you have any history of genetic problems in your family?

We aced the test. All nos. Congratulations, you're having a healthy baby.

The waiting room began to fill. There was a Hispanic couple with a three- or four-year-old daughter. There was an older couple. Waaaay older. I felt sorry for them. I nudged Karim and whispered, *There must be something wrong with their babies. They must have failed the questionnaire.* He nodded in agreement.

We went in and met the doctor. Bald and unfriendly and delicate, he performed the ultrasound silently in the cramped, dark room. He didn't make small talk, didn't point out the baby's body parts.

He kept the screen to himself. We thought he might have social problems.

He left the room (my belly sticky and exposed) and came back with a nurse in pink scrubs. She ran the machine. She left the room.

He came back. *The prognosis is not good.*

I was still smiling to encourage the doctor's social skills.

There's very little amniotic fluid. Terminate. Soon. You're young. Have another baby later. Are you leaking fluid?

I wasn't.

Your outcome won't be good, you have to decide soon. Before it's too late to be legal.

At some point, I dropped my smile, refused to accept it. Demanded a rematch with another ultrasound machine. They worked us into the schedule for Monday. We walked out through the waiting room, tears streaming. And the couples waiting must have felt so sorry for us.

The hours after you get bad news are like airplane turbulence. The weightless rise on the first impulse to convince yourself that you misheard, that the information was faulty. The grasping and scrambling on pure air. And then the downside, the drag: when you're yanked down from your gut and you just want to fold.

I rested my head against the cold window of the car, letting it bounce against the vibrating, buzzing glass. Karim drove fast, expertly, left-handed. His right hand was in my lap, enclosing my left hand, almost touching my rounding belly. Several times words formed in my mouth and when I released them, they bounced between us, as hollow as tennis balls.

My oldest sister, Mona, picked Sam up from school that first day. She had made beef stroganoff (my craving) and bought sparkling cider to celebrate the inevitable all-clear. When she answered the phone, I echoed the doctor: "The prognosis isn't good."

When I hung up, she called our parents back from vacation, called our aunt and uncle in Baltimore, put away the sparkling cider.

It was dark in her living room. Mona had recently moved, and the room was empty aside from an ornate bench and an opulent rug. I sat on the edge of the bench and dialed my aunt the pediatrician.

When she answered, I stood and traced the edge of the rug with clockwise steps. I told her what the doctor had told me and then answered all her questions. *The fluid is low. Five cc's. Eighteen weeks. High AFP. Dr. Khrusey. I'll have another sono on Monday.*

She didn't offer her classic you-are-overreacting irritation, didn't explain how it was really not such a big deal. Just told me to prepare for a difficult journey.

I canceled the follow-up appointment scheduled for Monday. I went to better appointments with prominent doctors arranged by family and friends; doctors with websites and publications.

We saw the beautiful doctor whose waiting room was packed full of pregnant women grumbling with discontent at Food Network on the television. When she performed the ultrasound, she turned a little screen toward me so that I could see as well. With the fluid so low, there was only gray, with the steady pulsing of a small heart in its midst. Then she held my hand and cried; she had lost a baby of her own just months before. Her nurse cried too. Karim kept his eyes wide and dry and asked questions.

We had another appointment after that, with Johns Hopkins doctors— *the best of the best.* The Hopkins doctors were narrow and intellectual and striking. They didn't wear make-up, didn't seem to brush their hair. They wore sweaters and socks of thick, practical wool with their scrubs. They gave us a jewel of hope and put me on light bed rest for a month. Karim gave a homeless man a twenty on the way home, succumbing to superstition after years of cocky agnosticism.

On bed rest, I watched every movie anyone recommended: *The Royal Tenenbaums, The Life Aquatic.* I fell asleep during *Star Wars* three times until Karim gave up. I wet the bed a few times, woke hopeful, and went to the doctor thinking the fluid leak mystery had been solved, that we might finally know where it was going.

While I was inert, a tsunami in South Asia caused hundreds of thousands of deaths and left families devastated. I avoided the news, but Mona was obsessed, so the stories reached my ears. Against my will, it put my woes in perspective, all these people drowning on land.

But inside my body my child was withering, the amniotic sac clinging to its limbs like a plastic bag.

According to the internet, some babies with oligohydramnios in early pregnancy do make it. The baby was active, that was unusual, surely a good sign. I was drinking bottles upon bottles of water. I lay on my left side, removed caffeine from my diet completely. Pomegranate juice was supposed to be good, and I drank a tart cupful every afternoon. I tried anything that was recommended. Except for God. *If* he existed, he was clearly overwhelmed.

After my month was up, I went back to Johns Hopkins. Nothing had changed; my baby was still alive, the fluid was nearly nonexistent. A decision might have to be made after all. During the ultrasound, the doctor found that the baby had a cleft lip and palate. That was the first solid thing wrong with the baby.

Before that it was the fluid, only the fluid, and so many guesses on how the low fluid might affect the baby. The bladder appeared to be filling and emptying and "practice breathing" was evident, and we saw sucking motions and the baby was moving, moving. So it seemed like maybe the fluid was *their* problem, not ours. But the cleft lip and palate made three things wrong and miracles more elusive.

I underwent genetic testing. The testing rooms at Hopkins are cavernous, sterile cubes of gray. They rubbed iodine on my belly and in dim light punctured my abdomen with a long needle and, guided by ultrasound, led it into the placenta and pumped in and out. Hard. I welcomed the pain. Everyone was so nice, so compassionate. But I remembered the things I'd done wrong:

- I hadn't been off the pill for long before I got pregnant (two weeks)
- I had a couple of drinks (five weeks)
- I had to stop to breathe during a tough bike ride (ten weeks)
- I lost control in a fight with Karim (fifteen weeks)
- I went to a concert in a smoky bar (seventeen weeks)
- I was bad about prenatal vitamins (most weeks).

The apricot placental tissue was sucked into the syringe, and my uterus cramped. As the iodine was wiped from my belly and the lights were turned up, the doctor said:

"Take it easy today and back to normal activity tomorrow."

"No bed rest?"

"It didn't seem to help, so no."

Even the best of the best were giving up.

After putting Sam to bed, I brought the CD player from my bedside table into the bathroom and plugged it in next to the sink. I pressed play, turned the volume up, filled the tub halfway with warm water and climbed in. I held my breath and lay down face first, checking that my ears were fully submerged, balancing my weight on my folded elbows to keep the pressure on my belly minimal. The edge of the drain plug pressed into the top of my head. I could hear long notes of music playing through the water and the garbled lyrics. When I pushed myself up on to my arms, the air felt sharp against my face and neck, the music seemed too loud. So I took another breath and lay back down.

Seema. SEEMA.

I turned on to my side to see Karim kneeling at the side of the tub on one knee. I pushed the wet hair from my face and smiled at him.

He put his face in his hands and shook his head, then looked up. I could see white all the way around his brown irises. "Why?"

"Oh. Sorry." I realized what he thought he had walked in on. "I wanted to hear what the baby hears. There's not really this much fluid in there, but there's fluid in the rest of my tissue. I think the baby can hear me singing. I think it hears you too." I pulled the knob and hot water rushed into the tub. When the water level rose to the overflow drain, I raised my foot and pushed it off. "I'm not suicidal. Are you?"

He furrowed his brows. "No. Why would I be?"

"Why would I?"

Karim sat on the lid of the toilet. He gave me a half smile through the rising steam and I missed him. I missed the crinkles at the corners of his eyes when he laughed and I missed hearing what he really thought. I missed his old confidence, his I-can-solve-anything attitude. I missed making plans. We scheduled only as far as dinner tonight, what movie we should watch next. Each unwilling to bring up the topic our lives spun around lest the other be reminded of it in a rare moment of peace.

I unplugged the drain. Karim passed me a towel and steadied me as I stepped over the side of the tub. I stood in front of him and he rested his head against my damp body.

I protected my baby—there wasn't any fluid there to cushion my movement. I walked slowly to avoid jostling. Karim suggested tying pillows around my middle. I laughed. He wasn't joking.

My cousin was getting married, so rather than risk slipping in heels, I ventured out to buy flat dress shoes, a first in my adult life.

In the mall I felt absurd, conspicuous. Like a bear posing as a person. I felt certain that someone would stop me and tell me that I should be home crying. Karim walked beside me, his hand at my elbow. Within fifteen minutes I bought my shoes and left the mall. Another first.

My mouth always tasted unwashed, my hair lay flattened on one side. Deep circles had carved space under my eyes, and my cheeks were swollen from so much unearned sleep. A fog clung to me. I donned silk, lipstick, jewelry. The reflection of the sequins on my clothes made me wince.

The wedding was held in a plush ballroom adorned with chandeliers, yards of tulle and vases of flowers set on pedestals. At any point, the doctors told me, I was likely to become a tomb. I hadn't felt the baby move for a day and a half by the evening of the wedding. I smiled in pictures, ate what was served, congratulated the happy couple—all the while moving through syrup. I avoided adult conversation, and when it found me, my responses were mumbled and peculiar. Karim spent the evening taking photographs of our nieces, nephews, and son. Each time our eyes caught, he tilted his head to the side and I shook my head.

And when finally, on the car ride home we played music loud and I felt distinct kneading against the inside wall of my abdomen, I was not entirely relieved.

We met with a genetic counselor. Her office had two tweed chairs for us to sit in. I noted the placement of the tissues. There were tissues everywhere these days. Everyone expected me to cry.

While she asked us about our families' medical history, Karim sat at the edge of his seat, jiggling his far leg. I couldn't feel it, but it annoyed me. We offered my grandmother's cancer, my father's thyroid, Karim's grandfather's heart attack and early demise. Karim offered an autistic cousin, which seemed to pique her interest.

She showed us a chart of neatly arranged tooth-shaped chromosomes and told us about trisomy 23 and spina bifida. She told us adoption was an option.

At home it was back to the internet. We googled cleft lip. It's not a big deal, it can be corrected. There'll be a little scar above the lip, but so? Cleft palate gets trickier.

I drew my tongue across the roof of my mouth. The joint jutting out would be missing in the baby's mouth. So the baby wouldn't be able to drink milk without a feeding tube. Breastfeeding—my magic trick—would not happen. A chunk of my resolve broke off and floated away. We began to divide.

When you die, Karim would tell me, *I will have you cryogenically frozen.*
When you die, I invariably responded, *I will have you buried.*

In eighth grade, I told the class that I was pro-choice for everyone, but pro-life for me. In tenth grade, a friend of mine was on her second abortion. I hit the prayer mat, reaching out to a God I had been on the outs with for years. In eleventh grade, I took a pregnancy test in the girls' bathroom at school and was relieved to have no decision to make. The following year my grandmother, watching my trash can like a hawk, noticed that I hadn't had my period in two months. I used tampons, which she did not recognize. She offered to take me for a quiet abortion. In college, I discovered science. I pored over the laws of chemistry. For once, it made irrefutable sense. I took astronomy, calculus, physics—with each course, guilt over my doubts lifted until I was finally free of God. And then this.

Everyone told me to pray. There is a special prayer, the *Istikara*, that Muslims use to help make decisions. A specific Quranic verse is recited just before bed, and the correct path is revealed in dreams. In short, have a nightmare and forget it. Have a happy dream and go for it. I wanted to believe that if God wanted my baby, He would take him. That I just had to wait and it would all unfold. If I did lose the baby, we would eventually be reunited and I would see it take its first steps in heaven. But I had seen a fair bit of His handiwork and had no confidence in His thought processes. So the decision would have to be mine.

Karim and I discussed it gently, one of us retreating when the other became agitated. He brought me articles from the internet—babies who had made it. I carefully highlighted the differences between their cases and ours. I was *not* leaking fluid, our baby was younger, my fluid was lower. I had pored over these same articles, had asked the doctors many of these questions. I pointed out that while *the doctors said the baby was going to die horribly and then he did* was not a particularly compelling or interesting story, it was probably the more common one.

The uncomfortable truth was that it was ultimately my decision. While Karim was pleading with me to keep his baby alive, I thought of the baby, gasping for air like a fish out of water. I thought of Sam, burdened for life with a younger sibling who wouldn't be a companion. I thought of Karim, already stretched, trying to juggle the added expense and stress of a very sick child. I thought of myself, consumed forever with childcare and destined for a ponytail and untamed eyebrows.

One day, between movies, my cousin and I happened upon an episode of *Oprah*. Her guest that day was Mattie Stepanek's mother. Mattie was born with muscular dystrophy and passed away just shy of his fourteenth birthday. His mother spoke of his last moments; the intensity of his pain, the deterioration of his body as his muscles distorted and twisted him from within, causing him to lose his hair and fingernails while she begged him to stay alive for her. She spoke of his amazing accomplishments, his poetry and speaking engagements and the lives he touched. She didn't regret a moment of it. All I could think of was Mattie's fingernails falling off.

When I finally made the decision, it seemed so sudden—they told me it was a boy, they told me he was starting to get clubbed feet, they told me there was no hope. Hope was starting to feel like a selfish luxury and so I succumbed. I wanted this over. I wanted to be with Sam, to make pancakes with him and enjoy his four-year-old wisdom instead of shuffling him from family member to family member. I wanted it to end.

I had seen all the pieces before—the low-fluid ultrasound, the sharp, stark line of the needle as it enters the image on the screen. Though they turned the screen away from me, I could see it all. Karim watched the screen. He held my hand, but my guilt and his uncertainty made the motion feel automatic.

I wanted to shut my eyes, but I forced myself to look at Karim's face. His jaw was clenched, his eyes wet. The needle went in, full of adrenaline. I imagined it piercing through the soft, unformed fetal breastbone, entering the heart that I had seen pulsing rapidly at my first prenatal appointment, the heart that I had lain in examining rooms listening to.

Oh. The doctors (residents really—doctors are reserved for life *saving*) whispered among themselves briefly. They prepared a second needle.

It didn't work? I considered reconsidering. Was this a sign? Should I just get up and run, leave my shoes, my purse, my pants? In went the needle again, and this time it worked. Karim let go of my hand. I shut my eyes and they cleaned me off, turned on the light and began to tidy up. I put on my maternity jeans.

They led me down a long hallway with no doors. Behind me were the series of passageways that led to the ultrasounds, the examining rooms, the genetic counselors' offices. Before me, the nurses' station in the blue tiled labor and delivery ward shone.

Pulling a twenty-three-week-old fetus from the womb is not simple. First, a steady drip of Pitocin is fed into the bloodstream to induce contractions. One thousand milligrams of Tylenol are also administered to fight the inevitable fever that arises when the body resists relinquishing the baby. Next, to begin the dilation of an unwilling cervix, toothpicks of seaweed are forced into the tight tissue every hour or so.

I watched CNN during my first seaweed treatment. With studied focus, I read the ticker tape to the doctor and nurse, and we discussed current events like friends.

Karim stood by the bed, folding and unfolding his arms and staring at the television. When the doctor and nurse left the room, he sat next to me on the bed, and I pressed my face into his neck. His warm skin smelled of home.

I felt the baby twitch and brought my hand to my stomach. *Rigor mortis?*

After a few hours, the Pitocin began to kick in. Another drip was attached, this time with morphine. The nurse handed me a button that would release the painkiller into my blood. My fever spiked and I began to vomit.

Mona, who had brought our mother along after arranging child-care for Sam and her own daughters, tied my hair back with a child's turquoise flowered tie pulled from the depths of her purse. My mother looked frightened and hollow. Karim held the kidney-shaped bedpan under my mouth until I laid back.

I opened my eyes needing to vomit again. *Karim, the thing. I need the thing.*

The room was amber and blurred. I heard only shuffling and mur-muring. They couldn't understand me, and I growled louder, frustrated, my mouth felt full of rocks, my jaw twitched. The effort to speak exhausted me, taxed my diaphragm. I had a faint impression of the bedpan being passed from hand to hand until Mona or Karim or my mother was holding it in front of me. I retched and lay back.

Time passed. One nurse left, and another began her shift. The con-tractions started to come. I still had not used the morphine. I was in control of that, swallowing the pain.

A few times I opened my eyes and the room was quiet. Two people had left the room and the third was snoring softly in the chair in the corner. I had nothing left to offer the bedpan, so I sat in the dark with my hands folded under my belly until sleep took me again.

As night began to give over to morning, the contractions came closer together. Karim had just fallen asleep, and I hated waking him. He stood and rubbed his eyes with his fingertips, disoriented. The shake of his head, the crush as he brought himself to the present made me fully conscious for the first time in eighteen hours.

This is usually the exciting part. He came and stood to the right of the bed, pressed the back of his hand against my cheek.

My sister and my mother stood behind him, near my head and I heard my sister whisper to my mother: *You can stay, but do not gasp.*

I pressed the button twice, ready for the morphine.

The gentle doctor who I had seen while I still held hope arrived. She and the nurse assembled in the room with a timid resident. The doctors stood at the foot of the bed, and the nurse stood to my left.

The nurse put her hand on my left leg and told Karim to put his on my right, as he had nearly five years earlier. I looked at the ceiling, pushed once, and hardly felt the baby's body pass out of mine. My mother gasped.

The doctors rushed him to the edge of the room, away from me, and the nurse began to massage my belly for the afterbirth. *Hardly any fluid at all*, she mumbled. And I was relieved.

My mother and sister left us alone. When the doctor brought him back to me, he was bundled in a hospital blanket, shrouded.

She gingerly peeled back the edges of the blanket uncovering his face, like flower petals. I was as eager to see him as I had been to see my live baby. I studied his small, pointed, and beautiful face, his cleft lip. As she transferred him to me, she explained that the right side of his body was open, had never closed.

The bundle was light, like a nightmare in which your baby has disappeared. But he was there, and when I pulled back the blanket to see his body, his inky purple intestines were spilling out of his right side and sticking to the cotton. His entire body was the length of my forearm.

I opened his mouth, gently pushing down on his chin with my forefinger. There was no cleft in his palate. The roof of his mouth was whole and joined. He could have been fed without a tube.

His tiny tongue lay neatly behind his lower gums, pinkish gray and pointed like a cat's. He had faint eyebrows and eyelashes. His eyes would not open. His hands were gummy and curled, his brow furrowed.

My mother returned with a croissant and attempted to force bites into my mouth. I turned my head away and golden flakes fell onto the receiving blanket enveloping the baby. I laughed hoarsely through tears. *Imagine when they do the autopsy. They'll find cafeteria croissant all over him.*

Karim took the baby from my arms, and my mother continued to feed me, both of us shivering with the laughter that comes too close on the heels of tears.

I held him one more time before the nurse came to take him. I kissed the tiny concentric swirl of fine hair on his cold, yielding forehead. And then he was gone.

For Micah, My Neverborn

Mahtem Shiferraw

I don't know how to live in this body
without you. I don't know how to go back

and bear fruits with a lovely shade. The day
you came to me in thought, I found myself

at crossroads, the word of God supple
in my mouth, a light I once knew

combing through the windows. You were
my prophecy, my bearing, my salvation.

It was you I saw, before everything
turned cold. I remember smiling a new

smile, cradling my belly as if it contained
gold, wearing my hair down so my demons

wouldn't see this newfound joy. I
penciled you in my body, created paths

for you to follow, hand in hand with my daughter,
where she would be your shield in the world

outside of me, she made of bone and steel
and so much joy. I don't know how to think of her

without thinking of you. It seems cruel to feel
anything but sorrow in your absence. I remember

drinking so much water, thinking this body to be
a tree, thinking I could summon it into nurturing you,

slowly, slowly. I remember naming you, knowing
you before it was so, eating enjera dusted with berbere,

shiro and firfir, thinking this seed would need to survive
the spices of my ancestors in order to grow.

How foolish of me to think you would be made whole,
how foolish of me to keep hoping, even after the absence

of a heartbeat. I wanted to build you, construct you
bit by bit, make a home for you where there was none.

But this body keeps housing wars that show up
unannounced. I have trained myself to wear
armors made of metal, to embalm myself with honey

and eucalyptus leaves. I have known ancient wars,
wrestled them free from myself, tore up this body

inside out, so it can reshape itself into something new.
But you, I had seen, and this seeing blinded me,

fractured me into my bones. I don't know how
to do this, how to continue carrying with me

a body riddled with new wars. I don't know how
to bear the wars of other women—mothers, grandmothers,

aunts, sisters—our language is that of dying.
I had so much to tell you, so much to give you,

this is when I finally learned to be free
with myself, to be generous, when I finally learned

to be kind to this body. And then, you,
the weight of you, the sudden knowing, carrying death

inside of me for so long. The decisions afterwards,
the incisions, foreign things going through

where your head would've emerged. The sound
of vacuums sucking me dry. My silence during

all of it, counting backwards, to where I started,
to the thirst, my bones brittle with sorrow.

I have done so much leaving before—leaving
my lands, leaving my body, leaving my family—

but this, I don't know how to leave this,
how to leave you, even when you are far gone.

Who will know your name, who will remember
your smile, your brilliance, who will keep

your memory alive, if not this body? Grief
has finally found a home. At night, when

the world is quiet, and all has gone to sleep,
this body unfurls and leads me to new waters;

here, I rest, beneath rivers that cross small cities
thinking of you, naming you out of invisibility.

Patient

Shaina Phenix

After Bettina Judd

Black women's sexuality is often described in metaphors of speechlessness, space or vision; as a "void" or empty space that is simultaneously ever-visible (exposed) and invisible, where Black women's bodies are always already colonized. In addition, this always already colonized Black female body has so much sexual potential it has none at all.

—Evelynn M. Hammonds, "Toward a Genealogy of Black Female Sexuality: The Problematic of Silence"

> I am sacrament
> unforgivable sin and reprieve   practiced
> in the dark ghetto of my body.
>
> — Bettina Judd, "The Opening"

Dear Akil,

I begin this letter with my spine pressed against the cool skin of a leather table. I am writing to you because I know you won't get it. Because I know even though we seemed to have made amends, I am a part of the reason that you don't trust women, trust men, or yourself.

The gynecologist is a Black woman. She is likely midfifties with a thick and gray-speckled scalp of hair, sporting black flips-flops, a thin coat of ash on the heels of her feet, and she names medicines for her assistant like an auctioneer at work. The nurse who assists is a white woman—midtwenties, a round rosy face, a frantic pen racing against a prescription pad. I am naked underneath this paper dress. Doc says, *Scoot down a little more.* I rattle the film stuck to my butt on top of the table—I scoot down toward her light, her blue-gloved Black hands, the tools shimmering in their plastic packages.

A little more.

Relax.

Almost there.

Okay.

You'll feel a little pressure—first with just my fingers—now where's that darn cervix?

There she goes.

More pressure, this time with cold metal and goopy lube. A speculum opens its arm inside of me. I dig my fists into the table's mouth.

* * *

"The idea for the *speculum* **came** to J. Marion Sims while **treating** a *white* **patient** who had been thrown from *a horse*. After he **helped** her 'reposition her *uterus*,' he **had** an idea. He **fetched** a *slave*, had her **lay on her back with her legs up**, and **inserted** the *bent handle* of a silver *gravy spoon* **into her vagina**. The very first modern *speculum* was **made** out of a bent gravy *spoon*."

* * *

I wince. Doc pats my foot. Doc says, *I wish there was a better way to do this.* Doc says, *Sorry honey.* I don't need you to tell me that I am nothing like Anarcha. I don't need to hear how lucky I am—that Black women with their pussies exposed on examination tables seldom get foot pats and apologies. I swear I am trying to be grateful. I am writing with a needle poked into my uterus. I don't mean to cry. I know how lucky I am. Soon it'll be numb; soon Doc will extract a tiny cone-shaped piece of flesh from the *hystera*—Greek for uterus; root word of hysteria—historically used to categorize a loss of a socially acceptable emotional consciousness or exaggerated or uncontrollable emotion or excitement in people with wombs—perhaps suggesting that because I can build a life inside myself, the way that the state can't trust me with my own body is completely warranted. Doc takes the tiny piece of hystera and places it into a small test tube. In a lab, they will look for cancer; while I await the results, I should tell you that I want children more than I want to live.

* * *

One time I was pregnant. I am no prisoner to my past or my grief so I won't keep this letter here long. But one time I was pregnant. One time, I was on a leather table like I am on a leather table today and a doc, not Black, not foot patting, rushed through all of the terminations scheduled for that day. Doc said, *Count down from ten*—by five I had stopped counting—started screeching *No, no, no, I changed my mind.* I guess one thing those medical shows got right is that by five, the anesthesia is already doing its work, by five you are already gone. By zero, I woke up empty. No doc. No baby.

A new nurse escorted me to a room where I swear one of the girls had a face I imagined our daughter might have. She was beside me, drinking apple juice, nibbling saltines. I couldn't find the arms to comfort her.

If asked, my mother's greatest hope for her children is to do better than she did. If asked, our bloodline's generational curse is young pregnancies and births and mothers, followed by indefinite obligations to live a life beneath our potential because of it. I am twenty-five years old and my right hip is bare of a small butt resting on it. I wonder if I've at least broken the curse.

* * *

I wonder how many bits of Anarcha, Betsey, and Lucy float around inside us. Perhaps we should have an idea—create a test—after having buried countless Black mothers who are twelve times more likely to die than white mothers in childbirth or postnatal care—fetch a billionaire white man lawmaker, age fifty, have him come in for his colonoscopy, lay him on his back with his legs up, swab as far up as we can get in his insides, see what of these women the speculum has carried and if their unanesthetized yelps crept up into amniotic sac before his mother emptied of him. If any of them are there squalling in his cells, diagnose him with hysteria. Rework the word uterus to be derived from Dutch word *üteren* meaning to speak, to make known—connect this new meaning to their ability to speak themselves into living. Rework cishet men to be derived from the Greek word hystera—connect this new categorization to their inability to make conscious and emotionally sound decisions about anatomical parts they do not possess.

* * *

I am writing from the follow-up appointment. Since the biopsy, I've developed an unsightly and bodily fear-response to silver things—car lettering, eating utensils, faucet knobs, the cuff my mother gave me after the eighth time I left my ex-girlfriend inscribed: Happiness can be found in the darkest of times, if one remembers to turn on the light.

At fifteen, I saw my rapist at church a week after—he said hello, I said it back, proceeded to sit three pews behind him, prayed, *God let him lose his phone in the train station or a house fire. There are photos that might speak on my behalf, saying I got what I asked for and only you know my heart.* Meanwhile, I am a grown woman and afraid that the fork carrying food to my face will somehow end up lodged inside of me, shoveling away tiny cone-shaped chunks of reproductive organs. I am still writing from the follow-up appointment where the fork is on the exam room counter, staring at me through the plastic covering. Doc reports, *STD panel, blood work, and biopsy confirm the following: negative for STDs and STIs; no cancer; still polycystic ovaries. Do you want to get started on birth control?* At this point, Doc is clear that I will say no, she has asked this a million times. Because one time I told her I don't really sleep with people who can get me pregnant through sex anymore. A statement that is mostly true—hence, the *really*. Because I've been to her a time or two with a missed period and peeing in a plastic cup. Because every time we talk about my sexual health, I ask how likely it is that I'll be able to get pregnant a second time. I am not a liar; I am just doing with this sliver of freewill that I have, what my foremothers could not. Sue me.

* * *

I am writing from inside my body which means I am writing as blood. Anarcha, Betsey, Lucy, and other unnamed selves are here blessing my will-be healthy babies into an already existence. The women of my cloth, they dance and worship and prepare a table in my fallopian tubes. My once-and-almost baby, a gatekeeper at the bridge between my legs. Foot-patting, sorry-saying Doc sings onto a history of this bright and curved thing looking into me—*Come by here, my lord, come by here, oh lord, come by here.*

Constant Kiss of Contractions

Mahogany L. Browne

The baby is moving. Pushing her legs into my ribs. It is my twenty-first birthday and I'm too busy being pregnant to taste my first legal toast of champagne. I use the open palm of my right hand to massage the taut brown skin of my exposed belly. Clockwise. Counterclockwise. Clockwise. Counterclockwise. This act is a white flag. The little girl growing inside my womb graciously concedes.

Before I ever have sex, I decide I dislike the word *womb*. Soon after my eighteenth birthday, after the first pregnancy came and went, I recognize and reconsider the word: womb. I decide it is a powerful term of life/span/sphere. I will never again challenge the word's position in the world. Because the womb can be forgiving, even when the guilt will not let me sleep. The womb can be forgiving, restorative in its nature. The womb can be forgiving, it harvests so much. Children. Fibroids. Empathy.

I am eighteen and living in my grandmother's spare bedroom. My mother is battling substance abuse somewhere in the shadows. Recovering and failing. My father is housed in prison for the third time. My high school boyfriend, still deceptively sweet, abides by my wishes. He wants whatever I want. I want my dreams. I touch my belly. I speak it loud enough for only the two of us to hear, "I don't think I can be anyone's mother now." We are by a man-made lake. The sadness fills the car, and I have to open the window to let in a breeze. I sit with the severity of the situation. My dreams to graduate high school, to be a writer, to survive everything that tried to end me are reason enough to call the clinic and make an appointment for termination the next morning. After the procedure, I wipe dried tears from my face. When

I am awake and moving so slow, I am so sick, I cling to the cool porcelain of the toilet. When I am not sleeping, shrimp-like, in the full-sized bed, I am too wracked with not-guilt and resolved sadness to cry. I don't tell my best friend. I don't tell my sister. I don't tell my mother. My boyfriend leaves me alone for days. I think, This is what I deserve.

It is my grandmother who learns the truth. Months later, after my despondency urges her to look through a set of envelopes stored in my nightstand drawers. She asks me. And it's the first time since its happened that I acknowledge the forever change in my blood. My grandmother's face is brown and full of worry, but she says nothing. Nods her head slowly, resolves whatever questions she has and returns her attention to the stove. She slow stirs the pot of porridge bubbling on the stove top. Turns off the fire and wipes her hands.

It is my twenty-first birthday and the baby is moving. This is the first time I realize I am alone. This childbirth experience is nothing like the films. There are no Lamaze classes. There is no one to rub my swollen feet. I attend community college until the very last class. Earlier that morning, my water broke. While sitting on the toilet my mucus plug falls into the water with other fluid. Clean and contained. The contractions are so far apart that, an hour later, I kind of forget I am in labor. I call my nurse, she says, "If you come too soon, we'll have to send you home. If it doesn't hurt, wait it out." I hang up the phone and decide, "This makes sense. I might as well take the finals test for my Economics 101 credit."

Seated in the back of the class at a makeshift desk constructed out of a folding table and aluminum chair, I answer questions between contractions, now separated by twenty-two minutes or so. An hour later, I finish my test, and acknowledge the pains lightning striking across my abdomen have lessened from twenty-two minutes to eighteen minutes. I call the father who now lives across the country. I call my mother and grandmother. I call my sister and cousin. Everyone is a lightning bolt of love. Acknowledging my pain and asking if I want company. I do not. I want to be alone for one last time in this life. Hours later, my sister and cousin suggest we walk the mall to speed things up. Hours later, the baby is unimpressed with the red Slurpee, the smell of Cinnabon, and the Tupac movie about addicts that we watch in the air-conditioned movie theater. I retreat home after thirteen hours of labor and resign to sitting in the shower alone, again.

The movies about pregnancy piss me off. The mother and father fall into each other and decide a baby is the most beautiful way to share their love with the world. They plan their future. They paint the nursery walls. The mother is coddled. The mother nests. The father is smitten. The father is present. The birthing story always has the scene of animal grunts and hospital gowns. Of women who yell and scream and say mean things that they know will be forgiven once the baby is born. The birthing story always has the scene of a father and mother, holding hands and counting together: *one, two, three, four, push!* The birthing story on the screen always featured the father slightly flustered and the mother sweaty with both heels in stirrups. There is so much commotion, but when the baby is born, the screen goes into focus. The world stops moving so fast. The father cuts the umbilical cord, holds the bloody, writhing frame so close to his own. The birthing story in my head, always included a baby with both parents. The movie fades to black.

But my birthing story is different. Eighteen hours later, I sit home alone. I barely climb out of the shower in time to sit on a cream-colored loveseat, just in time to push through the quickly returning contractions. The loveseat was purchased by the father of my child, back when we were living together. When we were still sweethearts graduating high school together. Now, three years after graduation, we are together, barely. And after the contractions grow closer and stronger, resembling a grip on my lungs and lower intestines, I push the spring out of the frame of the love seat. The pain is a sea of faces that have forgotten me. My father. My first best friend. Myself. The pain is so definite, I wonder if it is more honorable to suffer alone. But the cooling wind that sweeps across my face, a gesture of grace from the air conditioner's insistence, remind me that I've got something bigger to concern myself with. I rock up, sloppily, look at the damage, laugh at the metaphor and call my sister to transport me to the hospital.

It's October in California. I am the age I am, but now, I have to sign away my right to sue if the epidural shot paralyzes me. I am nineteen hours into labor, and my sister, who is also pregnant and nearly ready to pop with her second child, sits comfortably across the room on top of a rollaway bed. Upon our arrival, the staff thought she was in labor, not me. She likes this kind of attention and sprawls across the mattress like a queen. When it is time to check my vitals, the nurses come into the mute-colored birthing room, go to my sister's rollaway castle and are surprised to find she's not in labor. This happens twice before I start crying from the constant kiss of contractions.

Initially, Lamaze class made me believe I was prepared for a natural birth. But the movie on the hospital screen reminds me that I was alone during those classes. Who will count and breathe and cheer me on? My sister and mother have gathered me here. But nothing is like the movies I watched. The father of my child is attending a college program in Florida, over 2,500 miles away, and cannot afford to finish his studies and attend the birth of his firstborn. I am the age I am when I realize I will soon have a daughter who will have to learn that disappointment can feel as forever as death. I do not want her to have abandonment issues, like me. I do not want her to be like me.

When the anesthesiologist administers the catheter into my spine, when I think the eight-centimeter epidural needle will end me, I am reminded sternly "do not move" as he pinches my skin and keeps his eyes on a grainy rerun of Star Trek playing nearly mute on the television screen. One tear betrays me. Slides down my stone-jutted cheekbone like the traitor it is, and I pray to stay still long enough to hear her first cry.

Fifteen minutes of active labor. Three full pushes. And I don't feel the vaginal tear as my daughter, all pink and clean, slits the skin of the room with the sound of her arrival. I forget who is not in the room. I have my mother holding my hand, a first for us in years. She is clean today. She bears witness to her third grandchild's introduction to the world. I don't cry like the movies. I don't think of who is missing from this frame of the film. My sister waddles in shortly after my daughter is born and says, "Hi Amari." I have already determined my daughter's name. It means "God is highest" in Swahili. It means "lovely immortal girl" in Hebrew. It suits her perfectly. We all note how quiet Amari is. I notice I can feel my toes and I say, "Amen." I note that I cannot feel my stomach, not even when I push my finger two inches above my belly button. I whisper to myself "Amen." But I can feel the sadness pull a chair close to the foot of my bed and take a seat. I nod and bargain "Later, later."

I focus on my daughter. Her tiny pink hands, her fingers tightly around my own. I smile. Today, we have cheated death. My daughter's big brown eyes conquer me.

Life Signs

Andrée Greene

1.

When you are very young, unmarried, and pregnant, everyone wants to talk to you about Mary. And by everyone, I mean my grandmother. Mothie was the everyone, my everyone, the matriarch of our family, and I had spent more than half my childhood in her house, reared by her or near her. If it was good enough for the mother of a god, no need for me to be ashamed, was her logic. But Mary did get married in the end—she "all's well that ends well"ed me to a point. I didn't have the strength to remind her—that was not the ending of *that* story, that it wasn't a rom-com for the biblical ages.

Less than a month before my due date, there'd been a gentle rap on the door to my very first apartment of my own, the second floor of a duplex. There, without warning, Mothie stood; my belly, a globe spanning the threshold, jolted us both as if we'd been kicked by the tiny foot within. The magnetic field created kept us bobbing at each other without touching. I didn't catch her look down at my belly, but her breath drew in softly and her eyes clouded with the hot-house humidity of the past. She stepped around me with her well-worn shopping bags from New York City visits rattling and set them down in the center of the spare living room. She was in her tan spring overcoat despite a hundred-degree heat wave; an air conditioning chill was her kryptonite. I was a little thankful that not much furniture was in the place so that my usual habit of clutter and the piles of clothes didn't look as bad. I sat on the folded-S futon, watching her clean with one eye on the small TV atop some boxes, and was startled and grateful by the relief and comfort her familiar movements radiated. I could never fall into the hyper-neatness that was practically genetic with the women in my family. "Dust knew my name" was a refrain I heard often growing up.

Slowly it sank in that my mother had driven her the forty-five minutes from Elmira up to Ithaca, dropped her off, and fled without coming in, which, after a quick minute's thought, I accepted as fair. After all, I'd had my younger sister tell my mother I was pregnant after putting it off for four or so months rather than face her myself.

I felt foolish but not ashamed and, at the time, I was proud that I could discern that difference as a victory, a tiny flag on a shimmering new moonscape. I'd been using a diaphragm—I didn't like taking pills, being reactive to medicine and prone to side effects. Maybe I should have tried it out. I didn't understand that stupidity is often shame's stylist for the book smart, those who believe they should always know better, that they should be the exception and not human. How else will you survive? My mother was the polar opposite, blunt and flat.

... And you waited to *not* get an abortion beeeecause ... wha—?
I was not prepared for that choice of life or not life. My grandmother, soft spoken and whose true anger was rare, was a master of wielding a teacher's approval where her disappointment felt like a quiet little death, and you worked hard to rise again and again in her sights with its enormous pride and satisfaction, two tent poles I had not quite pitched into terra firma for myself. Not yet.

I had shed much religiosity by this time, except for my habit of seeking signs. At night, from a young age, I would lie in bed and not ask for things or luck but for peace of mind. And I asked for signs. It was the only living prayer that sustained me because I deciphered answers and there was always an answer. Suddenly there were none. I tried to convince myself that this choice was not about disappointing a holy father but rather it was a holy mother—Mothie that kept me guessing and so much more, an explanation that could fill my own new testament.

2.

The older white ladies in tight polyester culottes and straggly ponytails at the bus stop in front of the senior citizen towers, who were going to the mall, looked at me like I knocked them down and snatched the money hidden in their slouchy bosoms when they saw me coming with my manila envelope of paperwork. It was the closest stop for the bus up the hill to social services. "Wel-fare?" In Mothie's island mouth, sounded like a festival in the town of Well.

"You've worked jobs, your taxes paid, I pay taxes," when I told her where I was going when she called.

They murmured to each other loud enough for me to hear, "She's a baby having one," or the bold ones said it right out like they're the first ones to think that shit up.

I was twenty years old, but I had the plump, thumbprint-dimpled face of a fifteen-year-old on a good day, thirteen more usually—a family trait that I was assured again and again that I'd be thankful for when I was much older. The bus only came once an hour, and if you missed it you had no choice but to wait—not only was it too far to walk, but also more than half of it was up, the steep, narrow, and winding North West hill, or you could take an expensive cab to save not a lot more time—all part of reminding you of the bed you so obviously made.

The fifteen-minute interview took more like forty, because I kept interrupting her in disbelief. I wasn't married, she asked me about the date, time of day, the place, the very room I believed conception occurred, where it happened. The questions getting progressively more intimate as they went along.

"I don't understand. The father isn't contesting paternity."

"It's a required question in case he does after the birth."

"But what does that matter . . . I mean that's no one's business. He was only my second real boyfriend," I said, as if inexperience would get me an exemption.

"Can I see the questionnaire?" I snapped.

"Look. If you want this money, it's government business now."

"Having a baby is not a crime." I impersonated my mother's best salty voice in my head, but I'm pretty sure I sounded like a string of hiccups. Or worse, a whimper.

Without looking up from her form-filling, "Ma'am, please." I blinked. I am a ma'am now? I thought.

Ahhh, now I understand. Oh Mary, don't you dare weep.

3.

Mami was just finishing her graduate studies after years of research, towing us around the state. I attended two elementary schools, two middle schools, and three high schools. You understand a lot about people and how they don't want to trouble themselves over difference, how deeply they want you to be just like them. You can see how ranks fall in, and faces fall down as they misread you, or read you just right for their uses.

Now, guilt ruled my hours; doubt could numb my days. I was not unaware of sacrifice, history. While I had babysat regularly for extra money at one point as a teen, my younger sister was the one who loved dolls, babies, and small children, and they her. I wondered if mine would like me.

I was not the first person in my family to go to college, not even the first woman. But I was expected to do it right, the American way, with dorms and parties, straight through, with no postponements, early marriages, no babies. No night school, no war, no struggles beyond the money to pay for it (not a small matter). They trusted that my becoming would be completed in that place. My grandmother, an elementary school teacher, taught me to read early, so early they wanted me to start school at second grade. But my mother, herself freshly returned to college postdivorce, offered her Psych 101 theory that her already too shy, self-contained daughter might not adjust well. So I only skipped kindergarten to first grade.

My path was clear, as if Mothie had tacked down her plastic rug runner herself. I had known and heard of all kinds of mothers. Many are mine. I am the eldest Caribbean daughter. I worked retail and waited tables. I could cook, iron, garden, refinish wood, knit, crochet, sew, iron, and even darn. I was at a loss but not for capability. Nevertheless, and somehow, I was not terribly afraid. If nothing else, reading is its own religion, instills a specific kind of anticipatory patience, seeking quiet intimations and meanings in the silence and the signals within the sounds. Change and revelation are only a page turn away.

4.

Barely two semesters and I was through. Academic probation technically, but I wouldn't be returning to that Massachusetts college. I passed through that campus like a hologram. That's how college life is anyway. Who are you when there are no witnesses, no one to vouch for you? My dissolution had already begun before I arrived on campus. The goody-goody church girl rent in half, cicada dormant, for years. When I lived with Mami, I'd sneak off during school for joints and beer. No curfew 'cause you are never allowed to go anywhere. Repent, begin again at Mothie's. Rinse repeat.

In the throes of teenage depression, I cut classes and school regularly to play huge spades tournaments in the cafeteria or, after cards were banned due to a distracted student body, stay home to read and watch soap operas. Alternatively, I read and slept in the NYC public libraries, dodging the library's homeless police (sleeping not allowed!) while my mother commuted to Long Island for her graduate work. I could catch up fast, retain information easily with my strong memory. It was a new move to the state's biggest city, a huge specialized high school, taken along because Mami feared I was too much under my grandmother's religious thrall. I had friends, Brooklyn West Indians who lived too far, but not a bestie—my central New York–accent, schoolteacher-imprinted speech was both novelty and source of mostly friendly ridicule of the country mouse. I was used to my own company, and did not fully recognize loneliness.

At college, the sheltered upbringing and instability finally caught up to me, the sheer variety of people, the unstructured time, and events overwhelmed my coddled circuits. I found a best friend, one always more extroverted than me, a Jamaican artist from Dorchester. Celine had taken a year or two off and returned to school, and lived in a huge single. We drank and partied, went to concerts, citified me. I still read compulsively from the syllabi I was interested in and argued ideas, but barely did anything else that was actually academic. Students were protesting apartheid in cardboard shanties and my white sociology professor taught *Violence in America* by day, and sang Paul Robeson as a kind of sonic-cosplay blackface in the coffeehouse by night.

Mami, of course, was not impressed with my performance. She could sniff failure across state lines. She'd have to, as I never called home. Over winter break, when my academic standing was officially mailed, Mami tried to reason. She'd put money down on a subsided low-income house, not far from the public housing where we once lived. One step forward, two steps back.

"Ask for help if you need it. Have you contacted minority affairs?" I was sitting in the living room; she was standing beside my chair, willing me to look at her

"Minority affairs," I snorted. Ha! That's funny. But she was seeing a completely different joke.

I remembered Dad's shadow over me as Mothie made me play the piano for him the one or two times he visited. I'd considered myself lucky to have missed living under it. I could never make myself feel connected to him. An ex-athlete from a family of five very athletically gifted boys. All he could ever say to me was how much I looked like my mother, always calling me sweetheart or baby, asking whether I had a boyfriend.

. . . and when I learned he wasn't my real father, not the same person as my siblings' father, what my mother's old love letters informed me of one truant school day afternoon as I sat in the middle of reading her past. (You wouldn't believe me if I told you how I found them. Piles and piles of their clandestine letters, during my junior year of high school.) You can't miss what you never had, I told myself. What I will say is that if you are raised in silence, sometimes it will stand up, take your hand, and tell you who you really are.

There was a confrontation, furtive and quickly stifled. Not to be spoken of again for a decade.

At that year's Christmas dinner, the rest of the family hadn't yet been informed of my home permanence. Mami hadn't told them. The "Hallelujah Chorus" magnified the season—a holdover from our island Anglican roots, now cum holy-roller Pentecostal—Handel played on, Mami and her siblings sisters sang their parts, segueing to gospel. Conversation brought the usual cherished remembrance chatter. The aunts and Mothie told me to keep working hard and that nothing worth having was easy.

Besides, everyone was in a fit over Bryan, a younger cousin who'd gone joyriding in a stolen car and gotten busted. It turned out alright, his buddies had his back, verified that he hadn't been in on the actual lack of permission to use his friend's uncle's or brother's or cousin's car, and he was let go without being charged. The situation was retread in clandestine discussions, murmurs about "permanent record," *the place* (aka jail), and "bad company," in the kitchen or bedrooms over plates jammed with food—"pass the yams" was a sticky translation. We were all accustomed to eating our words as if they were our hearts.

5.

I'm telling this wrong. All inside out, backward. But I guess that's the kind of story it is. King Solomon had been right, way, way too early in human history. Same old same old. Yet full of surprises, all the same. Here we are.

I had my beautiful baby. My obstetrician was out of town. Thirty-eight hours of labor—hours of combat boots stomping my lower spine and pelvis, only to have my cervix barely dilate over a centimeter. The doctor had warned on my last visit that my pelvis was a bit narrow, if the baby was close to or over eight pounds, I might have problems.

My mother had to return to work, and she once again delivered my Mothie.

Mothie hovered. Upon her arrival the nurse updated her, "Back labor….Thee. Worst. Poor girl. She is so tired. Did you have labor issues?"

Mothie who was squinting hard with intense concern, surveying me head to toe and back again as if she really could beam restorative rays from her eyes. She looked up, straightened her own petite back to softly flex, "No no, they just came right out really." She almost whispered.

I glared, "Really?! Now?"

"How many?"

Then Mothie smirked, you'd miss it if you did not know her, looked the nurse in the eye. "Six."

I never heard my grandmother's accent growing up at home or took note of her deep darkness until we were around institutional whiteness. She was diamond bright under the hospital fluorescence, despite staying at my side out of the way. The staff moved around her.

The twenty-four-year-old father-to-be was banished from my room for whining to his mother, who happened to be near the hospital that day, about why it was taking so long and why was I in so much more pain than the amount that he obviously had planned on coping with.

And then the heartbeat started to go way down with each contraction. It sounded as if the sonogram heartbeat itself was alive, blubbering breaths through scuba gear in syrup. And each time, everyone in the room held their inhale as they listened each cycle. Mothie's eyebrows were in her hairline in alarm—only my huffing through the strain and the nurse's "Breathe" filled the room.

An emergency caesarean was ordered.

I woke long enough to see him, give him his first feeding. Even in the haze, his bindle warmth, a revelation unimagined. Isn't a baby nothing if not the weight of the world? And I knew I was the luckiest mother ever. Seven fifteen, one ounce off from eight pounds. My mother said later that when she returned, his head was coned, the way it does when it's in the birth canal, that I had probably dilated. Who can say?

Before the next feeding. The second time I was to see my son, the nurses brought me the wrong baby.

Looking skeptical, "Are you sure he's yours?" as if I'd been too drugged earlier to be able to recognize my child. His father a light brown–skinned man whose mother was white, my baby was pale at birth except for his brown ears, the augur of the change to come. They brought a baby they thought matched me without reading the card.

When they returned, wheeling him in the clear baby bin, his jittery arms cycling to escape the loose blanket, his eyes wide, alert as dots on dominoes but direct like we were on a raft on a calm sea. Who comes first, mother or child? Many people would point at me and say giving birth worked out—an argument for the pro-life movement—and many have. Close readings are difficult if you are accustomed to believing all the worlds on this planet were made for your spiritual perspective. This sign is the one I chose.

In a postpartum single room, I felt all of the nurses studying the comings and goings of cousins, aunts, mothers, and Mothie. And then one recovery morning, my main nurse asked if I was going to get out of bed any time soon. I hadn't noticed my lack of movement, the heaviness to my natural, closed-mouthed way, because my family had been gauging and caring for my well-being, and so I instantly burst into sobs.

"Hmm yeah. I thought so," she said with a coldness and stare I still haven't shaken from memory.

One thing's for sure, my son stayed in my room until we left that hospital room together.

I told her, "Leave him with me."

Ode to Kale

Hope Wabuke

when my son is young I make him
kale popsicles: one pound of kale

shredded ginger lemon squeezed apples & water blended
he eats them two in hand as fast as they come

but I cannot take credit recipe copied from his favorite juice
bar in long beach california where we

would sit before catching the bus
back to the domestic violence shelter we lived

that first year of his life our windowless tiny apartment after that—god
how my mother was so proud of my fighting back

to the surface in tiny little motions prouder than
she has ever been of me in my whole life

as if she could applaud in me something she could never
name in her own being

      but we never saw any other brothers & sisters at the juice bar

even though we saw them next to us on the bus & through its windows
to other places like kfc & outside   after dark

when gunshots & cruising took over the farmer's market greened streets
shaking the veterans & other shattered survivors awake

& I would turn my blender loud with kale &
add to everything blend again
                                        my mother hates
kale she says because after that gun-splattered night

they escaped from the dictator & his genocides
kale grew everywhere like a weed she says & they ate it for days

breakfast lunch dinner   she says organic & locally sourced from
the camp yard or the side of the road & so

when she got here my mother worked in school kitchens & ate
what the kids were given & thought them delicacies—mega muffins
& giant cookies

fruit jelly popovers juices & syrups &
hamburgers & fries & five different kinds of pizzas & sugar &

her body used to vegetables beans & lean meats could not
take it but kept trying until now the diabetes

spread the heart attack scarring
spread she is all the american sicknesses fed; fermented

—*& what does this say about a country that does that to its kids by the way*—

& then medicated my father also married to stress
in the myth of advancement through horation work ethic

until there is nothing left when there is nothing
left *kale is good for you* I tell my mother *it will help you*

feel better but she will not eat it *here, kale is a delicacy* I tell her
a hipster organic treat at whole foods higher priced

per pound than the special coffee or cuts of meat she enjoys but
no she says then & again even when I feel

my own heart stutter after my son's birth when I have
become so busy that I do not take care of myself

I eat fast on the run do not exercise &
I lose my balance dizzy spinning light-headed only understanding one
thing:

this is how you are going to die your heart
like your mother is going to die

& I start to eat kale & other things beloved back
home as if I could eat enough for the both of us *mom* I tell her

no she tells me *it is a weed the starving eat*
in kenya & I will not

                                    my mother is already dead or we know how
my mother will die each tiny growth of scar tissue encroaching

with each pump of the tiny slick red bulb in the six years since the
first surgery now half
way across & still we do not talk about

            how we do not do mat   how we are silent

this is how you deny your mother is dying &
                    to everything: what is the point—

kale will not stop it now even when I make my mother's peanut stew
& matoke & I sneak in the rich handfuls of leafed green

life my sister always asking *mom, please*
her voice enough like mine to make me think

for a minute it is me speaking instead even though I do not know
what either of us would plead for anymore so

I tell my sister it is not hard to make if I can make it she can
but she brushes me off the point I suppose not in the eating of the
matoke & peanut stew

but in the wanting of mama whole again making her stew in the
kitchen &
us unaware & small our whole world held in mother's body

on just another unremarkable day when we would all wake up
& all go to sleep & then all wake up again

5

Questions for Mamas of Sons

Emily Raboteau asks Angie Cruz

What did you crave when you carried him?

What did you ask him when he was inside you?

What were the mothering myths you were told, in the voices of the women who told them?

What were the truths you weren't told, in your voice, to the women who are pregnant now?

How were you served by the medical system?

Who was the woman who helped you when birthing him was hardest and what did she say?

What did it feel like to almost die when bringing forth life?

What song did you sing to him when he was small?

How did your body change after you had carried him inside of you?

How did your partner fail you?

How did the comadres reveal themselves?

What do you wish you knew then about when he was new that you know now?

Tell about the birth trauma.

Tell about the joy.

Where was your mind when he was an infant?

Who was the woman who helped you when breastfeeding him was hardest and what did she say?

Why did he choose you to be his mother?

What do you miss from before he was here?

What did you want for him that you did not have?

What do you want for him that you do not have?

What has he given you that you did not know you needed?

What do you fear for him?

In what cloak do you protect him from harm?

When My Son Came to Me

Angie Cruz

And I asked him...
  Baby, baby, be easy, so easy, because your father is hard.

And I craved things...
To fuck, but not his daddy, and so I ate peanut butter-banana sandwiches for breakfast, lunch, and dinner and vanilla ice cream inside of
espresso cups. Because the protein made the baby strong, because the
ice cream, with all its fat, was good for the brain. His brain. My brain.
  Craved the days to go slow so time was mine. And in Texas the days
were slow and the air thick. The cicadas, the frogs, the javelinas, the
deer, the possums, the snakes, the scorpions all had their clocks tram-
pling, buzzing, screeching, in and out of the land I occupied. Swayed
on the hammock on my porch listening to them mate, fight, and call
each other as I savored the sweet vanilla Blue Bell ice cream.
  Baby, baby, be easy on me, please.

And the mothering myths ...
And *they* said...the love affair is instant. It wasn't. Your body will know
what to do. It didn't. Your maternal instincts will kick in. Ha! don't
worry about money. I did. babies bring fortune. So much debt.

And the truths I wasn't told ...
Babies want to live. They will meet you halfway, always. They don't
need all the bullshit you buy them. Babies listen if you listen. Breastfeeding hurts like a motherfucker. And no, I didn't do it wrong. I did
everything right and still...

And the women helped and said things...

Baby came late and large. I had a birthing plan and was set to go natural. Took Bradley Method classes and watched videos of women squatting in the forests and pushing out babies like they were taking a shit.
Women having orgasms as the baby pushed through the birth canal.
That will be me, I said. I am that kind of woman who would trust her
body to do the work it had to do. And then the contractions came and
they didn't repeat but went continuous, one long piano note of steady
ache. No water break. No dilation. And I could feel the baby's head
wedged in the canal in a way that I could barely walk or stand. But I
have a birthing plan, I said to anyone who would listen. I printed multiple copies for everyone who would read it.

And then this nurse in her eighties, it was the last day on the job,
said, Kid I need you to do some squats.

I can't!

Do it with me.

And so I did. And my body, a closed fist, was open, palms up.

You're gonna have an emergency C-section. You can make it hard
for yourself and try to follow your plan or tell your doctor you want a
C-section.

Can I trust you, white lady?

Countless articles say that hospitals push C-sections on women.

My doctor, a Puerto Rican from New Jersey who grew up in the
projects had yet to arrive. She was someone I trusted. She knew how
racist medicine is.

The spry nurse had bright white hair and high-top white sneakers.
She had started nursing school in her sixties after her husband died
and college was free for seniors. She had a stern voice and the softest
hands.

That nurse saved my life.

I almost died.

When they opened me up they found an infection. I went to ICU for
three days. Had a blood transfusion. My son in NICU being monitored: ten pounds four ounces. A giant among the preemies. My husband and mother were allowed to visit thirty minutes, two times a

day. My terrified husband who spoke no English and did not have the capacity to keep track of doctors, the medicines, the bills, instead took photos of the alien baby attached to the machines and printed them out, taping them to the wall by my bed.

Isn't he beautiful, he said.

No.

I want to breastfeed. I said repeatedly to the ICU doctors who did not care that I needed to pump. And dump. Pump and dump—la leche de oro was now toxic because I was on so many drugs.

I will never be able to catch up with him, I said.

My plan—to be a natural mother, unlike my grandmother, who famously rubbed her nipples with camphor so that babies rejected her milk.

My plan was to recover from birth in a day or two and strap him on my back and go on with life as usual.

My plan was to have them dim the lights of my room and play my soothing playlist with some Lauryn Hill, India Arie, and Si*Sé. And have my mom feed me ice chips, and the baby was supposed to come out like it did for my friend Tamara, who said that when it came, it slipped out like a bar of soap slips from one's hands in the shower.

For months, friends would visit and call me and say, OMG Angie, you almost died.

I almost died. I almost died. I almost died.

And when my son came to me . . .

I was thirty-five, and my ob-gyn called my pregnancy geriatric. At the time, I loved my childfree life. But you see I had made a promise. When I was twenty-six, I was pregnant, and I told that baby who appeared to me in a dream and who happens to look a lot like my son does now . . . I said, Baby, baby, I am sorry but I'm not ready for you, come back, okay?

And he did.

[I turn the hours into a love note to myself]

Mariahadessa Ekere Tallie

I turn the hours into a love note to myself
calligraphy of burning sandalwood drifting
hot water filling the tub
5 tall yellow candles encased in glass
deep exhales

water and salt whisper
to my muscles,
the softness
Yes.

Simple Bath Salt Recipe

1 cup epsom salt
¼ cup Himalayan pink salt
2 tablespoons baking soda
Handful of dried rose petals
5–15 drops of essential oil (such as rose maroc, ylang ylang, wild
orange, jasmine, or lavender)

Stir the ingredients together in a bowl while singing your favorite
love song to yourself. Add to the tub after it is full. Store remaining
salts in a glass container.

Conception

Celeste Mendoza

For ninety-six months so many attempts to conceive
the results are negative. A vacuum of conception. Blood—
a spot becoming nothing like a her or him—drops
breaking apart that function of woman
to pricks, shots, pills—whatever to make her fertile
ground for IUIs and IVFs. Mother—

nature, a landscape of rocks. Barren mother
earth folds her knees to her head, says: conceive.
The mantra taking over her motions. She says: be fertile. Affirmations
like sage surrounding, pumping like blood
pulsing through me, through me, through me. Only a woman not a
God. No miracle in my hands. Nothing but prayers, drops

of hope I whisper into rosary beads but every month, drops. Could it
be? It's not to be? Is it foolish to mother
this dream, nurture it, breathe it into being? I am a woman—want it
so bad, the tears never drying; I can't conceive
a day I haven't thought. Said. Cried. Blood.
Crystals. Oils. Mandalas. Vision boards. My body fertile.

Full. It could be happening right now. Maybe I'm fertile.
Only imagination, close my eyes. See her and him. Drops
in a bucket of loss. Hear how full it is? So much blood—

and questions. Did I wait too long? Could I've been a mother earlier?
Will my eggs be healthy? Am I? Can I conceive? Isn't this all part of,
can't it just be part of, is this my mother's

voice or his? When did obsession become me? I am a woman who is
full of questions that ache. Am I fertile
with the futility of negative, negative, cannot conceive,
have you tried or maybe did you hear—drops
of conversation—it's taking them so long. The mothers
must be so angry, no grandchildren, no extending blood

line. The name stops here. Every month. Blood
comes to me, lamenting that it must fall. Woman—
why can't you just do your job? And yet, Mother
earth runs around and through us—Fertile.   See the water fall,
cascade—there seeds drop
and become trees. Thoughts. All which I now conceive.

"Fertile" lullabies me to sleep as the blood
dries, and a fact takes root inside me. I am still
a woman even if I may never hear the word, "mother."

Artist Statement VI

Laurie Ann Guerrero

> "'tis revolution all . . . . The eye that directs a needle in the
> delicate meshes of embroidery will equally well bisect
> a star with the spiderweb of the micrometer."
>
> —Maria Mitchell, first female American astronomer

I cannot afford to think of this as chaos. The red of spine, and the red of hands, and the red of shock, and the red of love, and the red of silence, and the red of anguish, and the red of birth, and the red of sex, and the red of campaign, and the red of that small bird and sinister beet, and the red of rare, and moon, and the red of snapper and shovel, and the red of leaving, and the red of feeding, and the red of release, and the red of mending and trigger and root. And, too, the red of kiss, and the red of virus, and the red of fire, the red of kitchen and cleaver, and the red of now. 'Tis revolution all.

This is the redwork.

This is not a metaphor.

How to Arrive

Ellen Hagan

Alarms shoot forth from the monitors connected to my stretched and taut stomach. The doctor on call, who is not Dr. Su, the one I trust and love, is frantic at my side, giving me a look that says *I told you so*. An hour earlier telling me that I am absolutely not in labor and that I might as well just *get it over with. A C-section is so easy*. Telling me lies in the labor and delivery room looking out over the Audubon Ballroom in Washington Heights—the tip-top of Manhattan. The skyline erupts outside our window. And I know she is lying, because my firstborn was a planned C-section since she was breech and standing straight up in my uterus and the major surgery, recovery time, constipation, aching, wrecked body of it all was not *so easy* as she suggests.

Someone is shouting to *move, move*. At least seven bodies pile into the delivery room. I immediately wave goodbye to our view and all that sky, as the nurses rush in, panicked and fast. One guides me to the bed and checks my vitals, while another nurse pulls up my gown and begins to shave the top of my pubic hair. The new doctor (the one whose name I will promptly file away and forget) tells me I am in distress, and we will need to move to an emergency C-section. She is talking seriously and focused, her brow furrowed. There is an instant bustle all around me, as they rush with alarm and frenzy. Beeping and loud back and forth, their voices ricochet around the hospital bed while David stands back in panic and shock, a jolt and rush as he watches us in motion, suddenly blushing and shy with embarrassment and pleasure both, all, at the same time.

I lean back, my face and body flush in the same exact same way, because I have just had an orgasm. Self-pleasure with him right beside me. Small death inside of me. Meant to move the baby forward and out in the old-fashioned vaginal-canal kind of way. Anything to avoid a second C-section. So we followed the young nurse's instructions when she told us that nipple stimulation and squats and anything that contracts the uterus would truly help us along. She spent a year in Nicaragua and told us the way they deliver babies there is much more humane than in the United States. We believe her as I amble around the room connected to an IV and a machine meant to keep me safe and alive. Instead, I have been "in labor" since 9:00 A.M. this morning, when I arrived for my weekly check-in. Already three days over my due date, I had imagined this baby staying inside of my body forever. Possibly attending my close friend's wedding and shaking it hard on the dance floor, maybe starting work in the fall with her attached to me still. Still, she had felt both close and far away. They sent me weeping and dizzy to the hospital that day, Columbia Presbyterian being a behemoth that sprawls from 165th Street to 170th Street, from Broadway to Fort Washington Avenue, each building connected by corridors and loopholes. I call David and tell him the baby will arrive immediately, so he runs with superhuman speed from our apartment to the waiting room, where he finds me flipping through some type of Baby & Me magazine.

Guess I'm not quite in the danger they thought I was in. We both smile, sweating and ready and scared of the long haul.

* * *

Time is fluid and changes around me. How will we live now—now responsible for two, this addition. Now that we cannot be afraid of the small things or of everything that is. The gigantic water bug in the kitchen that crawls the whole of the wall all cocky, like it owns the place, god bless. How will we live now with the loss of control—all an illusion anyway. Because once a body arrives, there it is. The always reminder that nothing is controllable. Predictable. Not even one moment of it. That ashes and destruction are always possible—wings and Bigfoot and dragons maybe, the Loch Ness Monster I obsessed about in middle school. Could be real or not, but my fear then certainly was—as it is now. And my curiosity, too. *How will you choose to live now?* A question I keep on asking myself.

When the first nurse asks me, *Is this a Hurricane Sandy baby?* I think, Sure? Hurricane, absolutely. But did we have sex in October of 2012 at all? Yes, yes, that, too. And a child is a hurricane for certain. Rapidly rotating, a simple cyclone in and outside of me. Winding winds in a circle, all circulation and whirl. I am so ready, is what I think, but suddenly there is no moving now. We sit and wait.

* * *

Waiting for the Storm—the title of my whole life.

* * *

Another one of the nurses, and there are so many, tells me the hospital is full of birthing bodies and that every room on every floor, delivery or otherwise, is occupied. *Hurricane Sandy babies*, she says with a wink. We will have to wait. So that's exactly what we do. Hidden only by a small curtain with other laboring or nonlaboring bodies and the partners or family members with them. We chitchat, look through the IKEA catalogue on David's phone. It is morning still, and I am easily hooked up to over a dozen cords and pulleys. A needle in my right arm. Monitored up. They think I could be in labor but are super suspect. One doctor agrees to let me "labor" a while longer. All the time it is said in quotations. My stomach makes no clenched moves. I feel nothing like the labor I have read about in countless online blogs and watched in Ricki Lake's documentary *The Business of Being Born* or read about in Ina May Gaskin's *Guide to Childbirth* that promises I could squat in a field and deliver both pleasure and a human body if I just try and believe hard enough. That's not really fair to the natural birth movement, which I absolutely wish I was a part of, but that's how I feel now, disconnected from my physical body, made to pretend I need bathroom breaks so I can deep squat next to the public toilet and try the nipple stimulation I read about. They deny me any food, except for an applesauce and saltine crackers that I devour greedily and then deflate in the makeshift hospital bed. All I have is time to think and panic and obsess and wonder what I could have done differently.

* * *

Ten days before, I sit underneath the giant whale in the Natural History Museum with a college class called Nature & Poetry with twelve students from Long Island. They are here to write poems and think about the natural world. I am here for the air conditioning and to help me digest the chocolate ice cream cone I had for breakfast and to discover that 4.3 billion years ago, rains flooded the earth, creating the oceans. Life on earth began in the ocean 3.5 billion years ago. I feel like an ocean. Oceans hold the greatest abundance of life on earth. Shrimp. Amoeba. Anemone. Coral. Sea turtles. When pregnant, it is like holding earth and the ocean too. In a way. To sit here in the calm darkness, most quiet with the weight of a whale directly above me in the dead heat of a three-day ninety-plus-degree heat wave at over nine and a half months pregnant is to know—is to kind of, somehow, in a way I've not known before—life. City. City of bodies. City of my body in all of its oceanic tides. I have never been this deep into the museum, or known this much about my body, have never sat below a great sea creature, feeling myself somehow like a great sea creature. No clue of arrival. Animal. Or otherwise. Feeling both myself and otherworldly too. How much is lost and found on the ocean floor. How I spent every summer of my life becoming buoyant in saltwater, learning to ride, skim, body surf through each changing tide. Tumbling and roughhousing my way through who I was and who I wanted to be—all of me shifting and turning—orbiting around myself and everyone I come from.

How then, do I show up in the world? And how do I deliver someone else into it? Having spent forty-two years navigating body, skin, existence, whole lives of people I arrive from. Lineage. Ancestry, but more complex. Weird. Wired. Kaleidoscope. My mother descendent from Turkey by way of Assyria, her father renaming himself Albert from Aziz. Assimilation. New Jersey by way of Turkey. Alterations. Made his life rearranging items of clothing to fit just right. Always I am rearranging my answers of how to exist. How to carry a child and bring them into existence. Am I enough of? How much is enough? My mother, descendent of the Middle East. And Dumont, New Jersey. Ocean girl of waves and deep dives. She claims the color of her skin, shape of her nose, the Arabic my grandfather's family spoke. What is existence anyway. Search: *Assyrian*. Search: *Assyrians*. My mother is Brown, her skin a collective history she wears. Appear, disappear. Magician. Now you see me. Now you— Search: *What do Assyrians look like?* See a photograph of yourself, your mother, your grandfather, your unborn daughter. Google search finds: *Claim White, but just look at them.* Clinging onto some part of myself I want to appear. Disappear. And again, I am treading water, beneath the riptide, flipping and trying to catch breath, catch body, catch weight, float to the surface, survive. Not trying to hide, pass, fly by unnoticed but also not trying to pretend I don't exist. That part of me is all of me. Same for the child I'm hoping will be birthed from the very canal of my body. Back to the whale. Back to the ocean. Back to the body carrying the ocean and every single turn of tides.

Araceli, my oldest daughter says, *I am a Brown girl. That is what I am.* And I know her sister will say the same. Their mouths moving double time, twin girls born in different years—moons apart. But same, same. Their father, Filipino-American. "Classic Fil-Ams," my students from Manila will say when I show them photographs many years later. What does it mean to raise girls who know themselves better than I knew my own self. Body. Delivery. Exalt. Exhilaration. Identity. Own who they are: mixed race, Brown girls arriving. Know what it means to show up who and how you are in the world. To know yourself before you even arrive. Yes, that is what I would have loved. To know myself then. How I am all the time learning and knowing myself now. A study in always. I am learning all the ways to love.

* * *

Flash, back again, back to the story. Back to the waiting area/labor holding space/IKEA catalogue viewing station. *We have found a room for you*, a nurse tells me. *They will let you labor just a little bit longer.* Wheel me upstairs, show me the view. David sneaks hummus with pretzels from the cafeteria, which I scarf down greedy and wild. *I'm gonna have this damn baby*, is what I think. Begin to dance and twirl in the room, visit our own private bathroom, pee, jump in circles, rotate, shimmy, hip shake, sigh, cry wildly into his arms, admit finally that I'm likely not even in any type of labor. I go on and let out the biggest sigh of all. And almost give up when the final nurse comes in to remind us that there are alternative ways to get a baby moving, and that's when we know that an orgasm could be the only/best way, so we kiss and hold and imagine ourselves a whole planet outside and moving.

My whole body becomes core. Sediment. Rock and oasis. Measurement of the unit of all electricity. Electricity itself. Define all. You define definition. All hemisphere and heat. Hydroponic. Volcanic membranes and nitrogen. Becomes oxygen itself, and just when my body finally lets go and my uterus contracts and shifts, that's when the alarms go off and they all rush to my room. Arriving. Arriving. And it's then that I know. A C-section is inevitable. Already in the books. Tied up neatly in this hospital complex that takes up whole city blocks. My body is a harbor, and it's time to give it up.

* * *

There is nothing sentimental about delivery. A woman's whole work at producing lungs, ribs, femur, and collarbones. How to produce another body inside of yours, then deliver. That's not sentimental. It's transformation.

* * *

Quick, quick, we need to move, they say in my ear, while I am laid out, having just been spent, having just released and felt all the pleasure a body can bring. *Bend over*, one of the nurses says to me, *and hold perfectly still. Do not move one muscle*, is what they must say since an epidural in your spine could cause paralysis, death. Couldn't everything cause death at this point?

I stay perfectly still.

You help me breathe—become my breath. Helium, too, all of you. Geology. The story of my bones—body transforming into you. Every second and always. A child is a planet inside of you. This, I know now. A whole solar system. Mercury. Earth. Venus. Mars. Jupiter. Moons. Saturn. Neptune. Volcanism and atmospheric storms. A baby is a planetary system. The atmosphere of a womb. Continents. Oceans. Vast. Deciphering celestial motions. How craters are formed. Planetary. The sun, of course, is always a star, massive sphere of luminous gas, hydrogen and helium. I'm lift, lifted. Most of its life, a star is balanced between the inward pressure of its gravity and the outward pressure of its internal heat. Both at the same time I think, as Miriam is lifted from me. Abdomen sliced fast, and she is star shine for sure. Screaming she arrives, as the doctor or the doctor in training or whoever is closest to the gaping wound of my body holds Miriam in the air. She clenches both fists and bellows out. I smile a *hell yes* at her volume and rage. How twin we are, both of us in this antiseptic delivery room. Not the birth I imagined: swaying, singing, squatting to open my vagina as a child slipped seamlessly out and into space. None of it the way it was supposed to be. But somehow exactly right.

And then—there I am. Holding my daughter for the first time. And aren't we both so high, high. Me, stoned, still on the constant drip of morphine, numbed from the waist down. And her so new, adjusting to fluorescent lights, swaddle, the hot pink fingernails of the recovery room nurse; her search for breast and curl of arm. How do I get back inside, she must be wondering? And me, with silver hoops in both ears, hair still done, and glossed lips. All heavy with sedation and pain medication.

Miriam. Gem/mineral that you are. Gypsum, halite, opal in your soft yellowed glow. Graphite and copper, smoky quartz, biotite, serpentine, amethyst, rose quartz, rock crystal, agate, properties, and all. Energy and minerals. Radiant. You radiate inside of me. Diamond, fluorite, and beryl. Topaz. Axinite. You are what it means to ignite; become stone and gem. Rock the whole quarry of me. Endless.

On the Origins of O.

Nelly Rosario

Etymology: Adriana, Athena, Kahlo, Martine, Monet, Paloma, Patria, Trinity, Violet

1/20/99

Hi page,

It's been a while since I've written on fancy paper with fancy ink on a moving train. All's well, then. It's so hard to keep this handwriting worthy of quality paper (my L's have become like [the father's]).

Baby happy. Good, weird dinner: rice and squid, mung beans, plátanos, apple, compliments of Mami. The kitchen's become a hearty health food place since Papi went on his cleansing diet. I'm enjoying the most I can.

I spy: a man and woman by the door; a girl telling her friends, "Make him change," Hebrew written on a baseball cap (in foam letters!).

I like being pregnant.

Now I walk like my grandmother. And I walk like a duck.

8/31/20

Hi page,

It's been a while since I've thought of them days. The train is always moving, each stop on this journey more unreal than the previous. Here I am, standing on a chair, pulling down the last of the boxes containing old journals from the top shelf of my closet. They're heavy. Plastic bins full of unfinished notebooks, many of which I'd curated (burned pages in a backyard bonfire) before moving back from Texas to New York over five years ago. Here I am, in my parents' house, after over five months of quarantine, trying not to go batshit crazy. "What are you doing now?" says O. And when I tell of her of the piece I'm working on about her birth, about the next-day deadline, and

I'm wearing my favorite outfit: striped maternity top (thanx, Mami); black leggings; combat boots; peacoat; Merlot lipstick.

Six months and counting. Another soul walking with me. I don't want this feeling of expectation and intimacy to end.

A woman has asked if I want to sit. I forget I'm showing. That I waddle. The severe thirst, especially in the morning. Oh, and the mood swings. I hate him. I love him. The extreme horniness. Who is this child? Anger. Sadness. I am full clouds and little rain. My mind, a universe and a blank. Fatigue and energy. Hunger and fullness.

I'm radiant. Alive . . . sea syrup. No sailing south, "That's the baby's," he says. Ours. But soon I'll be all to the baby, my breasts, my attentions, my love.

Out of breath. Diaphragm compressed, they say. My sighs are cosmic. No more seats on this train. I'd refused the last two offers. Out of breath. Heels hurt. But if I sit, nosy folks will try to read what a bellied woman is writing.

Here we are at 66th Street. Baby, who are you? I feel you're a girl. A knowing.

show her the tattered pages, she says, "Oh."

Last week, it was she who wanted to look through old albums and relive a childhood that grows more distant each day. The kid who loves *Call the Midwife* and all other British shows. The premed student who wanted to study embryology but switched to an interest in epidemiology and public health, even before the COVID-19 came to snuff out futures.

I'm wearing my favorite outfit: a *bata*, now gentrified by pandemic fashionistas as the "house dress." Stylo quarantino. The fibroid makes me look pregnant. I forget that I'm showing, but my father reminds me. And the mood swings. The fatigue. Fibroids are energy hoarders, an energy worker told me recently. Um, yeah. That's the unwritten novel, I told her. The many things unborn, unsaid. Too many blank pages in the journals, particularly between August of 1998 and April of 1999. But the few signs of life appeared like blips, spread across various notebooks, sometimes alongside doodles. It's as if that bellied woman were hiding from me, from herself—no, I remember her being overwhelmed by the sheer power of experience, knowing that all words would fail her. Still, she took deep breaths and pushed.

February 1999

Dear Baby New Soul,

I sit here at this milestone, picking pebbles out of my shoes and wondering where you will guide me next.

You, so small and mysterious at the center of me, guiding my life, pointing me to turn here and there. Who will you be? You will drop on a part of the planet where you may not always be welcome. Yet, in this corner, I'll make sure you explore who you are, grow, choose, come into your own. So much comes before you—then again, you may be an older soul than your parents combined. My maternal instincts are prepared to prepare you as best as I can for whatever your mission is in this world.

From "On Becoming," *Becoming American: Personal Essays by First Generation American Women*, ed. Meri Nana-Ama Danquah (New York: Hyperion, 2000).

A woman born in the Dominican Republic and raised in Brooklyn, New York, is expecting her first child. Having lingered in many communities but remaining firmly rooted in none, having named and renamed herself, she is like a stamped travel trunk. She needs to constantly rub the compass in her belly and look within for her true north. This woman has flat feet. Always a nauseous feeling of vertigo, disoriented on the land where she feels both native and foreign.

Balance is often difficult for this woman, but she keeps traveling.

2/10/99

Lots of activity. Belly becomes pointy, then round again. I feel an elbow or a knee poke. Who are you today?

I'm sleepy. Trying to stay up and do marathon writing, since I slept all day. But I'm so sleepy! Terrible to squander time the way I have, as if trying to enjoy the last few months of being alone, of not having this huge responsibility.

I like being pregnant. Yes, it has definitely been trying, especially dealing with [the father], but Baby is kicking softly to the music. Maybe I should be doing all these experiments on the fetus, like reading to it, playing an instrument. Playing lots of music, if only because I like it.

So he left last week. Moved out 'cause he "needed space" and to finish cleaning up the apartment we're moving into soon. Only after a fight does he decide to clean. It's been trying.

2/19/99
Waiting for that WIC [Special Supplemental Nutrition Program for Women, Infants, and Children]. PBS drones on above, though no kids are here. Is Woodhull a public hospital? Why don't I know this?

3/2/99 1:30 A.M.
I can hear the dying
Leaf by leaf
Of the fica tree
Tonight
With the flutter in my womb
And the ocean in the radiator
By the ticking of the cockeyed
clock
A quiet death
That intrudes enough
To remind you

8/16/20 8:44 P.M.
Acupuncture points in the ear correspond to the organs of an inverted fetus. The ear is the last organ to develop in a fetus; hearing is the last of the senses to die.

So when baby daddy nibbles the tip of your ear, he has your foot in his mouth. And when Baby is taken to her first ear piercing, gold studs are put in her eyes.

3/11/99

Birth Plan for O. [girl] or N. [boy]

Due Date: 4/20/99

Scheduled to deliver at: Elizabeth Seton Childbearing Center or St. Vincent's Hospital

Dear ESCCs:

We are excited by the prospect of having our first child. The following birth plan is to help you understand our preference for [the] upcoming labor and delivery. We are aware that in certain circumstances these guidelines may not be followed, but it is our hope that you will assist us in making this experience the one we hope for. Please let us know if you have any other suggestions.

Sincerely,

[Parents]

LABOR

- I would prefer to avoid shaving of pubic hair.

- I wish to be able to move around and change position at will throughout the first stage of labor.

- I would prefer to keep the number of vaginal exams to a minimum.

9/1/20

Life with Now-Twenty-One-Year-Old Daughter Under Pandemic, Black Lives Matter, Climate Change, Trump . . . Dystopia

Due date went down in history as the day of the Columbine High School Massacre, Hitler's birthday. While painting my toenails red, I watched the news in horror.

The ESCC closed its doors four years later, in 2003, after thirty years of catching babies. According to an article in the *Brooklyn Rail*, "The center's insurance policy expired . . . and because of the high cost of malpractice coverage—which the center can't afford—the insurance policy was not renewed." The article was titled "Eliminating the Middlewoman." And right now, the name of the first US-born citizen to be canonized by the Catholic church only brings to mind the St. Elizabeth Seton Catholic Church in Indiana, where, just two months ago, one Reverend Theodore Rothrock referred to leaders of Black Lives Matter as "maggots and parasites." Well, it was with the spirit of "maggots and parasites" that, weeks later, Planned Parenthood

MONITORING

- I do not wish to have continuous fetal monitoring unless it is required by the condition of my child.

LABOR INDUCTION

- I do not wish to have the amniotic membrane ruptured artificially unless signs of fetal distress require internal monitoring.

- I would prefer to be allowed to try changing position and nipple stimulation before Pitocin is administered. Should my labor need induction, I would prefer castor oil or an enema to be administered instead of Pitocin.

ANESTHESIA

- I do not want any kind of anesthesia offered to me during natural labor. I would prefer other methods of pain relief, such as breathing, water, massage, change of position, music, and meditation.

disavowed its founder, Margaret Sanger. The national organization removed her name from its Manhattan clinic building because of Sanger's connections to the eugenics movement and Planned Parenthood's "historical reproductive harm within communities of color," according to Karen Seltzer, the chair of the New York affiliate's board. The saints keep falling. My designated birth hospital was the now-defunct St. Vincent's. It was named after the third-century martyr who was tortured and killed under the Roman persecution of Christians in Spain. St. Vincent's Hospital was the major site for the triage of survivors of the Titanic, of the AIDS crisis, and of 9/11 attacks on the World Trade Center in 2001, two years after O.'s birth. In 2010 the hospital went bankrupt and closed.

God and I try not to laugh at "Birth Plan for O." The narrative tone cracks me up: *I would prefer to avoid shaving of pubic hair*, thank you very much. To the credit of ESCC, no speculum or rubber gloves got near my vagina during pregnancy. I did my own continuous fetal monitoring, which included checking for responses

- Should I be transferred to St. Vincent's Hospital, I would like anesthesia available in a small dose if I specifically should request it. No epidural.

CESAREAN

- I would like [the father] present at all times if our child requires a cesarean delivery.

- If our child is not in distress, s/he should be given to me immediately after birth. Should I be unconscious, s/he should be given to [the father] immediately after birth.

EPISTIOTOMY [sic]

- I would prefer not to have an episiotomy. Use perinium [sic] massage instead.

DELIVERY

- I would like a water delivery if possible.

- If out of water, I would like [the father] and/or midwives/nurses to support me and my legs as necessary during the pushing stage.

- If out of water, I would like a mirror available so that I can see our child when s/he crowns.

to Prince songs. Position changes, nipple stimulation, castor oil, and enemas all went out the window—labor progressed at a snail's pace, even after St. Elizabeth sent me to St. Vincent's, whose maternity ward sounded like a torture chamber. Neither saint was there to comfort me when a staff member informed us that a woman had just given birth to an eleven-pounder. Fuck the candles, massages, meditation. Who the hell had time to get purple and yellow flowers? Gone were my visions of pushing Radiant Baby into the jacuzzi of Birthing Room 1, surrounded by doting family members in a red-lit, warmly furnished room to celebratory clinks of wine glasses and teary blessings. The last thing I wanted was grape juice, miso soup, Triscuits—when did I ever like Triscuits?! Visualization did help. Each time the tsunami of pain came, I pictured the beach near my mother's *campo* in Puerto Plata, and I'd dive into each oncoming wave, letting myself dissolve into water. Women throughout millennia have survived this, I told myself whenever I wanted to drown. But there's only so much treading you can do. The baby pooped inside me. I had

- Even if I am fully dilated, and assuming the child is not in distress, I would like to try to wait until I feel the urge to push before beginning the pushing phase.

- I would like our child placed on my stomach or chest immediately after delivery. Should I express that I am in [no] condition to receive the child, I would like for [the father] to hold the child immediately after delivery.

AFTER DELIVERY

- I would like [the father] to cut the cord.

- We would like our child examined and bathed in our presence.

- Should I be transferred to St. Vincent's Hospital, if our child is taken from me to receive medical treatment, [the father] or some other person I designate will accompany our child at all times.

- Should I be transferred to St. Vincent's Hospital, I would like a private room, if available.

- I would like to donate umbilical cord blood.

a fever. My water had been broken for more than twenty-four hours. I pushed and pushed. The head remained stuck at my cervix. Time for an emergency C-section. *No epidural?* They brought in the anesthesiologist. "Move an inch and be paralyzed," he joked, apologizing for the Russian humor. His words. I wanted a popsicle. I wanted to kill him. I wanted to poop. I wanted my mother, who had called many times but wasn't allowed through by [the father]. I raged. I pushed. "Stop pushing," said the midwife. The surgeon was on his way. Stuck in traffic. In the operating theater, I counted three blue rubber fingers, then found myself swimming in deep sea, deep in the sea, seaing deeply. Rays of light filtered down to the depths from the water's surface, and the closer I swam up to that sunlight, the more intense peace engulfed my being. I reached a point of no return in the water, where I knew that if I swam another inch, I would die. Child— everything—to be left behind. The vision of an orphaned life flashed, I hesitated, and then: *"How many fingers do you see?"* my cheeks being patted by a hand, [the father] holding a bundle and crying,

BREASTFEEDING

- Unless medically necessary, we do not wish to have any bottles given to our child (including glucose water or plain water).

- We do not want our child to be given a pacifier.

PHOTOS

- I would like to have pictures taken of labor and/or birth.

OTHER

- My main support person is [the father]. I would like him present during labor and/or delivery. At some point during labor, I may request the support of [sister] or [mother].

- Articles I would like in the birthing room: books on birth, eucalyptus candle, journal, cloth doll, music (Cassandra Wilson, "Blues & Stuff," water sounds, aboriginal), purple and yellow flowers.

- Foods I would like during labor: grape juice, popsicles, miso soup, Triscuits, seltzer water, wine, chamomile and detox tea, oranges, bananas, peaches.

a fat little pink face blinking back at me, the corner of an ear bent from being stuck at my cervix. A 9-pound, 11.8-ounce girl born at 9:10 A.M. on April 29, 1999, a feast for numerology. But all I wanted was water and sleep. When I asked for both, a nurse gave me an ice chip and told me to stay awake. I wanted to kill him. I wanted my baby. I wanted my mother. The baby had a fever. The baby was in the NICU. My mother was on her way.

None of it had gone my way. Way to go, [the father]. Way to go, me. No episiotomy, perineum intact—I was still a virgin! Lucky you, said my roommate later. She had torn from A to Z, from Monday to Sunday, from here to China. Her baby cried 24/7. Mine had to be in NICU for forty-eight hours. There, she was waging a hunger strike, refusing glucose water, formula. Way to go, O! I'm on my way. But until then, I had to learn to pee again. My mother taught me once the catheter was removed. She brought me fish soup to stimulate breastmilk and the lavender bata I wear as I write these words. It's full of holes but has gone everywhere with me.

- Clothing: robe, slippers, sneakers, baseball cap, sweatpants, T-shirts, nursing bra. For baby: home outfit, blanket, car seat.
- I would prefer Birthing Room 1. If not available, 2 or 3 will be fine.

The nurses would force me to walk so that I wouldn't fill up with gasses. Through the windows of the hospital hall, past the Monet (hence, her middle name) prints along the walls, I looked down at the impressionist streets of the Village. Through tears, I people-watched, marveling at the sanctity of each and every one of those tiny lives. Everyone, from the man at the hot dog stand to the girl emerging from a taxi, had come from a woman who had, in one way or another, experienced the catastrophic magic of childbirth. I remember also thinking: "Mama, you gotta write better characters."

4/29/99

[Wrote Dr. Rocchio:]

> *Rosario [girl symbol]*
> *9:10 A.M., C-sec*
> *9 lbs, 11.8 oz.*
> *20"*
> *38 cm head*
> *A+ mom*
> *Mom:*   *febrile predelivery*
>   *6 doses 11 antibiotics*
>   *baby to NICU – observation*
>   *blood cultures (-)*
>   *transferred to WBN 4.30.99*

4/30/99

[Note at the hospital-room door:]

> *10:20 A.M.*
>
> *Nelly—*
>
> *I stopped by to say hi & see how you were doing. CONGRATULA-TIONS! Please call the birth center if you need any breastfeeding help after you go home. You'll see Dr. Matheson for your first postpartum visit, but you can come back to us for your 6-week visit.*
>
> *[heart] Carolyn*
> *and all the midwives!*

5/1/99

Sitting in the postpartum unit, [the father] resting. There's an orange glow on the brick building outside our window as evening arrives. Almost no visitors today. A baby cries out in the hallway. O. rests in her bassinet, quiet, fed. She takes some, then sleeps. Sucks hard—a good latch ... This door in my life just opened, and whatever I left behind is blocked, just beyond this door.

I love her so much. Just looking at her pulls everything in me. I fell in love last night, when the NICU finally let her come and stay with me for good. She's a healthy, resilient baby. I try not to doubt her, attributing to her all of the negativities I've been holding. I want to simply love her. Scared of her, too; know she knows the things I feel.

"Arrival." *Meridians: feminism, race, transnationalism*, vol. 4, no. 1, 2003.

It was in the platinum light
that you were conceived
Long ago, I think
when apples grew on stems
and potatoes flowered
Silver metal water drops
you came to me
dripped low waiting to fall
stretching long until
you splashed alive

All of Yourself

A Conversation between aracelis girmay and Elizabeth Alexander

ag: I have a note as a way of beginning, which maybe can be a little doorway.

It's always seemed to me that you are someone so deeply curious about the inner world, your own inner worlds, and the inner worlds of others. And so I wanted to bring you this tiny excerpt from Olga Tokarczuk's Nobel lecture. She's talking about a photograph of her mother and she writes:

> When as a little girl I would look at that picture, I would feel sure that my mom had been looking for me when she turned the dial on our radio. Like a sensitive radar, she penetrated the infinite rounds of the cosmos, trying to find out when I would arrive, and from where.

And then I think of your deeply moving, exquisite poem "The Dream That I Told My Mother-In-Law," in which you write, close to the end of the poem:

> She began to dream
> of childhood flowers, her long-gone parents.
> I told her my dream in a waiting room:
> a photographer photographed women,
> said her portraits revealed their truest selves.
> She snapped my picture, peeled back the paper,
> and there was my son's face, my first son, my self.

I wonder if you could talk about how you, as a young person, first came to imagine, and then later understand, the processes of pregnancy and/or birth, and how this touched or shaped your imagination?

E: When I used to think about my future life, before I knew that I was going to be a poet, I knew that I wanted to be a mother. And it's funny—I never had fantasies about marriage, not really. It was about being a mother. That seemed to be the thing that I had a great deal of certainty about. Was that because I was the championship babysitter on the block [laughter] for years and years and years? Was that because little people were always very interesting to me—what they had to say, what their inner lives looked like? But people are interesting to me, so I don't know that it was that. It felt more like a cosmic certainty, which was also kind of interesting because as I came of age in my teens I very much had a clear feminist ideology. You know, raised in a civil rights and equal rights and movement home in that regard. Raised in years when Black studies and feminist studies and all of these questions [were] live and in the air. I became a feminist in large part because I spent a lot of time in a bookstore in my neighborhood called Lammas Bookstore, which was a feminist bookstore, and I used to go there most Saturdays and sit and read, so I was a hundred percent the "Our Bodies Ourselves" generation. And my mother worked on reproductive rights issues, so the whole idea of your choice and the sanctity of a woman's body was something I really came up in. The inevitability of marriage and a kind of conventional idea of having children was not in my developing consciousness, but children were a certainty—that's why I say maybe a cosmic certainty.

And to that excerpt that you read from the poem, leaping absolutely forward to when I was pregnant with that child, Solomon, and when he was born—he's here now, we're spending some time together... he graduated from college, and he's moving to Montgomery, Alabama to work at the Equal Justice Initiative. So right now I feel like my first son, my self, my best friend, the person who made me a mother, is heading out into the world. We always say Solo made me a mother, made me who I was supposed to be, filled me out in that way. And then what we always say about Simon is: "And Simon completed the family." That those two powerful things were things that they did. And thinking about another poem, "Neonatology," which came out of the space of nursing Solo and thinking (and I'm still answering your question about the imagination), I imagined that because I was 34 almost 35 when I had my first child, and I thought, *Okay, I've written books. I have a PhD. I have a job. I have a rich professional life and I'm not anxious about whatever's going to come next.* And I really thought that when I had babies I wouldn't write for a long, long time, and that felt okay. But what I found was, when I went into that deep space with Solo, and in the middle of the night when I would get up to nurse him, I would write. And that in the intimacy of my space with him, what felt like such profound radical acceptance by a human being, that even in the best of love I had never experienced consciously, the profundity of that self-acceptance with my baby—my imagination just felt like a garden. It just felt like everything was in it and everything could be in it, and it was dreamy, and it was surprising, and that also this pregnancy came, this child came. I had chosen abortion earlier in my life, and it was an unpleasant but untragic experience. It was an experience of self-deter-mination, and again, being a feminist in this time period, saying, *Okay, this has happened, and thank God I live someplace where I can safely take care of this because it's not the time in my life.* And it was not much more complicated than that; an unpleasant and difficult experience, but not a tragic experience. So coming to this moment where here is the chosen moment, and here is the chosen child, and here now, at almost 35, my circle is complete. And that was an experience of the body, but it was also an experience of the imagination.

ag: Mm. Mm. Can you say more, Elizabeth, about the word "accept-ance," that radical acceptance?

E: I think so often of the first night home from the hospital. The baby's nursed and the baby's down and everyone's exhausted and falling into a void of sleep, and then lurching up out of it at the baby's cry, and really, really honestly thinking, "I must keep that baby alive."

And the first time that you realize, *Oh, this is the enormity of the responsibility. This is what it means to be responsible for another. And this is different from any other human relationship or any other human responsibility.* I mean, you know, babies are complicated people too [laughs] but it felt like nothing had been messed up yet [laughs]. You know? Hold him, feed him, laugh with him, keep him clean, put him in the fresh air. The simplicity of the tending and the loving and the care was just tremendous. And just to look at this face and just think, *It's not just that he's mine—I am his.*

ag: Yes.

E: I just keep thinking of the movement of a circle and that's what the acceptance felt like.

ag: I'm thinking about histories of pregnancy and birth in your family and I'm wondering what your relationship to those histories was. If you thought about those histories of birth or labor or pregnancy in your family?

E: Yeah. I thought about them a lot. My parents are both only children. I have a brother, but cousins, sisters, aunties—I did not grow up in that. So there hadn't been anybody proximate to me who was having babies or doing anything like that. But what's interesting on my mother's side is that her father was the youngest of nine, and her grandmother was an amazing woman who lived in Tuskegee, Alabama—we're talking, middle-19th century; she died in 1915. She was a suffragist. She helped build Tuskegee. She was an astonishing woman who had nine children, was the wife of the treasurer, struggled with mental illness. My mother, who's a historian, has exhaustively researched her grandmother, for whom pregnancy, childbirth, too many children and overwhelmedness—being someone who fought for women's rights—were her paradox, and she had children throughout her entire reproductive life. The last one, my grandfather, coming when she was maybe 47 years old. And she committed suicide, and part of the theory was always that all of those things converged: there were political unhappinesses, there was mental illness, and there were too many goddamn children. And here was someone who was working at Tuskegee, building it, educating Black women... Black people who are, by the way, the first generation out of slavery. She was providing for those people, and yet she was worn down. By breeding. You know? And the even deeper thing was, of all of those nine, most of them did not have children. And none of the girls had children. Now, how unusual was that? So it meant that a great deal came to my mother. With all of these aunts and uncles, she was a beloved child of her family. But also, how did my mom start to think about what it meant that all of these women said that the choice to have children is part of what we are eschewing because it'll take you down? It'll take you down. And that's not a Black woman story that we always tell.

*   *   *

ag: I have another question about imagination. I'm thinking about your work in African American Studies and thinking about whether, or how, that work intersected with your imagination specifically when you were pregnant. For example, when I was pregnant I felt suddenly and newly terrified. Knowing everything I know of history. My imagination, I had to grab hold of it. And I'm wondering about whether your imagination or your relationship to your studies and work changed while you were pregnant or in the early years of your children's lives.

E: I found pregnancy itself to be just a fascinating human experience. What I really loved about it was that—this is so dramatic, but it's true—I felt that it connected me to something ancient.

I went to a very, very wonderful practice run by a really fabulously old school Black gynecologist, a man, and two midwives, and Dr. Holley had just been birthing babies forever and ever and ever and ever and ever. And he was very avuncular and very Black and funny and loving. I was in New Haven at the time. He had two offices: one was in Branford, Connecticut, so, you know, kind of like an upper middle-class suburb kind of strip mall place to go, and the other was on Dixwell Avenue in the Hill District of New Haven, in the most economically challenged neighborhood in New Haven. And you would book wherever you wanted to go, and we pointedly would go to both offices. As I said, I was 34 at the time, and I could be in one place with a 48-year-old professional white woman who had done in vitro and was having her first child and there was that, and then a 14- or 15-year-old Black girl on the other hand. Just the whole spectrum of what it meant to be having this experience. And I just found that very humbling and edifying and powerful to think that in some way, we are all sisters in this moment. We will all have children who are born in April 1998. We're all adding to the planet's load in April 1998. That activated my imagination very, very powerfully as well, even though I didn't write about it that much.

Thinking and teaching in African American Studies and our history, I think immediately of something like: how is a Black woman pregnant when she knows about Margaret Garner? I think there are certain experiences in life that sort of let you stare into the abyss a little bit, and for me, giving birth was one of them, witnessing death was another one of them. Those moments that are so primal and galvanizing and enormous that it sort of blocks out everything but what you have to do. It kind of raises you and makes you, or at least that's how I experienced that.

I had a natural childbirth for both kids—I didn't have any medication and they were big boys—

ag: How big were they!?

E: Oh my god. Solo was 8 lbs. 8 oz., which was normal big. But Simon was 9 lbs. 12 oz. and I remember thinking, You know what? There are a lot of things I may not have done, but I did that. I did that. And it really did make me feel like there is this sort of primal power that it just gave me for other things I had to do, including some of the hard things of learning and knowing our history.

ag: Thinking about labor and healthcare, it sounds like you had a great doctor and midwives so I don't know if this question is relevant, but when you engaged health professionals did you have strategies for being seen or for ensuring that you had what you needed? Was that something that you thought of?

E: Fortunately that was what came with choosing that practice. Those things were a given, and philosophically we were aligned. I had a friend whose sister ran a birthing center in the Bronx and I actually do sometimes think—I just said this to Solo the other night—that if I have another invention I've thought for a long time that midwife would be that reinvention. I just have so much respect for, and interest in, that work. Even understanding that it can be very dangerous and it's not always snowy and pretty and beautiful. But I value and respect deep experience. And that's what sort of blew me away about these people who I chose. They had just brought babies into this world a million different ways, and they had brought thousands of Black women's babies into this world. I chose upfront so that there were no negotiations down the line.

ag: We've seen the statistics and we read about Black women's health and maternal health disparities and in some ways, for many people, it affirms what maybe we knew from the stories or have experienced or imagined. Was this all part of your conscious choosing? Of the doctor and midwives you worked with?

E: Oh, yeah. And also that they served a Black community with that office on Dixwell. And were committed to being completely affordable. Some of their healthcare was free. That was just very powerful. It was their integrity. And, as I said, these people were incredibly experienced and experienced with Black women. I felt privileged. As you know, you have a lot of visits when you're pregnant, so I felt really privileged to be in all of that space.

*   *   *

ag: I think of this part of our conversation as The Tellers section, to borrow from Gwendolyn Brooks. Who were the people of your youth who seemed to know about reproductive health and pregnancy? Did you talk about these things with friends? Who were The Tellers?

E: Yeah, I love that. When I was growing up and when I was a teenager, I used to dance very seriously. That was what I did every day after school, that was what I did all day Saturday, and that was my favorite community to be in. Part of what I loved about it was that there were some women older than the teenagers. There was a junior company, and then there was a senior company, so we had grown up dancers, and when I performed with this group, we would travel together. We spent so much intimate time with each other's bodies. It's something I really loved about coming up in dance: little teeny tiny studio or changing room, not thinking anything about undressing in front of other people, being efficient about it and efficient about our bodies. And then the kind of in-between time, when you're waiting because your piece isn't being rehearsed, and you're sort of flopped and trying to keep warm on the side, and you're stretching and you're talking. Those low-voiced conversations. I remember two of the women in their 20s. They had lovers and had been pregnant, and they were very knowing about themselves. And so it seemed like they were The Tellers. They were extraordinary creatures and one of them, to make money, she worked as a belly dancer, and one night she told us that she was raped where she was working. That was the first time that anyone told me that story.

There was something about the intimacy of our being proximate to each other and doing this work with our bodies—the deep woman talk and queer man talk about sexuality that happened in that space.

ag: Would you say that it affected the way you came to speak about your own body or sexual experiences? Is it that clear?

E: Well, I'm pretty frank. [Laughing] Though I have decorum. [Laughing] But, here's what I think: I think about you and I know also that Ruti has three children. I think of the multi-generational joy of my students, and then my students becoming my friends as I would become friends of my teachers, and of something about feminist practice. With graduate students, I always say, "Have your damn baby. There's no proper time to have a baby. You can plan this thing forever, and then you'll be 100 and have no baby." Always having the example of myself, which was, you know, at the point when I was about to go up for tenure, I met Ficre, fell in love, left my job, moved across the country, and started having kids. It was at a stage in life where it was, like, *Okay, well, yeah, you know, might've been more sensible to stay and see that tenure thing all the way through, but then, it wouldn't have been Solomon. Wouldn't have been that human.* So I don't know if it's from that dance phase or what it is. Maybe because I didn't have a sister and I didn't have these aunties and I didn't have a cousin, I make those relationships with women. I always have. Wanting to be someone you can bring all of yourself to, bring mind and body and imagination. And bring hopefulness and fear, and bring it all and be helpful. It's how I like to be, but it's also such a profound gift to have all of these people in my life in such an intimate way, even as we go in different directions.

* * *

ag: When you think back to your pregnancies, all of them, are there things that you wish you had known or that you would've loved to hear other people talking or wondering about?

E: One very practical thing. [Laughter] So I was a formula child, and I was born in 1962. Formula was newfangled, formula was supposed to free women, and so that was how I was fed. I breastfed my children and I had *no idea* that it could be hard, let alone excruciating; that it could take days and weeks to get it right; and that there was a right and wrong, as far as not putting yourself in a situation where the baby's not latched properly so you can get injured. And I remember thinking to myself, *Where's the village?* [Laughing] *Why didn't anybody tell me?* And so I wish I'd known that.

And now it's really interesting. I have, in my immediate circle at Mellon, a lot of the people I've hired, I have a lot of women of color and we got pregnancies right and left. Yasmeen just came back from having her baby. And Ehsan—with my witchy sense, I think it's Saturday. That's what I think. For her second child. And then Alexis had her first child. And with Julie, my chief of staff who I work with, so we manage that space together, and she has two small kids and we both have a similar feminist mindset of *we are going to normalize this, and we are going to be, you know, supportive feminist employers.*

When I was pregnant I went to the chair of the English Department—I was at Smith College—and I had my whole plan, you know. I said, "So, I'm pregnant, and he's due in April, and I can teach all year and at spring break grade all my papers..." I had the whole plan. And literally, this guy, an older white man, he literally gasped. And when I said I was pregnant, he said, "What will you do?" And I had the presence of mind to say, "I know you have children, what did you do?"

But just thinking, *You've made this a problem. You've made this a problem, you've made this a weird thing.* And to now be running a workspace where when someone's pregnant, they come and they tell me and I hug them and it's a beautiful thing—we all have our stages of life.

I should say that that experience at Smith was mitigated by another. Ruth Simmons was the president of Smith at the time, and I was pregnant all year long, more and more pregnant. It's a smallish place, as you know, and she said to me once, crossing campus, and, you know, not a lot of Black women faculty at all. She said, "Come and see me after you've had the baby." She said, "When you're ready, just come and tell me how you're doing." And I didn't know her, really. And she said, "And bring the baby when you come."

And that profound, profound feminist act...

And then I had the baby. He came in April, there was the summer, and then in September her office called me and said, "President Simmons wants to see you, and she wanted to remind you to bring the baby."

ag: Oh, wow. Wow!

E: And then, the next stage, which was incredible, was: we went to the meeting, I dressed Solomon up in a sailor suit. [Laughing] Flawless. And he was very chatty. And she, you know, she admired him, and then she *turned* from him.

And she talked to me.

And what was also deep is that I think Solo recognized an authoritative Black woman elder, so he was quiet. And she was like, "Let's talk about your work."

It was a tableau. "Many things are true at once." No contradiction here. Okay. Got it all. We've done that, now let's do this. You are still that person, and now you're another person added to that.

Lucille [Clifton] was like that too at Cave Canem, where I brought Solo when he was 10 weeks old.

I brought him and then I didn't know what the hell I was doing, and it was in the monastery. I didn't have the nursing down, but I was nursing him in class and workshop. There were so many people who were encircling, but I remember: I went into the cafeteria, and I had books, baby, tray, and Lucille just took him. And I had never... He was 10 weeks old and I had never let anybody just take him. Ever. And that was when she said, "Eat fast." She said, "You have to eat, but eat fast." Lucille Clifton and Ruth Simmons, these great Black women elders, who were like, "Okay, having babies is so very normal that I'm actually not going to coddle this. [Laughing] There are a lot of cute Black babies out there. [Laughing] You know, it's what we do. But we have a lot of things to do."

ag: Yes.

E: And there's a great picture, you've probably seen it, it's a picture of Toni Morrison, Alice Walker, Toni Cade Bambara, Sonia Sanchez, when all those women were living in Brooklyn and Harlem at the same time, and all of them were having kids. And in Hilton Als' profile with Toni Morrison that was just reprinted in *The New Yorker*, she says, "We were all more or less single mothers, we all had these kids, and we would sort of do for each other. We would watch each other's kids." She said that when she got a little money, she would write Toni Cade a check and a letter and say, "You have just won the so-and-so grant." So there's a picture that has this community of Black women being writers, being brilliant, being struggling, being figuring-it-out, being mothers, being everything—and being practical. And I always just felt, even though I didn't have that exact village when I had my kids, that that was a dream.

Motherhood Is a State of Hypervigilance

Simone White

Open arms gathering all so wide to hold everyone horizontally
growing, this way, flat in this way capturing each
pellet   stream
danger, failure to possess
holding what cannot be held
natural, weightless impact of pressure in tons
separate,   prostrate time
the weather of wails
appetites
a thin sliver of wax or wood between one time and another what is
the impact
between one time and another more time and more succeeding
separations caroling he is coming

State

Simone White

It is a fish It is a whale   the only food I have eaten
is from the floor   as not from the floor
The wicked carport, it is hell, it is hopscotch
It is a gash It is forever falling on your right knee It is smooth It is
white and
      glossy with pure bright blood
It shines on the lip of a milk-sated infant soft like a kitten
white kitten soft baby It is a fish It is a whale It is cold
It wants to be touched   like you It is soft you cannot imagine
Imagine I am saying   do it
Fish, whale, ship
Caducity, the falseness of TV, the food I could still eat in Casablanca
It is a truck, it is a grain
It is a fish, It is a whale, It is a garbage truck   the only word I
know
is garbage, ice cream, gorilla

You are, baby
the fish the whale the skylark
you you you you you you you you you you you you you you you you you
you
You have
It is
The naturalized beast
The scar

We are
It is
soft
do it   I am telling you
I announce
It is

1994

Vanessa Mártir

When I think about the year 1994, I hear a line on loop in my head from Pete Rock and CL Smooth's "They Reminisce Over You": "Irresponsible, plain not thinking..."

I was eighteen, a freshman at Columbia University, in love with a drug dealer from uptown.

I met him when I was twelve. He was twenty, one of the guys who hung out on the corner of the block where my grandmother lived. I passed by that corner every chance I got. I made sure that when I did, my long hair was neat, half-up, half-down; shirt fitted against my budding breasts, pants hugging my ass. I batted my lashes. Pursed my lips. I was so hungry for attention, and those guys were more than willing to quench that hunger. They commented on how beautiful I was, what a nice body I had. "Que nena tan linda."

I was also rageful in that adolescent angst way that happens as a result of trauma. I didn't hesitate to sneer, "Get the fuck away from me," if they got too close. One grabbed my hand and I shoved him away, "Don't fuckin' touch me." They said I had that Brooklyn-stank attitude. I didn't care. But I still wanted them to want me.

Then there was him. Bottle-bottom glasses, missing front tooth, deep, scratchy voice. He didn't get too close. Knew he'd get a hard glare and a "véteme de allí." He'd always smile and say, "Hi, Vanessa." I'd roll my eyes and keep on walking, but I couldn't hide the pull at the corners of my lips. I was pleased by his worship of me.

I was walking by their huddle one day, the summer after my freshman year in boarding school. Being away on my own made me even more ravenous for attention, but I played it off better, or so I thought. I didn't see him coming.

He put his lips close to my ear. Whispered: "You're gonna be mine one day." I pushed him away. Said: "You wish." He laughed and watched me saunter away.

I was fourteen. He was twenty-two.

When I was sixteen, he got me like he said he would. He was twenty-four.

He came to visit me the following March in Boston. I was a senior, awaiting college notifications. I took him around the city, though all he wanted was to hole up in the hotel room I'd reserved for him on Boylston Street. That's where he showed me what he could do to my body. I learned a pleasure I didn't yet know.

That was also where he shat out the pellets of marijuana he'd swallowed on the trip to Jamaica that he'd just returned from. I watched as he unwrapped them from the latex and plastic wrap. I thought I knew what I was getting myself into. I thought I was old enough and had seen enough. After all, I'd already been on my own for four years. I thought I was worldly and wise. I claimed myself a woman.

I didn't know shit, and would spend the next five years learning just how much.

All I knew in 1994 was that I loved him and wanted him to want me. I'd do whatever, things that still make me cringe, to make him love me.

It was the second semester of my freshman year at Columbia University, and I was living in campus housing. He stayed with me every night. On the morning after Valentine's Day, I snuck out of the twin bed we shared to go to the student health center, conveniently located on the ground floor of my dorm.

"The pregnancy test is positive," the nurse said in a deadpan tone that shocked me more than the news. I couldn't stop staring at her wrist, so thin and fragile, it looked like it belonged to a child. She handed me a pamphlet and said as she walked out, "You can find resources in there. Good luck." I looked down at what she'd handed me. "So you're pregnant . . ." stared at me in large, bold font.

I miscarried days later. It was too easy. I didn't learn my lesson.

When I went back to the health center in April, the nurse looked up at me after scanning my chart. "It says here you were pregnant in February." She stared at me over the glasses she had perched on the tip of her thin nose. She held my chart in one hand and a pen in the other. I imagined the pen poised over the note on my first pregnancy.

I stared at the white walls, the counter with its jars of cotton balls and tongue compressors, the box of sterile gloves.

"You're pregnant again," she said when she came back into the room. The door wasn't fully closed behind her. It felt like she was spitting the words at me. I hopped off the examination table. The tissue paper stuck to the back of my legs and ripped. I made to leave with it still stuck to my thighs. She reached down and pulled it off.

"Here," she passed me the "So you're pregnant" pamphlet. "Do you still have it from last time?" I snatched it from her and left.

There was no question for me that I couldn't have a kid. When my mother found out I was with him, she flipped out. Yanked me by my hair. Punished me by denying me her love. She was right about him. He was trash. But I didn't want to see that then. I felt so alone, I didn't tell anyone but him.

I had to do some shady shit to pay for the abortion. He said he didn't have it. When he showed up with brand new Versace glasses, I said nothing.

Later, he went with me to the clinic on Park Avenue. A lone protestor stood outside the revolving doors. She held a poster I didn't dare look at. "Don't do this to your baby," she yelled.

The waiting room was full of women of varying ages and ethnicities. Some talked. Some stared off into space. I buried my face in a book and cried before the anesthesiologist put me under.

A few weeks later, I was still healing when he started groping me. I reminded him that the doctor said I should refrain from sex for six weeks. He said something about having needs; that if he cheated on me, it was my fault. I let him have his way. It felt like I was being pierced with daggers.

That June, I had a period so heavy and painful, I swore I was miscarrying. I was too ashamed to get a test. I endured it by myself in the bathroom of his parent's apartment, where we stayed that summer. I flushed the blood clots and threw out the blood-soaked towels, and I prayed.

When my uterus didn't fall out, I thanked God, jumped on my rollerblades and hit the pavement. That was my escape for years to come. I'd blade down to the village, across the East River to Brooklyn, back up to the Heights. By the end of the summer, my legs were taut and I'd lost fifteen pounds.

The next time was that fall. I didn't go back to the health center. How could I face the judgment? I didn't need anyone to remind me.

One day, after class in early October, I walked into Riverside Park. I took my journal with me. I hadn't written in weeks. I could lie to myself in my head, could rationalize the truth away, but there was no running from what stared back at me on the page. I sat on the wall overlooking the highway and the Hudson River. Rats scurried below, dashing back and forth, while cars sped by just feet away.

I opened my journal. Wrote: "I'm pregnant again..." and slammed it shut. I wiped my tears roughly with the back of my hand and started walking north.

I didn't know where I was going. All I knew was that I had to get that fetus out of me. He had a six-year-old he didn't take care of. He gave himself props for buying him Gap khakis and a polo shirt for Easter; a shearling from Orchard Street in Delancey that winter. But I never saw him pay a cent of child support, and he rarely saw or called his son. I didn't say it out loud to myself, but I knew somewhere inside that I did not want to have a child with this man whom I loved so desperately and so naively it ached every time I looked at him. Every time he came home smelling of another woman. Every time I took him into my bed.

I sat on the top step of a set of stairs I came to. There was no one around, and the stairs were hidden from view by a tall wall of stone on one side and the greenery of the park on the other. I put my head between my legs and started gagging. I begged God to take those cells out of my body. That's when I threw myself down those stairs.

I didn't fully realize what I was doing. I learned decades later, in therapy, that I had disassociated. I did that a lot back then.

I tried to stop myself when I felt the stone steps strike my back and knees, but the laws of physics and gravity are what they are, so all I managed to do was twist my wrist, break a nail down to the root and scrape my hands badly. When I finally landed, who knows how many steps down, I curled myself into a ball and cried. I begged for forgiveness and kept willing those cells out.

I didn't miscarry right away. When I did, my roommate found me in the bathtub, the water red with my blood. I had passed out. When I came to, I was being wheeled out of the dorm on a gurney. I felt his hand on mine. My roommate had called him. I felt a mixture of relief and hatred.

I was a girl in an abusive relationship, and I was terrified. I didn't have the support system I needed. Was I irresponsible? Yes. Was I traumatized? Yes. Do I regret not having a kid that year? No.

It is twenty-seven years later. My daughter (not with him) is seventeen and the Supreme Court has overturned *Roe v. Wade*.

I think back to the girl I was, who made those fucked-up decisions.

Not having a kid as a teenager was not one of them. I did what I had to do. I was not ready nor was I equipped to be a mother.

I've sometimes thought of what my life would have been like had I had a kid back then. I thought about it when I was a single parent in my thirties. That time I took my daughter on a boat ride when she was seven. I hyped it up for days. Told her we would have a picnic in the park afterwards, cold cut sandwiches and juice boxes I brought from home. Told her I'd buy her her favorite ice cream cone, vanilla with chocolate crunchies. I took her to the Staten Island Ferry because it was free. I couldn't afford anything else.

Years later, when I told her the story, she said she remembers the excitement of the boat ride, but she doesn't remember feeling like she missed out on anything because of money. I did a good job hiding it from her. Poverty made me industrious.

I thought about it when that case worker shamed me when I went to renew the SNAP benefit I'd been getting for six months when my kid was six. I knew I qualified. I just needed some help feeding us. My salary and the child support I received were depleted after rent, bills, and childcare. I was drowning. I walked out of that office and didn't look back. I never did extend those SNAP benefits, though I qualified for years. There were nights I went to sleep hungry. I made sure my daughter never did.

I struggled as an adult with means. Imagine what my life would have been like if I'd had a kid when I was just a kid. There are people who will wag their fingers at me, call me all sorts of names. I have spent a lifetime punishing myself for the choices I made out of trauma, and a lifetime healing from that toxic relationship.

I think about my daughter, the decisions she may make out of ignorance, youth, longing. If she ever came to me in a similar situation, que dios me la bendiga, I would let her make a choice, and I would support her and stand by her, no matter what. I would be for her what I wish I'd had.

There are so many things I would do differently if I could. Having a child at eighteen is not one of them. I am confident of this at forty-six.

I'm still working on being gentler with the girl I was. I write her letters, talk to pictures of her, repeat like a mantra, "I forgive you. I understand." I am fiercely protective of her, especially when it's me chastising and judging her, because sometimes I still slip and do that too. When I cut off my long hair in February under the first full moon, the snow moon, on our land in the woods of upstate New York, I talked to her as I scissored, told her this was a symbolic new beginning. We cried for three days. It was a purge.

I pour all that care and tenderness into my daughter. This to me is my ultimate redemption.

You May Drift

Mendi Obadike

You may drift
and start to count
the women who chose
to dim that faint but
pulsing beam some
call *life*.

You may swim
straight to the island
of that certitude
or you may stop
midstream and tread,
and then swim on back.

You may dive
into those depths
and begin to sink.

You may never leave
the shore. You may
stand there, dipping
one toe into that ocean,
alternately finding it
too cool, too hot.

You may shift your weight.

This is not to say
a woman can't trust
her own robust mind.

I am talking
about this angle
of light, how little
you can know about
the water until you
touch it, a problem
of perspective. You
could drown out there.

If you feel the tide
come in, if you look
for someone else
to blame, you may
feel the current
of a woman
swimming
in the distance.

Try not to measure
how far she moves
away from you.
Imagine, instead,
the heavy arms
of that woman,
how weary they
must be by now.

Radical Intimacies

Marta Lucía Vargas

> ... I am trying to speak
> without art or embellishment
> with bits of me flying out in all directions
> screams   memories   old pieces of pain
> struck off like dry bark
> from a felled tree   bearing
> up or out   holding or bringing forth
> child or demon
>
> —"Blood Birth," Audre Lorde

> What kind of lover have you made me, mother
> —"La Dulce Culpa," Cherríe Moraga

After being sedated, my mother is alone in La Clínica Palermo when my father arrives, demanding to see his son. *You have a daughter. Look here, her earrings.*

Myth remains the starting point, surrender leads the way. Does desire itself, where various threads nest upon themselves, begin at birth?

At thirty-seven, I don't pay close attention to the ticking of my suns but J had been listening. He counts my eggs, and leans in, turns us toward them. That is the moment he becomes father. Together we make way for their coming, a terrifying and gorgeous priority.

Before I pee on the stick, I know the new life inside me. When I become pregnant, my forehead begins to buzz at random. I play with prayer, *Blessed art thou among women and blessed is the fruit of thy womb Jesus.* I'd never noticed that Mary's womb was Jesus-named. Am I now with womb? My womb is not named.

And what about this *womb*—anatomical or biblical or political or something archaic that enters the body upon inception? ... *Now and at the hour of our death* ... That jump from life to death is quick ... *and lead us not into temptation but deliver us from evil* calls forth images of baby Jesus on Mary's breast, long-fingered young man Jesus, Jesus flogged, dead Jesus wrapped in linens.

Deliver us from evil requires a surrender I do not yet possess.

Instead, J and I are flung headlong into cultural forces hostile to natural physiological birth. Both aware and unaware, we are caught in this nexus.

In the dream, I'm in a cave with J. Three men who we don't know join us. We sit together and speak via thought in languages I don't know. J says, *As small as a flea then as big as an elephant, in seconds. Only here.*

The wall behind us opens to the dark mouth of the sea. I dive in. I see C who's been swimming with fish. She says, *Once you get to the other side, it's unbelievable, the biggest blues.* I'm not afraid.

Trust is everything. During birth, I'm completely at their mercy.

I'm completely at your mercy, at the mercy of your myths and your memories. Of your beliefs, of your skills. How you see, who you hear, who you're conditioned to love. I trust my body, do you?

* * *

In Bogotá, Colombia, my grandmother birthed seven babies in her bed across twenty years and our choice for a homebirth makes our families nervous.

I am strong and the most vulnerable one in the hospital room.

I am enormous and strong and infantilized.

Birth is rife with unpredictability and anything that plugs into a socket, beeps, or flickers gives the veneer of certainty.

I feel contractions and they look to machines to determine what's happening to me.

I must fully relax and feel safe for my sphincters to open and am prodded, poked, and penetrated without permission.

I have rights and my rights are routinely violated.

I have choice and no agency.

I am in the throes of nature and surrounded by technomedical equipment.

I am in the throes of nature and you behave superior to nature.

At thirty-seven weeks, our baby is breech positioned. We'd been preparing for a homebirth. His hands, we're told, remember how to turn babes in utero. Unknowingly, I sign the paper out of our midwife's care, into the hands of the magician doctor.

I deliver myself into his hands. This paper permits him.

He pulls out the hypodermic needle for an epidural to prepare me for the external version. I refuse. I want the version without the nerve block. He rifles off reasons why I must accept and leaves the room. He leaves me with his resistance, with my resistance.

My now-ex-midwife leaves, too. Our two-year old runs around, squealing, hungry, pulling on cords. The overhead fluorescents sting. My husband and I try to make sense. Plot to escape.

When the omnipotent one returns, he demands my decision. The sonogram reports that the baby's no longer breech but transverse. His cold hand fists me. He breaks my water. His other hand maneuvers my belly, turns the baby. He gives the *this is what you wanted* look and says, *Your baby's head down*. The confluence of pain and joy almost take me out.

As nature and baby would have it, she returns to her breech position. The baby's heart rate is up. Of course it is. And though I was not in labor before, this twist results in a cesarean birth. It's Thanksgiving week, an untimely inconvenience made convenient.

Lost opportunities for women become capitalism's gains. A routine occurrence. And lost opportunities force women into cesareans. An empty choice. In a conversation, Al-Yasha Williams and Ina May Gaskin state that empty choice lacks political content, empty choice appropriates feminist language.

I learn years later that not offering a vaginal breech birth option is unethical and illegal.

During our first birth, I expect the unexpected. I'm going for sexy birth, demanding birth, the full release, the oxytocin spike, the shakes, kissing, and nipple stimulation. I'm excited when my cervix shows herself with the release of the red-brown mucous plug, which I catch in my palm.

But after my water ruptures, too many hours pass. The midwife on rotation says, *Look, it's just a tiny thing, a half dose. Trust me.* Cytotec to soften the cervix. Pitocin to induce. The contractions come unnaturally. No breaks, too strong, too long. She belittles my ability to endure, *What do you expect, you're having a baby.* I want to shit all over her.

Instead, I see myself grow huge, as big as my uterus. Vagina bubbles now hold my attention, pleasure overwhelms pain. My husband and I lock eyes, take turns breathing into each other's mouths. This back and forth and back calms me as I bring my left hand down to touch my baby's crown.

Riding my irreverence, my baby emerges, scooches up my torso and grabs my nipple like a beast.

To give birth versus to deliver a baby. To want touch and to be touched. To not want touch and to be honored. Bodily autonomy is a universal human right. To restore this right would return the physiological process to birthing. Could you imagine this restoring?

I interview women about their upcoming births for a breastfeeding research project at a Bronx medical center. Attending presentations on birth control are a mandatory part of prenatal care here. I also attend.

The main tenet of this talk is spent on tubal ligation. The nurse who delivers this pitch is Latinx. The majority of the women being treated are Latinx, Afrolatinx, and Black.

Every time I hear her spiel I am reminded of the forced sterilizations of Indigenous women, Puerto Rican women, Black women, Chicanas, women in prison. *Right after you give birth, tubal ligation is an option, a viable option...* as she waves the consent forms, ... *tubal ligation, tubal ligation*, as if the women here have single issue lives, *tubal ligation, tubal ligation* as if she were serving up some reproductive justice special.

How does this medical center's code of ethics reflect health and agency? What good are ethics or rights if the women served cannot access the full services or the rights provided? How do we learn true informed consent? Who carries bodily autonomy?

Heji Shin's 2016 photo project *Baby* captures newborns in their *holdholdhold* before first breath. A beautiful capture of the iconic struggle from amniotic sac to this world. Anguish, trust, and turning point are caught with her lens.

Shin's photographs push imagination. I envision images of fontanels and faces—squished, gooey, and bloody—writhing from engorged vulvas stretched across billboards, buses, flashed during trailers at theatres, in schools, the news, everywhere. Why not?

I run a local vaginal birth after cesarean (VBAC) group with a friend. We create safe spaces. We share birth stories. We read books and organize author events. We help each other make choices for desired birth experiences. We encourage getting needs met, even if it means switching providers in the eighth month.

Through stories we learn that women who have experienced sexual abuse can have a challenging time realizing or embracing vaginal birth. That option can feel fraught.

* * *

To garner sufficient evidence that your potential provider is not a gynophobe or madwife, a Bhanu Kapil and Ina May Gaskin medley:

Who are you and who do you love?

Where do you come from and how did you arrive?

How do BIWOC lives matter in your practice?

What does comprehensive reproductive justice look like in your practice?

How will we begin?

What shapes the body and how has your body taken shape?

Who is responsible for the suffering of your mother?

What are the consequences of silence for the mother?

What do you know about dismemberment?

Can you describe a morning when you woke without fear?

What would you say if you could?

How did you come to believe in birth?

What is your birth philosophy?

How does woman-care inform your practice?

In what ways do you place women at the center of your care?

How do you serve my emotions, my psyche and the erotic during birth?

How involved do you need to be in my labor process?

How do you manage fetal monitoring?

How do you manage IVs during labor?

How do you guide eating and drinking during labor?

How do you guide pushing and labor augmentation during labor?

How many episiotomies have women in your care received?

What are your rates of cesarean births?

What do you remember about the earth?

* * *

On a crisp autumn day, during a routine wellness visit, the family practitioner asks my fourteen-year-old daughter, as a matter of protocol, if she's had sex. Heading home, she points out that the question implies sex with a male partner, *Isn't that curious?*

She asks me when I first had sex. Her question, her questioning of the questions continues her threading of memory, of desires.

Nature is wild, violent and life-giving. Her paradoxes abound. The mind cannot separate from the body. Consciousness is sensual. Be physically strong and stay soft to open. Surrender and experience extreme heightened awareness with the body. This surrender can allow us to step into the erotic, into mystery.

My nature is to push against the limitations of mythic violence and push for mystery. I want to keep in step with wild dreaming, protect her from being silenced, forgotten, annihilated. I am at her mercy.

ACKNOWLEDGMENTS

Umniya Najaer: My infinite gratitude to aracelis girmay and Jakeya Caruthers for deep engagement with this work. Many thanks to my advisors at Stanford University, Deirdre C. Owens, Jasmine Smith, Ainsley Eakins, and Cornelia King of the Library Company of Philadelphia; the McNeil Center for Early American History 21–22 cohort and Nicole Eustace; the Essayists Collective; and Alyea Canada for carrying, each in their own way.

Ama Codjoe: "My Nothings" first appeared in the Academy of American Poets' Poem-a-Day on March 12, 2018.

Terese Marie Mailhot: "Indian Condition" as well as excerpts from "Your Black Eye and My Birth" and "Better Parts" first appeared in *Heart Berries*, Counterpoint Press, 2019.

Deborah Paredez: With special thanks to everyone who helped me push through the dark: Shirley, Amy, Cherise, Stephennie, Regina, Gina, Heather, Michelle, Katie, Claudia, Liz, Georgia, Eva, my mom Connie, and my beloved Frank Andre.

Seema Reza: "Pity" first appeared in *What God Is Honored Here? Writings on Miscarriage and Infant Loss by and for Native Women and Women of Color*, edited by Shannon Gibney and Kao Kalia Yang, University of Minnesota Press, 2019.

Mariahadessa Ekere Tallie: "What We Don't Say" and "[*I turn the hours into a love note to myself*]," first appeared in Tallie's booklet *Mother Nature: Thoughts on Nourishing Your Body, Mind, and Spirit During Pregnancy and Beyond*, 2011.

Simone White: "Motherhood is a State of Hypervigilance" and "State" were published in White's *Dear Angel of Death*, Ugly Duckling Presse, 2018.

With deep and abiding gratitude to each contributor for so profoundly sharing your time and part of your story. Your work is an act of love and language. You donated this work so that all royalty proceeds will go to reproductive health and justice organizations that center people of color. My gratitude forever. Alyea Canada, thank you for your keen, capacious attention and your brilliant copyedit work. Maya Marshall, my editor and collaborator: your sharpest eye, clarity, and support have brought this work into the world. I am so grateful to have collaborated on this with you, exactly you. Rassan, I thank you for your immeasurable support and time as I worked on this anthology. So much of my work here is made of up of your work. Naz, I still see us dreaming at the table.

To those, named and not named here, whose energies run all through this gathering: I cross my arms in deepest recognition.

::x::

aracelis

NOTES

Then They Came for Our Wombs, *Sandra Guzmán*

1. *Immigration* is intentionally used and not *migration*. Borikén is a nation, a Caribbean archipelago that includes 143 islands, keys, islets, and atolls. The name was illegally changed to Puerto Rico in 1521 by the invading Spanish crown. It is a colony under military occupation since 1493, first by Spain, and in 1898 by the United States.
2. From *La Operación* (1982), a documentary about population control and violent sterilization efforts of poor, Black, and Native women in Puerto Rico, directed by Ana María García.
3. Harriet Ryan, Lisa Girion, and Scott Glover. "'You Want a Description of Hell?' OxyContin's 12-Hour Problem," *Los Angeles Times*, May 5, 2016.

we participate in the creation of the world by decreating ourselves, *Jennifer S. Cheng*

1. The title is from Simone Weil's *Gravity and Grace*.
2. *Who are you and whom do you love?* is one of the interview questions from Bhanu Kapil's *The Vertical Interrogation of Strangers*.

A Conversation between Naima Green and Suhaly Bautista-Carolina

1. Moon Mother Apothecary is a practice at the intersection of plant power and people power. It is an offering of plant medicine and a place to share wisdom about plants and healing.

The Water Clock, *Vanessa Angélica Villarreal*

1. A term I heard at a Hoa Nguyen talk about her mother at Naropa University, 2015.

I Chose to Stay Awake, *Maria Hamilton Abegunde*

1. Thank you to LaShawnda Crowe Storm for not turning away and for reading multiple drafts of this essay.
2. Maria Eliza Hamilton, "Reflections on a Lost Childhood," *Mother's Underground Magazine: The Womb* (1993), 14.
3. Gwendolyn Brooks, *Blacks* (Chicago: Third World Press, 1994).
4. Maria Eliza Hamilton, previously unpublished, 1993.
5. This was my mother's favorite dish when we ate at a local Chinese restaurant every month.

6. I want to be clear: my father never sexually abused me. Deep in my soul I *know* that had I told my father, he would have taken swift action that would have led to great harm to those responsible. I would have been motherless and fatherless. Once, he told off a boy who had leaned on my shoulder at a family party. He did not yell at me, only at the boy for being disrespectful. I still remember his words: "Don't lean on or over my daughter, boy. You hear me?" To learn more about how survivors of childhood sexual abuse have approached telling their stories and initiated healing, please read *Love WITH Accountability: Digging Up the Roots of Child Sexual Abuse* (2019), edited by Aishah Shahidah Simmons, to explore the different ways in which survivors of such abuse journey through multiple processes.

7. My life at home was complicated, unsettled, frightening. My parents both worked. My father drank and, when he did, he was violent. My mother was sick for many years before she died. My father cared for her, and in the last years of her life carried her (by car and in his arms when she could not walk) to the hospital every six to eight weeks for blood transfusions. Fear produces many things in a person. The first time I saw my father cry. The first time my mother held me in the ocean. I have held on to these memories of tenderness. When my mother asked me questions about certain behaviors, I could not answer, and she took that as a sign of rebellion and recalcitrance and not abuse. As such, the threat to tell my father about my bad behavior silenced me. At ages six and seven, I had no words, my parents no imagination, for what was being done to me outside the house. I hardly spoke at home or at school. By the time I understood that my parents would have protected me, I had already learned to be silent and to fight my own battles. This, too, is a wounding and trauma from which I learned to heal with lots of compassion for myself. Still, I have no regrets. I have lived long enough to see my father outlive any member of his own family. And, I have lived longer than my mother did. Love and the ability to love through pain allows me to see all the possible universes I could have chosen. Only in this one do I live past the age of sixteen.

8. To learn more about why women choose to have an abortion, and the consequences of their choice, read Diana Greene Foster, *The Turnaway Study: Ten Years, a Thousand Women, and the Consequences of Having—or Being Denied—an Abortion* (New York: Scribner, 2020).

Tits and Ass, *Deborah Paredez*

1. Joan Wolf, *Is Breast Best? Taking on the Breastfeeding Experts and the New High Stakes of Motherhood* (New York: New York University Press, 2011), 66.

2. Wolf, *Is Breast Best?*, xv.

3. Wolf, *Is Breast Best?*, 14, summarizing Orit Avishai, "Managing the Lactating Body: The Breastfeeding Project and Privileged Motherhood," *Qualitative Sociology* 30, no. 2 (2007): 135–52.

4. Martha Sears and William Sears, *The Breastfeeding Book: Everything You Need to Know About Nursing Your Child from Birth Through Weaning* (Boston: Little, Brown, 2000), 60–61

5. Wolf, *Is Breast Best?*, 105.

Death to Breath: A Mother/Daughter Story, *Emma L. Morgan Bennett and Jennifer L. Morgan*

1. On the Black maternal mortality crisis see Linda Villarosa, "Why Americas Black Mothers and Babies are in a Life-or-Death Crisis," *New York Times*, April 11, 2018; on mortality rates in the 1960s, see Vital Health Statistics, *Infant, Fetal, and Maternal Mortality, United States, 1963* (Washington DC: US Department of Health, 1966).

2. On the proximity between Black life and death in the context of the reproductive body, see Ruha Benjamin, "Black Afterlives Matter: Cultivation Kinship as Reproductive Justice," in Adele Clark and Donna Harroway eds., *Making Kin Not Population* (Prickly Pear Press, 2018).

3. On reproduction slavery and the courts, see Jennifer L. Morgan, *"Partus Sequitur Ventrim*: Law, Race, and Reproduction in Colonial Slavery," *Small Axe* 22, no. 1 (2018): 1–17; on access to birth control and abortifacients, see Londa Schiebinger, *Plants and Empire: Colonial Bioprospecting in the Atlantic World* (Cambridge, MA: Harvard University Press, 2007), especially chapter 3, "Exotic Abortifacients;" on kinship and slavery, see Saidiya Hartman, "The Belly of the World: A Note on Black Women's Labors," *Souls*, 18, no.1 (2016): 166–73.

4. On the history of eugenics and the fights against it, see Dorothy Roberts, *Killing the Black Body: Race, Reproduction, and the Meaning of Liberty* (New York: Pantheon, 1997).

5. We use "radical doulas" in reference to doulas who practice and support their clients especially with the aim of countering racism and discrimination in reproductive healthcare. See Miraim Zoila Perez's www.radicaldoula.com.

6. Orlando Patterson, *Slavery and Social Death: A Comparative Study* (Cambridge, MA: Harvard University Press, 1982).

7. Leo Lopez, Louise Hart, and Mitchell Katz, "Racial and Ethnic Health Disparities Related to COVID-19," *JAMA*, published online January 22, 2021. doi:10.1001/jama.2020.26443.

8. On the criminalization of pregnant persons, see Lynn M. Paltrow and Jeanne Flavin, "Arrests of and Forced Interventions on Pregnant Women in the United States, 1973–2005: Implications for Women's Legal Status and Public Health," *Journal of Health, Politics, Policy, and Law*, 38, no. 2 (2013): 299–343.

9. On the concept of the afterlives of slavery, see Saidiya Hartman, *Lose Your Mother: A Journey Along the Atlantic Slave Route* (New York: Farrar, Straus, and Giroux, 2006), 6; on the roots of black radicalism in women's reproductive bodies, see Jennifer L. Morgan, *Reckoning with Slavery: Race, Kinship, and Capitalism in the Early Black Atlantic* (Durham, NC: Duke University Press, 2021).

10. Robin D. G. Kelley, *Freedom Dreams: The Black Radical Imagination* (New York: Beacon, 2002).

Radical Intimacies, *Marta Lucía Vargas*

Bibliography:

Norma Alarcón, Ana Castillo, and Cherríe Moraga, eds., *The Sexuality of Latinas* (Berkeley, CA: Third Woman Press, 1993).

Jennifer Bloch, *Pushed: The Painful Truth about Childbirth and Modern Maternity Care* (Cambridge, MA: Da Capo Press, 2007).

Jane Caputi, *Goddesses and Monsters: Women, Myth, Power, and Popular Culture* (Madison: University of Wisconsin Press, 2004).

Robbie E. Davis-Floyd, *Birth as an American Rite of Passage* (Berkeley: University of California Press, 2003).

Barbara Ehrenreich and Deidre English, *Witches, Midwives, and Nurses: A History of Women Healers* (New York: The Feminist Press, 1973).

Louise Erdrich, *The Blue Jay's Dance: A Birth Year* (New York: HarperPerennial, 1995).

Ina May Gaskin, *Ina May's Guide to Childbirth* (New York: Bantam Books, 2003).

Linda Hogan, *The Woman Who Watches over the World: A Native Memoir* (New York: W. W. Norton & Company, 2001).

Bhanu Kapil, *The Vertical Interrogation of Strangers* (Berkeley, CA: Kelsey St. Press, 2001).

Audre Lorde, *Sister Outsider: Essays and Speeches* (Berkeley, CA: Crossing Press, 1984).

Toni Morrison, "Woman, Race and Memory," in *The Source of Self-Regard: Selected Essays, Speeches, and Mediations* (New York: Knopf, 2019).

Michel Odent, *Birth Reborn: What Childbirth Should Be* (Medford, New Jersey: Birth Works Press, 1994).

Alicia Suskin Ostriker, *The Mother/Child Papers* (Pittsburgh, PA: University of Pittsburgh Press, 2009).

Cherríe Moraga, *Waiting in the Wings: Portrait of a Queer Motherhood* (Ithaca, NY: Firebrand Books, 1997).

Al-Yasha Ilhaam Williams and Ina May Gaskin, "Elective Cesarean as Reproductive Choice: Some Ethical Considerations," unpublished manuscript, 2004.

CONTRIBUTORS

Maria E. Hamilton Abegunde is a memory keeper, ancestral priest, and full-spectrum doula. Her writing is published in *Trouble the Waters: Tales from the Deep Blue, Fire!!!, Kenyon Review, Massachusetts Review*, and *Tupelo Quarterly*. She is the ritualist and commissioned poet for the Ancestral Masquerade and Sister Song exhibitions. She is a Cave Canem, Sacatar, Ragdale, and NEH summer fellow. Abegunde is a faculty member in African American and African diaspora studies at Indiana University.

Elizabeth Alexander is a poet, educator, memoirist, and cultural advocate who has served as president of the Andrew W. Mellon Foundation since 2018 and is a two-time finalist for the Pulitzer Prize.

Suhaly Bautista-Carolina, *Moon Mother*, is an AfroQuisqueyan herbalist, mama, artist, educator, and community organizer born and raised up on Lenapehoking in New York City. Her work lives intentionally at the intersection of plant power and people power and is lovingly guided in collaboration with her community.

Cheryl Boyce-Taylor is a poet, author, and curator. She is the 2022 winner of the Audre Lorde Award for Lesbian Poetry for her verse memoir, *Mama Phife Represents*. The book is a tribute to her late son, hip-hop icon Malik "Phife Dawg" Taylor of A Tribe Called Quest. Boyce-Taylor's five full-length poetry collections represent a lifetime dedicated to poetry. She is the founder and curator of the Calypso Muse and the Glitter Pomegranate Performance Series.

Mahogany L. Browne is the inaugural poet-in-residence at Lincoln Center, executive director of JustMedia, and artistic director of Urban Word. As a writer, organizer, and curator, her work centers Black women and investigates the result of mass criminalization. Named Kennedy Center's Next Fifty, Browne's bibliography includes more than thirteen titles including *Vinyl Moon*, and her first book-length poem, *I Remember Death by Its Proximity to What I Love*. She dreams in Brooklyn, NY.

Jennifer S. Cheng's work includes poetry, lyric essay, and image-text forms exploring immigrant home-building, shadow poetics, and the feminine monstrous. She is the author of *House A*, selected by Claudia Rankine for the Omnidawn Poetry Prize, and *MOON: Letters, Maps, Poems*, selected by Bhanu Kapil for the Tarpaulin Sky Award and named a *Publishers Weekly* "Best Book of 2018." Having grown up in Texas and Hong Kong, she lives with her family in San Francisco.

Ama Codjoe is the author of *Bluest Nude* and *Blood of the Air*, winner of the Drinking Gourd Chapbook Poetry Prize. Her recent poems have appeared in the *Best American Poetry* series and elsewhere.

Angie Cruz is the author of three novels, most recently *Dominicana*. She has published short fiction and essays in magazines and journals including *Callaloo*, the *New York Times*, *Gulf Coast*, *VQR*, and *Small Axe*. Cruz has taught creative writing for more than fifteen years and is editor in chief of *Aster(ix) Journal*, a dedicated space for literature, art, and criticism by and about women.

Dr. LeConté J. Dill was born and raised in South Central Los Angeles, California, the granddaughter of sojourners of the second wave of the Great Migration. She remains curious about sojourning, migrations, and landing and launching places and spaces. A scholar, educator, and poet in and out of classroom and community spaces, LeConté holds degrees from Spelman College, UCLA, and UC Berkeley and was a 2016 Callaloo Creative Writing Workshop Fellow. Her work has been published in *Poetry*, *Mom Egg Review*, and the *Feminist Wire*, among other places. Currently, she is an associate professor of African American and African studies at Michigan State University.

Shannon Gibney is a writer, educator, activist, and the author of the award-winning young adult novels *See No Color* and *Dream Country*. Gibney is faculty in English at Minneapolis College, where she teaches writing. A Bush Artist and McKnight Writing Fellow, her new novel, *Botched*, explores themes of transracial adoption through speculative memoir. With Kao Kalia Yant she coedited *What God is Honored Here? Writings on Miscarriage and Infant Loss by and for Native Women and Women of Color.*

aracelis girmay is the author of three books of poems, most recently *the black maria*. Her poems and essays have been published in *Paris Review*, *Granta*, *Black Renaissance Noire*, *World Literature Today*, and elsewhere. She is on the editorial board of the African Poetry Book Fund and is the current editor-at-large for the Blessing the Boats Selections (poetry).

Naima Green is at first a lover and a lover at last. Between those points are pictures and even sonic. Beneath those pictures and even sonic are dreams and spit containing a want. Naima Green carries the want inside her throat and drips it out with a lens. Often, light.

Andrée Greene is a graduate of Cornell and Columbia Universities. She lives in New York City, where she teaches creative writing, is a freelance editor, and recently completed her novel, *Nobody's Doll*.

Laurie Ann Guerrero, born and raised in the Southside of San Antonio, is a multidisciplinary artist and the author of four collections: *Babies under the Skin*, *A Tongue in the Mouth of the Dying*, *A Crown for Gumecindo*, a collaboration with visual artist Maceo Montoya, and *I Have Eaten the Rattlesnake: New & Selected*. She is the former poet laureate of the state of Texas and the city of San Antonio.

Sandra Guzmán is an award-winning journalist, author, and documentary filmmaker. She was a producer of *The Pieces I Am*, a film about the art and life of Nobel Laureate Toni Morrison. She is the author of *The New Latina's Bible: The Nueva Latina's Guide to Love, Spirituality, Family and La Vida*. She is editor of the forthcoming anthology *Machetes Under Our Beds: An International Anthology of Words and Writing by Daughters of Latin America*.

Ellen Hagan is a writer, performer, and educator. The author of six books including her most recent poetry collection, *Blooming Fiascoes*, she received a NYFA fellowship in poetry in 2020. Ellen is the director of the poetry and theater departments at the DreamYard Project and co-leads the Alice Hoffman Young Writer's Retreat at Adelphi University. She lives with her partner and children in New York City.

Kimiko Hahn is a writer focused on feminism and Asian American identity. She writes: "For my first political act, I sold *Our Bodies, Ourselves* (1972 stapled newsprint for 35¢) to high school classmates out of a friend's car trunk. These were the years when I began to write seriously, and feminism and Asian American identity became powerful themes. In *Foreign Bodies*, I revisit the personal as political—exploring the immigrant body, the endangered animal's body, and elegy. Honors include a Guggenheim Fellowship, PEN/Voelcker Award, Shelley Memorial Prize. I teach in the MFA program in Creative Writing & Literary Translation at Queens College, City University of New York."

Keeonna Harris is a writer, storyteller, mother of five, and prison abolitionist. She received her PhD in Justice Studies from Arizona State University, defending her dissertation, "Everybody Survived but Nobody Survived: Black Feminism, Motherhood, and Mass Incarceration." Her forthcoming memoir, *Mainline Mama*, draws from her experiences as a Black woman, teen mother, and twenty years of raising children with an incarcerated partner and building community in the borderlands of the prison.

Kenyatta A. C. Hinkle (Olomidara Yaya) is a multidisciplinary visual artist, writer, performer, and healer. She is the author of *Kentrifications: Convergent Truths & Realities* and *SIR*. She is the recipient of numerous awards, and her artwork and experimental writing have been exhibited and performed at the Studio Museum in Harlem, SFMOMA, and Páramo Galeria in Guadalajara, Mexico, among other places.

Jada S. Jones is a mother of four who was born and raised in Harlem, New York. She has earned a BS and MBA from Monroe College. She currently works as a compliance manager, but her passion has always been in writing and poetry. In her heart, she knows it's never too late to follow her dreams.

Shaina P. Jones: please see Shaina Phenix.

Bhanu Kapil is the author of six full-length poetry collections, most recently *How to Wash a Heart*, which was a Poetry Book Society Choice and the winner of the T. S. Eliot Prize. In 2020 she was awarded a Windham Campbell Prize and a Cholmondeley Award, both for poetry. She lives in Cambridge, England, where she is an Extraordinary Fellow of Churchill College.

Mendi Lewis Obadike makes literature, art, and music. Her publications include *Armor and Flesh*, and with Keith Obadike: *Phonotype*, *Four Electric Ghosts*, and *Big House / Disclosure*. To date, Mendi + Keith's collaborations include three albums and a series of large-scale sound artworks, including *Blues Speaker (for James Baldwin)* at the New School in New York, *Free/Phase* at the Chicago Cultural Center, *Sonic Migration* at Scribe Video Center and Tindley Temple in Philadelphia, and *Fit (the Battle of Jericho)* at the Metropolitan Museum of Art in New York.

Terese Marie Mailhot is from Seabird Island Band. Her work has appeared in *Guernica*, the *Guardian*, *Mother Jones*, *Medium*, *Al Jazeera*, the *Los Angeles Times*, and *Best American Essays*. She is the author of *Heart Berries: A Memoir*. Terese is the recipient of a 2019 Whiting Award, and she is also the recipient of the Spalding Prize for the Promotion of Peace and Justice in Literature. She teaches creative writing at Purdue University and VCFA.

Maya Marshall is the author of *All the Blood Involved in Love*. She is cofounder of *underbelly*, the journal on the practical magic of poetic revision. Marshall teaches at Emory University and holds fellowships from MacDowell and Cave Canem, among others. She works as an editor at Haymarket Books.

Vanessa Mártir is a writer, editor, educator, and founder of the Writing Our Lives Workshop and the Writing the Mother Wound Movement. Vanessa has been widely published, including in the *New York Times*, *Washington Post*,

Longreads, the *Guardian*, the *Rumpus*, *Bitch Magazine*, and the anthology *Not That Bad*. Her awards include a 2021 Letras Boricuas Fellowship, a 2019 Bronx Recognizes Its Own Award in Creative Nonfiction, and a 2019 AWP Kurt Brown Award in Creative Nonfiction.

Dominique Matti is a writer, a mother, a messenger, and plant worker. She lives in Philadelphia with her two children, her books, and her jars of potions, roots, leaves, and flowers. Through creative practice, spirituality, tending the land, and listening, she ritually strives to situate herself in the long story. Her work centers Black mysticism, ancestral inheritance, liberation, and recovery. She looks forward to discovering what arrangements of words will populate the rest of her sentences.

Celeste Guzmán Mendoza holds a doctoral degree in education leadership and policy, and an MFA in poetry. She was a cofounder of CantoMundo, a workshop for Latinx poets and led the organization for ten years with codirector Dr. Deborah Paredez. A fellow of both Hedgebrook and Macondo, she is the author of the full-length poetry manuscript *Beneath the Halo*.

Nina Angela Mercer is an interdisciplinary artist and scholar. Her writing is published in *Black Renaissance Noire*, *Continuum*, *Break Beat Poets Vol. 2: Black Girl Magic*, *Are You Entertained? Black Popular Culture in the 21st Century*, *Represent! New Plays for Multicultural Young People*, and *A Gathering of the Tribes*.

Jennifer L. Morgan is professor of history in the department of social and cultural analysis at New York University. She is the author of *Reckoning with Slavery: Gender, Kinship and Capitalism in the Early Black Atlantic*, *Laboring Women: Gender and Reproduction in the Making of New World Slavery*, and the coeditor of *Connexions: Histories of Race and Sex in America*. She is the past vice president of the Berkshire Conference of Women Historians and is a lifetime member of the Association of Black Women Historians.

Emma Morgan-Bennett is a scholar and filmmaker. She is interested in visual media, race, reproduction, and apocalypse. She is currently completing her MA in filmmaking at Goldsmiths, University of London as a recipient of the Marshall Scholarship. Emma recently directed the award-winning documentary short, *Mama, I'm Through*, which is about how four Black women in their twenties question their potential for motherhood having grown up during the time of the Black Lives Matter movement. Morgan-Bennett is a trained doula.

Umniya Najaer is a poet, scholar, filmmaker, and multidisciplinary artist and world traveler. She is interested in radically synergetic relations of being with each other, our world, and our cosmos. Her chapbook *Armeika* was published by Akashic Press in the New-Generation African Poets Series. She is completing her PhD in Modern Thought and Literature at Stanford University and is a Cave Canem and Sacatar Fellow.

Cynthia Dewi Oka is the author of *A Tinderbox in Three Acts* (BOA Editions), *Fire Is Not a Country* and *Salvage* (Northwestern University Press), and *Nomad of Salt and Hard Water* (Thread Makes Blanket Press). A recipient of the *Tupelo Quarterly* Poetry Prize, the Leeway Transformation Award, and the Amy Clampitt Residency, Oka's writing has appeared in *The Atlantic*, *POETRY*, *Academy of American Poets*, *Poetry Society of America*, *Hyperallergic*, *Guernica*, and elsewhere. Originally from Bali, Indonesia, she currently serves as Editor-in-Chief of *Adi Magazine*.

Deborah Paredez is a poet, essayist, and cultural critic. She is the author of the poetry collections *This Side of Skin* and *Year of the Dog*, and of the critical study, *Selenidad: Selena, Latinos, and the Performance of Memory*. She is the cofounder of CantoMundo, a national organization for Latinx poets. She lives in New York City and teaches creative writing and ethnic studies at Columbia University. Her next book, *American Diva*, is forthcoming from Norton.

Shaina Phenix is a queer, Black femme poet, other-art-maker, educator from Harlem, New York. She holds an MFA in poetry from Virginia Tech and is the 2021–2022 Jay C. and Ruth Halls Poetry Fellow at the University of Wisconsin–Madison. Her work has appeared or is forthcoming in *West Branch*, *Glass Poetry*, *Foglifter Press*, *Salt Hill Journal*, the *Pinch Journal*, *Puerto del Sol*, *Frontier Poetry*, the *Offing*, and *CRAFT Magazine*.

Emily Raboteau is mother to Geronimo and Ben, professor of creative writing at the City College of New York, author of *Searching for Zion: The Quest for Home in the African Diaspora*, winner of an American Book Award, and author of the forthcoming *Caution: Lessons in Survival* about social and environmental justice from the lens of motherhood.

Marcie R. Rendon is a citizen of the White Earth Nation. Rendon was named to *Oprah Magazine*'s 2020 list of Thirty-One Native American Authors to read and received the 2020 McKnight Distinguished Artist Award and the Fifty over Fifty Minnesota AAARP & Pollen Award in 2018. Rendon's award-winning crime novels are *Girl Gone Missing* and *Murder on the Red River*. Rendon also writes children's books and plays. With Diego Vazquez, Rendon received the Loft's 2017 Spoken Word Immersion Fellowship for work with incarcerated women.

Seema Reza is the author of *A Constellation of Half-Lives* and *When the World Breaks Open*. Based in Maryland, she is CEO of Community Building Art Works, an award-winning organization that brings workshops led by professional artists to veterans, service members, and healthcare providers. She was awarded the Col John Gioia Patriot Award by the USO of Metropolitan Washington–Baltimore for her work with service members. Seema is an alumnus of Goddard College and VONA.

Nelly Rosario was born in the Dominican Republic and raised in Brooklyn. Nelly's novel *Song of the Water Saints* won the PEN/Open Book Award. Her fiction and nonfiction works have been published in various anthologies and journals. Rosario earned an MFA in creative writing from Columbia University. She is an associate professor in the Latina/o Studies Program at Williams College.

Ruth Irupé Sanabria's first collection of poetry, *The Strange House Testifies*, was published by Arizona State University/Bilingual Press. Her second collection, *Beasts Behave in Foreign Land*, received the Letras Latinas/Red Hen Press Award. She is a CantoMundo fellow and works as a high school English teacher in New Jersey.

Deema K. Shehabi is the author of *Thirteen Departures from the Moon* and coeditor with Beau Beausoleil of *Al-Mutanabbi Street Starts Here*, for which she received the Northern California Book Award's NCBR Recognition Award. She is also coauthor of *Diaspo/Renga* with Marilyn Hacker and the winner of the Nazim Hikmet poetry competition in 2018.

Mahtem Shiferraw is a writer from Ethiopia and Eritrea. She is the author of three collections: *Behind Walls & Glass*, *Fuchsia*, which won the Sillerman Prize for African Poets, and *Your Body Is War*. Her newest collection, *Nomenclatures of Invisibility*, is forthcoming from BOA Editions Ltd.

Patricia Smith's eight poetry books include *Incendiary Art*, winner of the Kingsley Tufts Award and finalist for the Pulitzer Prize. Her writing has appeared in *Poetry*, the *New York Times*, the *Washington Post*, *Best American Poetry*, *Best American Essays*, and *Best American Mystery Stories*. She also authored *Africans in America* and *Janna and the Kings*. A winner of 2021's Ruth Lilly Poetry Prize for Lifetime Achievement, she teaches as a Distinguished Professor for the City University of New York.

Mariahadessa Ekere Tallie is the author of *Strut*, *Dear Continuum: Letters to a Poet Crafting Liberation*, *Karma's Footsteps*, and the award-winning children's book *Layla's Hapiness*. Ekere creates cinepoems with her husband and self-care posters and healing herbal potions with her daughters. She has a long-quiet blog called the Sage Honey. A proud New Yorker, Ekere is currently living in Rhode Island where she is a PhD student at Brown University.

Lena Khalaf Tuffaha is a poet, essayist, and translator. Her first book of poems, *Water & Salt*, received the 2018 Washington State Book Award. She is the author of two chapbooks, *Arab in Newsland* and *Letters from the Interior*, a finalist for the Jean Pedrick Prize.

Marta Lucía Vargas is a poet, teacher, and founding member/poetry editor of *Aster(ix) Journal*. Her work has appeared in various journals and anthologies, including *HTI Open Plaza* and *The Lake Rises: Poems to and for Our Bodies of Water*. She holds an MFA in Poetry from Drew University and lives in New Jersey.

Vanessa Angélica Villarreal was born in the Rio Grande Valley to Mexican immigrants. She is the author of the award-winning poetry collection *Beast Meridian*. Her writing has appeared in the *New York Times*, *Harper's Bazaar*, *Oxford American*, *Poetry*, and elsewhere. She is a doctoral candidate at the University of Southern California in Los Angeles, where she is working on a poetry and nonfiction collection while raising her son. Her essay collection, *CHUECA*, is forthcoming.

Hope Wabuke is a Ugandan American poet, essayist, and critic. She is the author of the poetry collection *The Body Family*, the memoir *Please Don't Kill My Black Son, Please*, and the chapbooks *her*, *The Leaving*, and *Movement No. 1: Trains*. She has won awards from the National Endowment for the Arts, SPACE at Ryder Farm, VONA Voices, and Fulbright.

Simone White's works include *or, on being the other woman*, *Dear Angel of Death*, *Of Being Dispersed*, and *House Envy of All the World*. She is the Stephen M. Gorn Family Assistant professor of English at the University of Pennsylvania and serves on the writing faculty of the Milton Avery Graduate School of the Arts at Bard College.

Kao Kalia Yang is a Hmong American writer and author of books for adults and children, among them the recently published memoir, *Somewhere in the Unknown World*. She coedited the anthology *What God Is Honored Here? Writings on Miscarriage and Infant Loss by and for Native Women and Women of Color*. Yang's work has been recognized by numerous communities and organizations, including the National Endowment for the Arts, the National Book Critics Circle Award, the Chautauqua Prize, the PEN USA literary awards, and the Dayton's Literary Peace Prize. She lives in Minnesota with her family.

Tiphanie Yanique is a novelist, poet, essayist, and short story writer. Her most recent work, *Monster in the Middle*, was published in 2021. She has received the 2014 Flaherty-Dunnan First Novel Award from the Center for Fiction, the American Academy of Arts and Letters Rosenthal Family Foundation Award, and the Bocas Prize in Caribbean poetry, among other recognitions. Tiphanie grew up in the Hospital Ground neighborhood in St. Thomas. She lives now with her family in Atlanta, where she is a professor at Emory University.

INDEX

ABOUT HAYMARKET BOOKS

Haymarket Books is a radical, independent, nonprofit book publisher based in Chicago. Our mission is to publish books that contribute to struggles for social and economic justice. We strive to make our books a vibrant and organic part of social movements and the education and development of a critical, engaged, and internationalist Left.

We take inspiration and courage from our namesakes, the Haymarket Martyrs, who gave their lives fighting for a better world. Their 1886 struggle for the eight-hour day—which gave us May Day, the international workers' holiday—reminds workers around the world that ordinary people can organize and struggle for their own liberation. These struggles—against oppression, exploitation, environmental devastation, and war—continue today across the globe.

Since our founding in 2001, Haymarket has published more than nine hundred titles. Radically independent, we seek to drive a wedge into the risk-averse world of corporate book publishing. Our authors include Angela Y. Davis, Arundhati Roy, Keeanga-Yamahtta Taylor, Eve Ewing, Aja Monet, Mariame Kaba, Naomi Klein, Rebecca Solnit, Olúfẹ́mi O. Táíwò, Mohammed El-Kurd, José Olivarez, Noam Chomsky, Winona LaDuke, Robyn Maynard, Leanne Betasamosake Simpson, Howard Zinn, Mike Davis, Marc Lamont Hill, Dave Zirin, Astra Taylor, and Amy Goodman, among many other leading writers of our time. We are also the trade publishers of the acclaimed Historical Materialism Book Series.

Haymarket also manages a vibrant community organizing and event space in Chicago, Haymarket House, the popular Haymarket Books Live event series and podcast, and the annual Socialism Conference.